Fundamentals of Child Psychology

FUNDAMENTALS OF CHILD PSYCHOLOGY

Dr. Deepesh Chandra Prasad

MD PUBLICATIONS PVT LTD
NEW DELHI

For information:

MD Publications Pvt Ltd
'MD House', 11, Darya Ganj
New Delhi - 110 002
Phone : +91-11-41563325 (Customer Service)
+91-11-41562846 (Editorial)
E-mail (orders): contact@mdppl.com
Website: www.mdppl.com

ISBN: 978-81-7533-145-7

Published and Printed by Mrs. Rajni Gupta on behalf of **MD Publications Pvt Ltd** at Times Press, New Delhi.

Dedicated to The Memory of

My Father

(Late) Shri Umesh Chandra Prased

&

Mother

(Late) Smt. Suniti Devi

CONTENTS

PREFACE

Child of any family is more important than other because he/ she is the futuristic man/ woman about the world which will be formed by their parents and other. So this is the moral responsibility of everyone of his/ her family to give a platform where he/ she can complete their developmental period with all necessities i.e. physiological, sociological, psychological etc.

Child Psychology is one of the integral branches of psychology, which deals with the development of a child from infant to maturities. The present book entitled Fundamentals of Child Psychology deals with two major aspects: first aspect says that all humans are similar to another in their potentialities, patterns of development, and behaviour; while second aspect says that, the difference between human beings in capabilities and in behaviour as these differences are manifested within this core of similarity. We usually see two forces operating to produce similarity. The first is our biological nature, which makes humans the moderately large, omnivorous, tough, stimulation seeking, problem-solving, symbol-using organisms that we are. The second is that necessary core of culture based on such aspects of the human condition as a long period of dependency which in turn demands a stable family structure, considerable instruction, and considerable psychological support if the highly immature organism is to survive. Within the limits imposed by these two forces, individual differences in behaviour occur as a result of hereditary and environmental variability. This handbook is packed with all the necessary child psychology topics viz., methods for studying behaviour of childhood, fundamentals of child psychology, child as an individual, basic instincts temperaments, growth, development and maturation, heredity and environment, learning and motivation, intellectual growth, personality integration and adjustment during childhood, sociological influences on child's behaviour, dilatory and precocious children, physiological considerations, nutritional values, child health and adolescent's behaviour and problem.

I have attempted to present a sound body of facts within the context of those ideas and theories that influence our view of development. We can discuss and raise questions, but the reader must interact with real children to understand the reasons for my interest, my discussion, and my questions. The basic motivation of any science is to understand those natural phenomena that are objective of the study within that science. We have tried to present data that will help the individual to understand the processes involved in human development. I have tried as best concerning to the evidence based on my interpretations and explanations related to psychological phenomena.

Dr. Deepesh Chandra Prasad

1

Methods for Studying Behaviour of Childhood

Why Study Child Psychology?

A study of the psychology of childhood, if conscientiously and intelligently pursed, provides a rich background of information about children's behaviour and psychological growth under a variety of environmental conditions. It provides information about psychological scales for appraising a child's development status; provides certain "norms" of behaviour and growth for comparative purposes; provides understanding of basic psychological processes like learning, motivation, maturation, and socialization; supplies knowledge of the general principles of development with to evaluate critically new trends and "fads" in child care and training; and offers practical suggestions for guiding the psychological growth of children who experience difficulties in adjusting to adults, children and other personal and natural components of their culture.

Furthermore, extended study in this scientific area promotes a better understanding of adolescent and adult behaviour. Familiar aphorisms such as "The child is father of the man", and "As the twig is bent so grows the tree" document man's belief in the major contributions of childhood experiences to the personality and behaviour of the mature individual. The principles of psychoanalysis, criminology, and psychosomatic medicine emphasize the importance of childhood experiences. It therefore seems important to understand the child because every stage of childhood is itself important, and also because an understanding of the child gives a better understanding of all the effective characteristics of the adult, as well as the foibles and idiosyncrasies of later years.

One of the many reasons a person seeks knowledge is to understand the world around him. By knowing the why of what he sees, he acquires some proficiency at discerning orderly sequences of events and predicting the future from the present. Through understanding the causes of events, an individual may at times change the sequence and produce a different end result. Understanding leads to prediction and often, ultimately, to control of the environment. But there is a great difference between common, ordinary, everyday understanding and scientific understanding.

The latter is achieved by application of what is widely known as the scientific method. Let us therefore explore this method to learn how scientific understanding, prediction, and control develop, in distinction to the more personal, day-to-day understanding of the universe which is shared by all manner of men. And then let us see how scientific techniques develop valuable findings in child development.

Scientific Method

Prediction

All scientific endeavour is concerned with making observations that do lead to accurate prediction-predictions ranging from what to anticipate from a change in the structure of a molecule to what new attitudes to expect to develop among race-prejudiced persons exposed to close contact with another race, as in an integrated teen-aged boys' camp. Prediction, however, is never certain. It is merely a statement of probability. The form in which it is used in all science is often called actuarial prediction.

This term is borrowed from insurance, whose actuaries can tell-barring great, unexpected catastrophes such as wars-the number of individuals in a given age group who will die in a particular year. An actuarial statement sets forth the odds, the chances that a specific thing will happen. In child psychology, for example, an actuarial statement might hold that a child of IQ 70 at age 12 has less than one chance in 100 of completing a conventional high school course curriculum by age 20. The chance is there, but it is a longer shot. This form of prediction is also known as nomothetic prediction-that is, arising from or based on law distinction noted by Allport.

A nomothetic statement like an actuarial statement asserts the odds; it is a statement of probability. A statement like "Republicans worry more about a balanced budget than do Democrats is a nomothetic statement. It may very well be true, based on a theory of budgeting which has influenced many Democrats, but it is only a matter of probability for any individual member of either party. Even though the odds in its favour are excellent, the statement is still not a certainty. A second type of prediction, limited almost entirely to the social sciences, applies to the individual case.

This is ideographic prediction, roughly a drawing or graphing an individual, and it is aimed at understanding a particular individual. Ideographic prediction makes use of nomothetic knowledge, but is concerned only with one individual. To the applied psychologist, it is the predictive technique par excellence: "Mr. X will not commit suicide; Miss A will do better in group therapy than in analysis; Mr. K is not a good parole risk. Such predictions are often wrong. They are based on knowledge acquired by nomothetic means which only imply the odds. Nevertheless, the social scientist must make these predictions, since though they often prove inaccurate they are frequently more precise than the predictions made by others.

Indeed, considering the present state of knowledge and the complexity of subject matter, the proportion of accuracy in prediction is remarkable. Whether nomothetic or ideographic, the accuracy of a prediction supplies cues to the truth of a belief. The most wonderful thing about science, believed M. R. Cohen, is that built into it is the notion that unless ideas accurately portray reality, they must be changed. If of two theories, for example, one makes more accurate predictions about the phenomena with which both deal, this theory is accepted and the other is rejected. If the two predict equally well, the more parsimonious theory, the one making fewer assumptions, takes precedence.

Should a new theory be developed that outshines either of the other two, both prior theories are discarded. No truth is sacred, universal, or immutable to science or the scientist. This attitude of disrespect for any authority other than nature, when observed systematically and without bias, is what has enabled science to change rapidly and relinquish old ideas for better-that is, more accurate or more truthful-new ones. Certainly this applies to many of the ideas discussed in this book; they are likely to be superseded in time by more reliable interpretations. If the goal of psychology is highly accurate prediction, how closely has this been approached? Not very closely, but progress is being made.

There are several reasons why success in psychological prediction has only been moderate. First, the subject matter of psychology is more complex than the subject matter of many other sciences; at least the psychologists claim this to be so. Second, psychology is a comparatively young science. One of the early American students of Wilhelm Wundt, a founder of modern psychology, died only recently. This makes one realize, as does nothing else, how young this science is. The youth of psychology cannot be changed until hundreds of years have passed and it has suffered the problems of growing up.

But there are aspects of the young science that can be changed, aspects which at present contribute to a deficiency in skill. One change desired by most psychologists and toward which they are working is an increase in the reliability and validity of measuring devices. In its simplest form, reliability means that a device used to measure a stable characteristic, such as the height of an adult, will give the same information on every occasion. If a yardstick expanded or contracted capriciously, what would measure five feet, ten inches today might measure three feet, six inches or nine feet, eight inches at some future date. Obviously this yardstick would be unreliable as a measuring device, and because of its unreliability, growth trends could not be predicted with any accuracy over intervals of time.

The reliability of many measuring instruments is indeed low, especially the tests for measuring personality. Perhaps personality characteristics are basically unstable and individual personality varies greatly at different points in time. If this lack of reliability is largely the fault of inadequate tests rather than of actual personality change, the continued efforts to increase the reliability of psychological tests should make their results more dependable and therefore better instruments for predicting behaviour. A test is valid if it measures what it set out to measure. It is invalid if it measures other things and not what it was designed to test. Suppose we measured the height of members of a psychology class and graded them on the basis of height.

The measurements would be highly reliable on the subject of height, but they would not be valid for achievement, since tallness is hardly a good measure of ability. Whereas a reliable measure may not be valid, as in the foregoing example, a measure cannot be highly valid unless it is highly reliable. As better testing methods are used and reliability grows, the validity of measurements increases. But more important, the validity of the measuring device can be checked by comparing its findings with reality. Does the person who does well in a test of creativity, for example, actually behave creatively? Only when behaviour in the real world is predictable from test results does as test become a valid predictive device. Development of tests at once reliable and valid increases the power to predict.

Phenotype and Genotype

Psychology also stands to gain in both understanding and predictability from an increasing awareness of genotypic variation as opposed to phenotypic variation between individuals. Genotype refers to the similarity in background forces that produce behaviour. One young man steals an automobile. Another holds down two jobs to pay for an automobile. Both are motivated chiefly by a desire to impress some young woman. They are genotypically alike in this specific aspect of their motivation even though their outward behaviour differs.

Phenotype, on the other hand, concerns the phenomenal or observable world. Phenotypically, or observably, these young men differ greatly. Psychologists and social scientists in general, have dwelt on phenotypes rather than genotypes and, further, have not done as good a job as they might on distinguishing between phenotypes. Consider the problem as it relates to the diagnosis and treatment of physical and psychological disorders.

A physical disorder entailing an increase in temperature is called a fever. Although various fevers differ in a number of secondary aspects, their major phenotypical or observable feature is the heightened temperature they all share. If physicians paid attention only to the temperature, no effective methods of treatment would have been developed, since a therapeutic aid for reducing one fever, such as quinine for malarial fever, is utterly useless in the treatment of many other fevers. Astute physicians managed, however, through keen observation to distinguish several sub-phenotypes within the general phenotype fever. These sub-phenotypes differed in genotype or cause-and, once separated from one another, also differed in the treatment effective for each of them.

This knowledge enabled development of individual treatment. By carefully examining subjects manifesting a common genotype, one can often discern systematic variations in their observable characteristics. Though superficially resembling one another, subjects in each group actually fall into distinct subgroups, each is a result of another genotype. How successful in this approach in psychology? Individuals with severe mental defects-say, below IQ 50 are phenotypically alike in being defective. Yet there are several rather easily observable distinctions among them. Some of these individuals have clearly suffered from brain damage during prenatal development, in a difficult birth process, or after birth itself. Others form the low end of the normal distribution of intelligence.

For every IQ of 160, presumably, there is another of 40, and its possessor is defective as a result of multiple genetic variation. Still others are defective from the effects of multiple genetic variation. Still others are defective from the effects of a single gene rather than the multiple-genetic deficiency responsible for the IQ of 40. More careful scrutiny divides these individuals into additional sub-phenotypes, suggesting the existence of still more genotypes than are casually perceived.

One variety of defectiveness resembles any other until the individual's urine is subjected to chemical analysis. This particular disorder with the formidable name of phenylpyruvic oligophrenia or phenylketonuria has an observable symptom in the excretion of phenylpyruvic acid in the urine when phenylalanine, an amino acid, is incompletely oxidized. When this acid is found in the urine, the individual is nearly always defective, presumably because of this unmetabolized amino acid in the system. The condition results from a double recessive genetic characteristic. Anyone may be a carrier of the disorder, though the probabilities are slight. The carrier who transmits the disorder has one recessive and one dominant gene, whereas the victim has a double recessive pair of genes.

If married, by chance, to another carrier, the original carrier has one chance in four of having a child with this affliction, two chance in four of having children who do not have it but who are carriers, and one chance in four of having a child who is neither defective nor a carrier. Here is an instance in which careful phenotypical observation led to the discovery of a specific genotype. Once the genotype was found, effective treatment was soon developed. With a phenylalanine free diet, especially during, the first year of life, a child could overcome the hereditary disposition toward idiocy. Without doubt, there are probably a number of genotypes of this sort hidden within the larger phenotypical category, "severely mentally defective," as there are in such widely inclusive phenotypes as juvenile delinquency, schizophrenia, or even shyness. But as long as psychologists continue to study individuals on the basis of broad phenotypes, there is scant likelihood for additional success in diagnosis, prediction of outcome, and treatment. A shift in interest to genotypes may very well improve the predictive powers of the child psychologist.

Observation

The raw data of scientific knowledge are facts, and scientific undertakings usually begin with their observation. Astronomy, the fist of the sciences, grew out of the keen observations of Egyptian and Babylonian priests. To them, the orderly sequences of day and night and of the seasons might have suggested an orderliness, that is, a predictability, in the physical world. Careful observation led to knowledge of planetary movement and of fixed stars; and this knowledge enabled these priestly astronomers to make practical predictions, such as the time at which the Nile would flood. Since they also believed in astrology, they made less valid predictions too-such as "Beware of a dark-haired man next Tuesday."

In all probability, the science of astronomy resulted from false notions about the influence of celestial bodies on human behaviour as much as from a belief in an orderly universe. Yet the information collected by these early observers was substantially correct, even when their interpretations feel short of the mark. Since these initial probings of the unknown, knowledge of the world has progressed a long way to its present state. In this advance, observation has played a major role: knowledge, in fact, has depended on observation. Although the ability to observe is widespread, scientific observation differs from ordinary observation in several respects. Scientific observation is systematic; it dwells on a particular phenomenon.

Thus phenomenon may be the movement of the planets as observed by the ancients, or it may be the social relations of two-year old as observed by child psychologists. In either instance, as in any scientific undertaking, the observation is restricted to one or, at the most, a few kinds of objects or events; it does not extend to everything. Moreover, this kind of observation concentrates on all aspects of the particular kinds of events, whereas everyday observation may take in only part of many events. Take the bias found in the casual observation of the relation between physical characteristics and behaviour. Redheads have hot tempers, we hear; people with big ears are generous; long fingers denote the artist.

If these views were valid, we could easily predict appropriate behaviour toward redheads, whom to approach for a loan, and which child would perform in Carnegie Hall. This is hazardous terrain. It leads from fallacies concerning the most observable characteristics of people with big ears to the quicksand of characteristics believed to be evident among members of racial or religious groups. These questionable beliefs result from the human tendency not to observe negative manifestations. People prefer to notice only those things that confirm their beliefs. If an event runs counter to a belief, they are more likely to forget or distort the event than change the belief.

This tendency may be seen in a vast number of studies cited by Rapport, and more recently in the work of Festinger, centred in his theory of cognitive dissonance. Scientific method, in contrast, is aimed at insuring complete, accurate observation and inclusion of even negative findings. The observation of these instances-the cases that do not fit the expectation-is the very essence of science. Observation leads to the formation of hypotheses, which may be considered "educated guesses" or suppositions. If these hypotheses are so linked that a test of anyone of them yields information not only about itself but also about the other hypotheses dependent in whole or in part upon it, a theory exists.

Sometimes the, information bears no essential relation to any specific hypothesis and hence to the theory. For example, the difference in average sentence length in the speech of two-year-old and three-year-old may have some value for other purposes, but it suggests no new ideas or leads no further to basic understanding of the child. Other data, however, may help to find out whether an hypothesis conforms to reality; such data permit new predictions which in turn provide new insights about the world. Scientific procedure benefits greatly from findings of this kinds and the experimental processes uncovering them, but all scientific investigations must start with the accumulation of from observation and then test their hypotheses against these facts. If a theory or an hypothesis does not fit the observed facts, it must be discarded, whether it concerns a folk belief like the temper of redheads or a cosmological issue such as the question of whether the universe is expanding or standing still.

The rejection of a theory generally results from systematic, close observation of all cases. Sometimes the facts fit the theory fairly well, but not well enough. Here, the negating instance indicate where a theory is weak and must be revised promptly to improve its accuracy. The next result is a fuller, clearer understanding of the world, which sharpens the skill of being able to predict the future more precisely.

Control

A basic purpose of prediction is control. However, prediction and control are separate aspects of science. In fact, control is not a necessary part of science, since some sciences exist for which control is clearly impossible. Many sciences such as astronomy, cosmology, volcanology, and seismology, for example, are reasonably adequate at predicting events, but they obviously have no control over the phenomena to which they attend. Predicting an eclipse is a simple matter for an astronomer, whereas causing or controlling one is indeed beyond human capability. One might contend that ability to predict without ability to control is essentially useless.

The argument depends on the definition of utility. If immediate, demonstrable usefulness is necessary, then, as Bugelski said, "Such a viewpoint might limit the work of astronomers to observations of the moon and the navigational stars since outside of these might be little of an immediately practical nature in astronomy. Most scientists, however, are unconcerned with practical utility. For them, knowledge is an end in itself. More cogently and more practically, knowledge that does not have immediate utility might be of value in the future. Bugelski noted that Faraday once demonstrated an elementary form of a dynamo to Disraeli. What good is it? Disraeli asked. Faraday retorted, Someday you may tax it.

The practical and concrete fact often arises from the impractical and abstract theory. From an interesting set of ideas proposed by a young man named Einstein evolved the atomic bomb. The justification for seeking knowledge clearly does not depend on the practical utility of the knowledge for controlling the surrounding world. In certain areas of psychology, notably clinical psychology, control of behaviour is often considered to be a major aim. As used in this sense, control does not mean forcing the individual to act in a desired manner. It rather means increasing the frequency of certain behaviours and decreasing the frequency of other behaviours through a manipulation of the environment. Suppose it is believed that a boy who sets fires does so because of neurotic difficulties stemming from his acceptance of the masculine sex role.

The clinical psychologist, using some form of therapy, tries to bring these problems into the open where they can be treated. If given some insight into the roots of his problems plus, perhaps, some form of training and support, the boy may indeed cease his arsenous activities. If successful, the clinician has controlled behaviour. Certain behaviours, such as setting fires, decrease in frequency whereas other behaviours, such as dating, increase. Even if the boy now starts stealing cars to provide himself and his young lady friend with transportation, the therapy quite likely has been successful.

It has discovered the sources of the arsenous conduct, and certain hypotheses have been formed regarding the efficacy of various treatment techniques. Behaviour has been controlled. Very often the child psychologist is asked questions pertaining to control. How does one increase a behaviour, such as eating everything on the plate, or decrease a behaviour, such as having temper tantrums? Psychology has some answers to these questions, and this book will attempt to deal with them. The scientist may not be sure that control should be attempted because he is not certain that control is desirable for human beings.

The parent, on the other hand, controls his children's present and attempts to control their future through manipulating the environment. Good or bad, this is parenthood. Any parent can do it to try to increase those behaviours that he values as "good" in a child and decrease those deemed bad. Like the clinician and the parent, the teacher too, must act. Since these acts have far-reaching consequences, parent and teacher, again like the clinician, should use what scientific understanding is available.

Research Methods in Child Psychology

There are several reason why knowledge of search methods is important for the beginning student in child development. Like other areas of the social sciences, child psychology is quite imprecise as compared with the more exact physical sciences. Yet in a relatively brief interval of time, the precision of research and, hence, the reliability and validity of conclusions have shown a remarkable advance. Moreover, the studying of research methods tends to foster a critical faculty in the student; he is better able to judge the value of research data and the conclusions by examining the methods that produce them.

This ability is perhaps more necessary in the field of child psychology than in any other scientific area. Here every layman considers himself an expert and is quite willing to proffer advice in such matters as child discipline, juvenile delinquency, and child growth. It is therefore of particular importance that the student of child psychology be well grounded in scientific methods. Only then can he judge, not on the basis of apparent meaningfulness and plausibility of statements, but by examining the source of the data, the correctness and appropriateness of the techniques employed, and the justifiability of the conclusion drawn. Four main questions will guide the inquiry into research methods in child psychology:

- Where is the particular method applicable?
- What are its advantages?
- What are its disadvantages?
- What does the method tell, and what kinds of information can it not provide?

Naturalistic Observation

The scientist, like the novelist, can gain his raw data from observing organisms in nature-that is, in their natural habitat, and not in any controlled or experimentally manipulated environment. Many psychologists believe that such naturalistic observation, which is relatively objective, will ultimately yield more information than better controlled but more limited techniques-limited in the sense of the amount of behaviour observed-such as experimentation.

Babv Biographies

Among the types of naturalistic observation the early diary accounts describing child behaviour have been of both historical and methodological importance. The biographer, usually an interested parent or relative, has observed the behaviour of a single child and recorded the observations in diary style. Often the biographers have been scientists in fields other than child behaviour. Charles Darwin, for example, was biologist. Thus, an individual of scientific bent, curious, yearning to know, to understand, to find out, approaches each new, unexplored area with a desire to observe and record the phenomena under study. Many criticisms may be voiced over the- "trustworthiness" of the information contained in these early biographies.

Darwin's attempts to separate the facts of observation from an interpretation of them were not always successful. A common weakness of such observations is the tendency to project onto the child the emotions, motives, and attitudes of the adult. Besides, there are other disadvantages and limitations to the biographical approach. First, the relevance of the observations depends in part on the adequacy of the observer's background and training. Since such observations are highly subjective, the biases of the observer may very well influence the types of behaviour recorded and the interpretations of these behaviours. Second, it is immediately apparent that the child cannot be considered truly representative of all children of his age and sex.

This limits the extent to which the date can apply to other children. Third, the type of parent who would engage in such painstaking observation and recording would not be likely to represent parents in general. So much for the observer and the observed, several things may also be said about the information itself. Since the baby biographies were usually initiated with no specific purpose in mind, no single type of behaviour was examined systematically. How representative any of these sampled behaviours might be is a matter for debate. Representativeness is imperative in research if the investigator attempts to conclude from his observations that a certain behaviour is typical or characteristic of a particular child.

As a final caution, the observer must remain alert to the danger of the observation itself interfering with the behaviour of the child under observation. More recent research, to be discussed in a moment, has dealt with this problem through a similar observational method.

Case-Study Method

A modern approach that shows much similarity to the baby biography is the case study. This technique collects a great variety of information about a single child usually to help a professional person understand the child's behaviour. Delinquency, school failure, problem behaviour are common subjects studied through the case method. School records, accounts obtained from parents, relatives, other interested adults, and the child himself, as well as the results of psychological examinations are among the sources of information consulted. The following case study was undertaken to obtain clinical evaluation of one child's behaviour problems.

Case-Study Report

Mr. and Mrs. Desouza requested an evaluation of their son, Tom, because they have become increasingly upset by his behaviour and have been unable to handle him at times. They are especially frightened of his rage reactions and are concerned about his lack of self-discipline and his inability to accept limits.

Interview with Parents

The parents described Tom as an intelligent boy who is overweight, has a quick temper, and is a chronic "tease." They believe that he is sensitive about his obesity and this prevents him for taking an active part in sports. They also noted that his rudeness, his unwillingness to cooperate, and his inability to accept criticism help to prevent his participation in organized sports. The Desouza feel that Tom hates to be frustrated, is rebellious, disorderly, and that he refuses to dress up.

He likes to work with mechanical things and is very interested in hot rods. Tom shows a great deal of animosity toward his eight-year-old sister. He becomes profane when angry and constantly threatens to leave home. The parents remember Tom to have been a relaxed and happy baby. They are rather vague about developmental history, but believe that he did everything early. Mrs. Desouza holds certain beliefs about food which do not have their basis in religious ideas. Hence, she has raised Tom as a vegetarian and he was fed soy-bean milk for approximately the first three years of life. Mrs. Desouza could not recall when he stopped taking the bottle, nor could she describe how weaning occurred.

She thought that Tom walked at nine months and talked at one year, but she could not recall his first words. She thought she began toilet training at about a year and a half and that Tom was easy to train. Tom fell out of a crib before age two, fell off a tricycle and hurt his chin at age four or five and he fell out of a car when he was four or five years old. His ears bother him; he feels as if there is wax in them and has had X-ray treatment for this irritation. He does not report hearing difficulties, however, nor does he hear peculiar sounds. Tom never sucked his fingers or showed evidence of masturbatory activity. Nightmares, sleepwalking, or enuresis were not present according to the parents. Sexual information has been obtained largely from other boys, although he is able to talk with his father about sexual matters. The Desouza have moved around a good deal; hence, Tom has attended a variety of schools.

There were no apparent difficulties about starting to school and no academic problems until recently. He attended Broad Hurst Elementary School, beginning two years ago, but was about to be expelled when his parent contacted the clinic. They transferred him to Edgewater Elementary School but Tom does not like this school. His recent school history indicates that he constantly disrupts the classroom with various kinds of attention-getting behaviour. The parents also described Tom as being somewhat belligerent toward younger children and as somewhat blustering in his approach to other children.

He has to have his own way, and at times it seems that he deliberately antagonizes his playmates. Mr. Desouza found it difficult to set limits on Tom's behaviour or to attempt to discipline him. Mrs. Desouza, on the other hand, feels that Tom should be made to conform to certain standards; she keeps after him to see that he does.

Psychological Evaluation

Tests Administered

- Wechsler Intelligence Scale for Children;
- Rorschach Inkblot Test;
- Thematic Apperception Test

Behaviour and Appearance

Tom is an obese ten-and-a-half-year-old boy who was quite belligerent toward the interviewer when first seen. At the same time, he seemed frightened about coming. On his first visit, he ran out of the building and across the street, and on his second visit, he sat in the car refusing to come into the building. On the third and last visit, however, he was able to talk about his anger toward the clinician, including his feelings that "what he was like was his business," and that he couldn't be helped anyway. He denied any fears about coming to the clinic, although he was able to talk about his concern with what his friends would think if they knew he was coming to see a "head shrinker."

Initially, he denied having any problems, but as the session progressed, he was able to admit that he was not very satisfied with his family. He claimed that his mother always nags him, especially about eating and about getting his hair cut. He said he likes his father and that they get along fine together when they are away from the rest of the family. He describes his sister as a pest who always gets her own way. In general, Tom's behaviour was quite ambivalent. He vacillated between ingratiation and direct criticism and between joviality and hostility. He seemed to utilize blandness and denial in attempts to handle his anger and fear.

Test Results and Impressions

On the Wechsler Intelligence Scale for Children Tom attained the following scores:

Verbal Scale IQ	=	*123 (Superior)*
Performance Scale IQ	=	*114 (Bright-Normal)*
Full Scale IQ	=	*120 (superior)*

Despite Tom' superior intellectual abilities, he frequently does not function at this level because of his negativistic approach to tasks and his tendencies to put forth minimally adequate efforts. Such tendencies reflect a lack of stamina and of enduring goals and are sufficient to prevent constructive planning for the future. Tom is able to see things as most people do; he is aware of conventionally approved standards of behaviour.

However, he maintains an active independence of thought and a stubborn insistence on the right to make up his own mind. Hence he finds it difficult to accept many conventional standards as being the appropriate ones for him to follow. Instead, his behaviour is most apt to be governed by his needs for immediate gratification. Tom has a great deal of anxiety about dealing with people and is unable to satisfy his needs by manipulating his environment in a socially acceptable manner. Hence he tends to avoid situations which require social conformity, despite his interest in achieving social adequacy. Furthermore, he has difficulties in forming close emotional relationships, and seems to vacillate between superficial emotional responsiveness and uncontrolled explosive outbursts. The test protocols suggest rather intense feelings of hostility which are not very well defended.

It appears that Tom's hostility steam largely from concerns about frustration of impulse gratification and particularly about frustration of oral-dependent needs. He is resentful of restrictions in general, and feels that social rules and regulations are unfair for the most part. For example, he told TAT stories about people who were put in jailor kicked out of school because they did not conform to certain standards, e.g., getting a license for a bicycle or getting a haircut. These attitudes appear to be related to Tom' attitudes toward parental figures. He sees mother figures as depriving, restricting, and making demands upon their children. He sees father figures as intervening in such situations, siding with the child and talking the mother into giving in to the child' wishes.

At the same time, he maintains strong underlying feelings of hostility toward father figures. For example, to TAT Card 8 BM he told a story about a "foolish" boy who shot a man accidentally and the man died; then the boy wasn't foolish any more and lived happily ever after. Then, too, in the story to card 12 M, the Lilliputians kill the giant. Tom' ambivalent feelings toward father figures as well as his apprehensiveness toward them is probably best illustrated in his story to TAT Card 13 MF: "This guy came in drunk, and he's wipin' shi eyes, cause he can't see. And he's an alcoholic and a dope fiend. And he's a teacher and well-he started all his pupils out on the dope and the alcohol and the principal found that out, so he shot him and then he shot himself and everybody laughed-no-that's not a good ending.

They died happily ever after. It appears that Tom is confused about the motivations of father figures and views them as destructive. Tom's sexual identification is primarily a passive, feminine one. However, he struggles diligently to maintain a facade of masculine assertiveness and becomes very anxious if others think of him as famine or refer to him as a sissy.

Diagnostic Impression

This appears to be the record of a primary behaviour disorder, passive aggressive type. Although the test record is not suggestive of brain damage, in view of the history of falls, etc., as well as the uncontrolled outbursts of rage, neurological and electro-encephalographic studies would seem warranted.

Summary Impression

Tom is an emotionally disturbed boy who is currently functioning at a superior level of intelligence. However, his motivation for achievement is sporadic and his behaviour is governed strongly by his needs for immediate gratification and his apprehensiveness about forming close attachments to others. Hence consistent intellectual efforts and effective achievement are minimal. The test records contain evidence of a passive, dependent orientation with hostility stemming largely from feelings of frustration. Ambivalent feelings toward parental figures are pronounced. Although reality awareness is adequate, there appears to be a lack of integration of conventional standards as guides for his own behaviour.

Some branches of child psychology have used the case study more frequently than others. Clinically oriented child psychologists employ it to a great extent. Although the case study helps to understand a single child, the method unfortunately suffers from some of the same defects as the early baby biographies. For example, the reliability of the information gained from informants may be questioned. Does the informant's relationship to the child colour his report? Do biases and emotional involvement could his memory of past events? Furthermore, how reliable are the test results in the case study? Often the very factors contributing to a child's failure at school also prevent him from scoring at his true level in an intellectual examination.

The IQ score on the test tells very little about his intellectual potential; it does not contribute to an understanding of the child's school difficulty. Perhaps an even more important consideration in evaluating the case study is the professional who interprets and assesses the data. His experience, theoretical basis, knowledge of research findings, and psychological understanding and skill all influence the value of the study. Finally, caution has to be exercised whenever one attempts to identify causes and effects. Was a child's rejection by his father the reason for a young girl's underachievement in school? Sweeping generalization and explanations are often made and conclusions drawn from unreliable, sketchy information.

A child's past can never be completely reconstructed. Rigorous safeguards are required in interpretation, and the person using case-study material must view his conclusions as tentative and subject to modification. Since the case study lacks many of the controls present in the experimental method, generalization of the data tends to be hazardous. No child' heredity or environment is identical to another child's. For this reason, factors causing a certain type of behaviour in one case may or may not produce the same result in others.

Psychological Ecology

Two psychologists, Robert Barker and Herbert Wright, have organized a Midwest Field Station in a small Kansas community, which they liken to a weather outpost or a biological field station. It has the purpose of collecting data about children and their daily lives, where they go, what they do, what they say, and with whom they interact. These two men argue that psychology, unlike many other sciences, began early and perhaps somewhat prematurely to gather data in laboratory situations. Psychologists manipulate and experiment with small isolated units of behaviour and with specific behaviour variables without first describing in detail some of the basic information of human life. They ignore such things as the frequency with which certain behaviours occur and the settings in which these take place.

It is different in other sciences. Geologists, biologists, chemists, and physicists know in considerable detail about the distribution in nature of the materials and processes with which they deal. Chemists know something about the laws governing the interaction of oxygen and hydrogen, and they also know how the elements are distributed in nature. Entomologists know the biological vectors of malaria, and they also know about the occurrence of these vectors over the earth. In contrast, psychologists know little more than laymen about the frequency and degree of occurrence of their basic phenomena in the lives of men-of deprivation, of hostility, of freedom, of friendliness, of social pressure, of rewards and punishments.

Although we have daily records of the behaviour of volcanoes, of the tides, of sun spots, and of rats and monkeys, there have been few scientific records of how a human mother cared for her children responded, what a family actually did and said during a meal time, or how any boy lived his life from the time he awoke in the morning until he went to sleep at night. The Study of behaviour in natural situations is given the name psychological ecology. This distinguishes it, say Barker and Wright, from experimental psychology which studies behaviour in artificially planned situations.

The Kansas work involves primarily observation and recording of everyday behaviour. To maintain some scientific precision and give some purpose to the observations, the psychological ecologists developed several categories. They call the stable parts of the physical and social milieu of a community, which by their very nature lead to standard and distinctive patterns of behaviour, behaviour settings. In their community, Midwest, U.S.A., these settings include the drug store, second-grade classroom, tavern, Methodist Regular Worship Service, cemetery, library, and Brownie's Regular Meeting. They designate the part of a stream of behaviour that describes a separate action and the situation in which it occurs a behaviour episode. Such episodes might include Painting the lips. Wiping paint off face, moving crate across pit.

A third category, the specimen record, is a collection of behaviour episodes. It is a detailed, sequential, narrative account by skilled observers of an individual child's behaviour through a more or less extended time. A book entitled One Boy's Day describes a day in the life of seven-year-old Raymond Birch. Eight observers took turns throughout the day observing and recording the boy's activities. Their objective was to include everything he did.

With some exceptions, the advantages, disadvantages, and usefulness of psychological ecology are the same as those of the baby biographies. One is impressed by the ability of a specimen record to capture the richness and complexity of the environment, the multitude of interactions which influence and shape a child's approach to people and situations, and the repetitiveness but yet apparent randomness of child behaviour. Moreover, the psychological ecologists seem to have avoided some of the shortcomings of the baby biographies. Well trained in observation and well grounded in the basic notions of psychology, they have deliberately attempted to separate the content of observation from interpretation; in fact, interpretation is indented and set off from observed data in a specimen record.

There is also the question of the extent to which the observer, as a result of his observation, changes or influences the individual being observed. Wright and Barker hold that children under the age of nine show neither sensitivity nor self-consciousness when being observed and soon adjust or adapt to the presence of an observer. This view seems to be supported by the relatively small effect an observer has on those being observed, especially when the observation continues over an extended period. Children tend not to act very long in ways differing from their usual behaviour. Finally, how representative is the group of children investigated? Although the community chosen was small enough to include all its children in the study, and its environment was undoubtedly less complex than that of a large urban area, it remains to be shown whether environmental complexity has psychological significance in the lives of children.

Controlled Approaches to Observation

Although observation lies at the base of all scientific research, "uncontrolled" observation, as we have seen, has many disadvantages. There is clearly a need for "controlled" observation of phenomena if meaningful comparisons and determinations are to be made. Scientists have developed many techniques for a controlled approach to observation, and in the following several pages we shall examine some of them.

Time Sampling

Arrington has defined time sampling as a method of observing the behaviour of human beings "under the ordinary conditions of everyday life in which observations are made in a series of short time periods so distributed as to afford a representative sampling of the behaviour under observation. The method was developed in order to overcome many of the weaknesses in the anecdotal descriptions of child behaviour. It was first used by Willard Olson to record the incidence of nervous habits in school children. Briefly, Olson marked off a record blank into five--minute intervals and entered a check whenever a designated behaviour occurred within each time interval among a classroom of children he was observing.

As originally conceived, time sampling yielded a score indicating the number of time intervals in which a specific behaviour manifested itself. Over the years the technique has undergone a great number of modifications. Most of them have resulted from a desire for finer precision in the sampling and recording of behaviour. The time interval has been shortened, often consisting of periods from 30 seconds to one minute. Only one child is observed at a time, with the observations distributed at random throughout the day as well as over a term of a week to several months. Symbols have been developed to record continuous behaviour instead of the occurrence or non-occurrence of specific acts.

For example, an elaborate set of such symbols has been devised to facilitate the objective description and recording of interaction between adults and children. This set use five-second time intervals and enters a series of category code letters on a prepared scoring sheet covering 16 minutes of continuous recording. Each square on the sheet represents five seconds of time, and the main categories symbolized by the code letters in this particular recording system include: non-attention, attentive observation, recognition, statement of condition or action, joint participation in activity, offering information, giving help, reassurance, seeking information, restricting, forbidding, disciplinary action, affection, compliance. Most of the time--sampling studies have been concerned with the social behaviour and social interactions of the young child.

Among the specific behaviours studied have been language frequency or content, ascendant behaviour, physical contents, quarrels, conflict, resistance, friendship patterns, cooperative and competitive behaviour, rivalry, and aggression. The principal advantages of this technique are the reliability and objectivity of recording. Attention is centred on a specific well-defined behaviour so that agreement about it among different observers can be achieved. Since scores are obtained usually in terms of frequency, the results can be treated statistically.

For example, the frequency, of quarrels can be related to age, sex, IQ, ratings of adjustment, and many similar factors. Time sampling will not work when the behaviour under study is neither overt nor readily observable. It is not feasible, either, for observing infrequent behaviour, such as the display of sympathy, compliance, or rare, private child behaviours, like fire setting. Because time sampling studies are restricted to the investigation of a specific behaviour, much of the richness and meaningfulness of child interaction goes unrecorded. Precision may be obtained at the cost of understanding. Moreover, data thus obtained can never of themselves yield information about cause and effect. If it were found that one child quarrelled more frequently than others, it would be necessary to draw on methods other than time sampling to determine the cause.

Psychometric Instruments

Although intelligence and personality tests are not customarily considered as vehicles for observation, they are, in fact, very short samples of behaviour and are extremely important in terms of their ability to disclose useful information. Knowledge of the results of an intelligence test provides insights into a child's ability in comparison with other children and into his level of intellectual performance. It also permits one to make predictions about how the child will cope with other tasks and other situations. The usefulness of a score on such psychometric tests that measure the speed and precision of mental processes depends on the meaningfulness of the theory on which the test is based, on the rigor of the procedure, and on the appropriateness of what is measured.

The object of a psychometric test is to provide in a brief interval of time information that would otherwise require hours of intimate contact to obtain. Tests, therefore, are shorthand observational techniques which enable us to make inferences about a larger body of data. For example, in administering a standard intelligence test to a five-year -old, we are not interested in his ability to answer the specific questions as such but in how these questions sample his general intelligence.

Questionnaires

Like the intelligence and personality tests, the questionnaire is a shorthand method for gaining a considerable amount of information on a specific problem in a brief interval of time. Its use, either written or oral, to obtain information about children has a long history. G. Stanley Hall is often credited with being the first to use this approach in child psychology. Under his supervision school teachers in the Boston area administered a general information questionnaire to beginning first-grade children. Although such a procedure seems commonplace today, it was a marked contribution at a time when unscientific speculation often substituted for the collection of data. One result of Hall's study was the realization that children's thinking did indeed differ from that of adults in terms not only of the quantity of information but also of its quality.

The following excerpt from Hall's original paper gives the content of the children's responses to certain questions included in the questionnaire. The chief field for such fond and often secret childish fancies is the sky. About three fourths of all questioned thought the world a plain and many described it as round like a dollar, while the sky is like a flattened bowl turned over it. The sky is often thin, one might easily break through; half the moon may be seen through it, while the other half is this side; it may be made of snow, but is so large that there is much floor-sweeping to be done in heaven. Some thought the sun went down at night into the ground or just behind certain houses, and went across on or under the ground to go up out of or off the water in the morning, but 48 per cent of all thought that at night it goes or rolls or flies, is blown or walks, or God pulls it up higher out of sight.

He takes it into heaven, and perhaps puts it to bed, and even takes off its clothes and puts them on in the morning, or again it lies under the trees where the angels mind it, or goes through and shines on the upper side of the sky, or goes into or behind the moon, as the moon is behind it in the day. It may stay where it is, only we cannot see it, for it is dark, or the dark rains down so, and it comes out when it gets light so it can see. More than half the children questioned conceived the sun as never more than 40 degrees from the zenith, and, naturally enough, city children knew little of the horizon. So the moon comes around when it is a bright night and people want to walk, or forget to light some lamps; it follows us about and has nose and eyes, while it calls the stars into, under, or behind it at night, and they may be made of bits of it. Sometimes the moon is round a month or two, then it is a rim, or a piece is cut off, or it is half stuck or half buttoned into the sky.

The stars may be sparks from fire-engines or houses, or, with higher intelligence, they are silver, or God lights them with matches and blows them out or opens the door and calls them in the morning. Only in a single case were any of the heavenly bodies conceived as openings in the sky to let light or glory through, or as eyes of supernatural beings-a fancy so often ascribed to children and so often found in juvenile literature. Thunder, which anthropologists tell us is or represents the highest God to most savage races, was apperceived as God groaning or kicking, or rolling barrels about, or turning a big handle, or grinding snow, walking loud, breaking something, throwing logs, having coal run in, pounding about with a big hammer, rattling houses, hitting the clouds, or clouds bumping or clapping together or bursting, or else it was merely ice sliding off lots of houses or cannon in the city or sky, hard rain down the chimney, or big rocks pounding, or piles of boards falling down, or very hard ruing, hail, or wind.

Lightning is God putting out his finger or opening a door, or turning on gas quick, or striking many matches at once, throwing stones and iron for sparks, setting paper afire, or it is light going outside and inside the sky, or stars falling. God keeps rain in heaven in a big sink, rows of buckets, a big tub or barrels, and they run over or he lets it down with a water hose through a sieve, a dipper with holes, or sprinkles or tips it down or turns a facet. God makes it in heaven out of nothing or out of water, or it gets up by splashing up, or he dips it up off the roof, or it rains up off the ground when we don't see it. The clouds are close to the sky; they move because the earth moves and makes them'. They are dirty, muddy things, or blankets, or doors of heaven, and are made of fog, of steam that makes the sun go, of smoke, of white wool or feathers and birds, or lace or cloth. In their changing forms many children, whose very life is fancy, think they see veritable men, or more commonly, because they have so many more forms, animals, faces, and very often God, Santa Claus, angels, etc., are also seen. Closely connected with the above are the religious concepts so common with children.

God is a big, perhaps blue, man, very often seen in the sky or in clouds, in the church, or even street. He came in our gate, comes to see us sometimes. He lives in a big palace or a big brick or stone house in the sky. He makes lamps, babies, dogs, trees, money, etc., and the angels work for him. He looks like the priest, Froebel, papa, etc., and they like to look at him, and a few would like to be God. He lights the stars so he can see to go on the side-walk or into the church. Birds, children, Santa Claus, live with him, and most but not all like him better than they do the latter. When people die they just go, or are put in a hole, or a box or a black wagon that goes to heaven, or they fly up or are drawn or slung up into the sky where God catches them.

They never can get out of the hole, and yet all good people somehow get where God is. He lifts them up, they go up on a ladder or rope, or they carry them up, but keep their eyes shut so they do not know the way, or they are shoved up through a hole. When children get there they have candy, rocking-horse, guns, and everything in the toy-shop or picture-book, play marbles, top, ball, cards, hockey, hear brass hands, have nice clothes, gold watches, and pets and ice-cream, and no school. There are men there who died in the war made into angels, and dolls with broken heads go there. Some think they must go through the church to get there, a few thought the horse cars run there, and one said that the birds that grow on apple-trees are drawn up there by the moon.

The bad place is like an over or a police station, where it burns, yet is all dark, and folks want to get back, and God kills people or beats them with a cane. God makes babies in heaven, the holy mother and even Santa Claus make some. He lets them down or drops them, and the women or doctors catch them, or he leaves them on the side-walk, or brings them down a wooden ladder backwards and pulls it up again, or mamma or the doctor or the nurse go up and fetch them sometimes in a balloon, or they fly down and lose off their wings in some place or other and forget it, or jump down to Jesus, who gives them around.

They were also often said to be found in flour-barrels, and the flour sticks ever so long, you know, or they grow in cabbages, or God puts them in water, perhaps in the sewer, and the doctor gets them out and takes them to sick folks that want them, or the milkman brings them early in the morning, they are dug out of the ground, or bought at the baby-store. Sometimes God puts on a few things or else sends them along if he doesn't forget it; this shows that no one since Basedow believes in telling children the truth in all things. The questionnaire has several methodological advantages over the earlier baby biographies.

Since questionnaires are designed to obtain information for specific purposes, their questions concentrate on a well-defined area. Besides, the researcher who uses them can obtain data from a large and representative sample in a relatively short time as compared with the baby biographies which were concerned with an individual child. These data can be related to several variables. For example, several researchers have administered Hall's questionnaire, with modifications, to children of various ages and related the subjects' scores to chronological age, mental age, IQ, socio-economic class, and sex noting the differences in total scores as well as in answers to specific questions. A wide variety of questionnaires has been employed with children and their parents, but one further example will suffice.

This questionnaire is directed to parents because knowledge of their attitudes and values is often essential to understanding the child's behaviour and personality. Questionnaires of this type may deal with statements of fact, such as the age of weaning the child, or with statements that tap attitudes and values that often relate to child-rearing procedures. In the following items excerpted from the Parent Attitude Research Instrument developed at the National Institute of Mental Health, the parent is asked to check the response that best represents his point of view for each statement.

Complete reliance on questionnaire responses has its weaknesses. Both "truthfulness" and unconscious falsification have to be considered. Some questionnaires contain a life scale designed to assess the respondent's willingness to falsify his replies. And there are researchers who believe that in assessing a parent' attitude toward certain topics, falsification as such becomes unimportant. Moreover, parents differ in willingness to divulge various kinds of information. Whether the parent comprehends the question as it was intended by the creator of the questionnaire is another matter of concern. In evaluating the findings emerging from a questionnaire, critical note must be taken of all these points.

Experimental Methods

One of the outstanding characteristics of this method is its control over the phenomena under investigation and the variables being observed. Scientific experiments are often called "questions put to nature," and the more precisely the questions are stated-that is, the more carefully the experiment is designed-the more exact and unambiguous the answers will be. Tracing a hypothetical problem of the kind, a child-development researcher might face may clarify various points. Shortly before the Second World War the effect of nursery-school experience on intelligence provoked an important controversy.

Some say that more heat than light was generated over the issue; if so, the fault lays with the methods used to examine it. Suppose we consider this problem. To begin with, the problem must be stated clearly and precisely or else the research will be neither well defined nor definitive. The problem is usually presented in the from of an hypothesis: nursery-school experience raises the IQ. Now the hypothesis needs to be tested. First, the IQs are tested of a group of children who have had a year of nursery school.

If their IQs are above 100 the hypothesis would seem confirmed, but the group chosen might have been well above average intelligence before going to nursery school. It might have been a biased sample. Therefore, the above-average IQs cannot be attributed to the nursery-school experience. Something has been learned, but it is necessary to test again. This time the children to be tested are selected at random from a large group of five-year-old to ensure an unbiased sample. The children are tested for intelligence and then re-tested after a year of nursery school.

If the measure of intelligence increases after the second test, the hypothesis would again seem confirmed. However, other factors than nursery-school experience might have improved the children's intelligence; in other words, the effects of other variables have not been controlled. The need is apparent for testing a similar group of children who are not exposed to nursery school. This leads to selection of a control group which does not undergo special treatment; the group accorded it is called the experimental group. Subjects for both groups are drawn from a large pool of children and assigned at random to either one. Often, to ensure the presence of no features that differentiate the two groups, both are matched on relevant variables, that is, other factors that might influence the results.

These might include such things as initial level of ability, sex of the child, or occupational status of the parent. Thus, only the one variable under investigation, the independent variable, is left to be systematically altered. Its effect on the dependent variable is then measured. To return to the problem at hand, the intellectual level of both control and experimental groups is measured by administration of a standard intelligence test. The experimental group is then given nursery-school training while the control group is not. Once again, intelligence tests are administered after a period of time. If the scores in the experimental group are significantly higher than those in the control group, the hypothesis is accepted.

If no difference in score exists, the hypothesis is obviously invalid. This method, then, holds all possibly relevant variables constant while identifying the effects of the systematic manipulation of the single variable under investigation. Although it is the most valuable method for research, this technique is not always applied in child development. In many important problems the researcher cannot manipulate the independent variable.

For example, rejection or acceptance by parents is thought

to have important bearing on child personality and adjustment. Yet it is manifestly impossible to manipulate this variable for research purposes. Under the circumstances, researchers turn to experiments in nature. They assess the adjustment of children who are thought to have suffered from parental rejection in the past and contrast this with the adjustment of a group of children thought to' be accepted. Even so, they can never be sure that the two groups do not differ in other variables, which perhaps helps to account for the difference in adjustments.

Nor can they ever be sure that parental rejection or acceptance does, in fact, affect adjustment, because they are unable to set up an experimental control, that is, a control group in distinction to an experimental group. The same criticism may be made of any studies that attempt to tie parental attitudes to a type of behaviour in the child when the parental attitudes are sought after the behaviour has appeared.

Interview Method

Although the interview has been used frequently as a clinical tool for understanding in individual case, it is now being employed increasingly as a research device for gaining information about a specific question under investigation. An interview is composed of several questions designed to elicit certain kinds of information. Often the questions are tested beforehand to find out if they do, in fact, obtain the information desired. Frequently the interview in tape recorded so that the interviewer need not rely on memory of sketchily written notes.

2

FUNDAMENTALS OF CHILD PSYCHOLOGY

The Need of a Study of Child Psychology

The teacher undertakes to co-operate in the education of the children committed to his care. He co-operates with the parent. The latter is expected to feed, clothe, and shelter the child, to look after his health, to see that he acquires a number of good habits, and to send him to school clean and tidy. Arrived in school, the child passes under the control of the teacher, whose chief duty is to instruct him. Education, then, includes instruction; but it embraces much more. In its widest sense, it includes all the influences which act upon an individual during his passage from the cradle to the grave. Now everything that happens to each of us leaves some trace.

But the occurrences of early life produce greater and more lasting effects than those of maturity. As we grow up, we become more or less set in the ways of thinking and acting to which we have been accustomed during the preceding years. Since the early part of life is so important, mankind almost everywhere takes special pains to influence the young. And usually the word education is reserved for these endeavours. Employing the word in this restricted sense, we may say that all young people receive some education during infancy and early childhood, most receive some during childhood proper, comparatively few at present obtain any considerable amount throughout adolescence. The object of education is to produce good behaviour, i.e. conduct which promotes the welfare of society.

I call therefore, says Milton, a complete and generous Education that which fits a man to perform justly, skillfully, and magnanimously all the offices both private and public of Peace and War. Now the teacher, with his thoughts bent on instruction, is apt to lose sight of the whole of which instruction is only a part. He is liable to mistake the means for the end. He is prone to think that the knowledge and skill which the child acquires under his supervision are things of value in themselves. But they are useful only in so far as they enable the child to act for the welfare of himself and the community. Knowledge is power only in so far as it can be applied.

Some boys who take high places at the school examinations are far from being successful after school life. Another reason why some teachers fail to recognise that good behaviour is the ultimate goal of their endeavours is that the meaning of the term is sometimes wrongly restricted. By good behaviour we should mean all that Milton implies in the passage just quoted. It includes the whole conduct of life-not merely punctuality, regularity, obedience, and respect, but what we do in every situation in which we find ourselves. It includes the way in which a man carries on his business, the part ne takes in public affairs, the manner in which he spends his leisure, the treatment he extends to his children, his wife, his relatives, his friends. Now it is obvious that all these things cannot be done well unless the individual in question has acquired considerable knowledge and skill.

The instruction, therefore, which the teacher gives is of great importance. It is, nevertheless, only a part of a larger whole-the education of the child. Both parent and teacher would do well to keep this ever in mind. At the outset, we attempted roughly to separate their functions. In practice, however, it is not advisable to make any such delimitation. The two should cooperate. What one does the other should appreciate, and what one fails to do the other should attempt to achieve. The teacher, then, must clearly understand that his instruction' is not complete in itself.

It should be most intimately connected with the other forms of training which the child undergoes. He cannot, therefore, draw a line round his instruction, and consider his work as ending with that. He must do what he can do further the whole process of education. The formation of good habits, the development of right tastes and inclinations, are even more important than more knowledge and skill. But thought and heart are not entirely separable. The right heart cannot exist without some considerable amount of thought. An idiot, for instance however harmless, can scarcely be said to have a right heart. And, conversely, without a good heart, sublime thoughts are to a certain extent impossible of comprehension. True, some scoundrels have been men of learning, men in whom the power of thought has attained an advanced stage.

Their knowledge and skill, indeed, have made them all the more potent as agents of evil. But it is doubtful whether such intelligent rogues, in spite of their learning, could ever really and completely think the thoughts of the just, upright, and honest person. There are, at any rate, some men who, on account of the depravity of their hearts, are unable to understand fully the point of view of the virtuous. Socrates of old went so far as to maintain that virtue is knowledge. He held that those who knew what were just and righteous acts would prefer nothing else, while those who did not know could not do them if they would.

The latter part of this statement goes no further than the couplet just quoted. But the former, whatever Socrates may have meant by it, can only be justified by reference to some such fundamental connection between thought and heart as we have attempted to emphasise. And even within the field of instruction, it is impossible to fix limits. Both in and out of a school a child learns a great many useful things for which the teacher cannot take credit. And it is the duty of the teacher to find out as far as possible what these things are in each particular case, and to ground his own lessons upon them. For, as we shall see more clearly later, we can only learn new things on the basis of knowledge already existing in our minds. Enough has now been said to show that no clear demarkation should be made between the instruction which is given in school and the remainder of education.

In pursuing his course of instruction the teacher should have ever in view the goal to which everything else is but a means-good behaviour. Knowing and doing are not to be artificially separated. We shall find, indeed, that they are most intimately connected, acting and reacting upon each other throughout life. If the teacher is to be highly successful in promoting good behaviour, he must know something of the processes involved. It is most dangerous to interferer with the working of natural forces which are not clearly understood. It is comparable to the rashness of a man who would undertake to sail a ship across the sea without any knowledge of navigation.

Put whereas in this case the perpetrator of errors would be likely to suffer in his own person, the ignorant educator often escapes scot free. He wrecks a ship, but he himself is not in it! Some educationists have been so impressed with the errors of the past that they have forbidden all interference with the process of early development. Thus Rousseau declared that nobody should be allowed to teach the child anything before the latter reaches the age of twelve. If we followed his advice, we should have to abolish all our elementary schools as at present constituted. But nature, left to itself, does not develop wholly on the lines necessary for man's welfare. Just as a garden when neglected by man soon becomes a wilderness of weeds, so a child left to himself would soon become a brutish creature of no use in any civilised community.

Such a case did once occur. A very young boy was left, by some misadventure, in the woods, where he managed to survive. When discovered and captured after many years, he was little more than a wild beast. And although a distinguished Frenchman attempted to educate him, the results feel far short of those obtained with normal boys. With respect to a great many things, he was already set, and little improvement could be effected. Rousseau has, however, in spite of his exaggerated statements, called our attention to the fact that we are dealing with natural forces. And, though we find it necessary to interfere with them, we must remember that they still obey certain laws. Just as in the physical world we interfere with the course of nature in order to produce certain results, so in the world of human nature we attempt to make various changes by educative treatment.

But in the latter case, as in the former, we must understand the forces with which we deal. We cannot alter the laws of nature. All we can hope to do is to utilise them in order to produce the results we desire. But if we do not understand them, our efforts are likely to end in disaster. The teacher, therefore, who desires to produce that kind of behaviour which we call good must understand the laws of behaviour in general. In other words, he must study psychology. For Psychology may be...defined as the positive science of the conduct of living creatures. It attempts to describe and explain our behaviour. But since much of our behaviour is due to certain inner or mental states of knowledge, feeling, and impulse, psychology endeavours to investigate these. Now each of us can experience only his own mental states.

In dealing with others, we see only the resulting conduct; the inner states which are often largely responsible for that conduct can never be directly examined by us. We can make inferences as to their character only on the basis of our own experience of such inner states. Hence the starting point of all psychology is introspection, of looking within. This branch of psychology is often referred as introspective psychology. Another name is analytic psychology. It is so called because we endeavour to find the elements of which each whole state of mind is composed. But introspective psychology does not explain all our behaviour. And, even if it could, it would not also completely explain the behaviour of children.

For introspective psychology results from the analysis of the mental processes of adults. Children are not naturally given to introspection. And one of the greatest mistakes we could make would be to project our own mental states into them. We must not think of children as adults on a small scale. Unfortunately memory is not sufficiently reliable, even with the best of us, to enable us to reconstruct the past. We do well to study the relics of our childhood, to read any of our early epistles which may have been preserved, to get our parents and other friendly elders to describe our former selves as far as they are able. But, after all has been attempted, we are still far from understanding the mental processes of the child. The only way to make further progress is to observe carefully the behaviour of the children around us, attempting to explain it in terms of mental processes like our own, but remaining continually on our guard against supposing that the mental processes of the child are the same as our own. Our present mental processes are possible only after a long period of development.

Those of the child are probably much more simple. They doubtless become more and more complex as the child grows up. The increasing complexity is due partly to a natural process of growth, partly to the kinds of experience through which the child passes. It is this latter factor which teacher and parent can most definitely modify. It is here, then, that education has its chance. And the more we can understand of the process of development, and ascertain what part of it is due to a natural process of growth, what part to the various kinds of experience through which the child passes, the more successful we are likely to be in our education of the child.

The examination of the processes of mental development which are possible from infancy to maturity is usually called genetic psychology. It is almost unnecessary to add that this branch of psychology, though it must always follow some discipline in introspective psychology, is by far the most important to the teacher. The young teacher, however, must not suppose that the study of a text-book on genetic psychology will by itself enable him to understand and successfully deal with all his pupils. In the first place, this science is still in its early stages. We know comparatively little of child nature. In the second place, it must be borne in mind that, in spite of many points of similarity, no two children are exactly alike. In such a book as this, it is possible to deal only with the points of similarity.

We shall note many principles which apply to children in general. And a knowledge of these will be of extreme value to the teacher. But no one can be highly successful in dealing with children who does not make a study of each one individually, so that variations of treatment are possible. Many teachers, indeed, who have never studied psychology as a science are extremely successful because of the keen interest which they display in each of their pupils.

3

Child as An Individual

It would be difficult to overestimate the effects of parental behaviour on children's psychological growth and behaviour. Home influences probably outweigh the effects of all other environmental impacts combined in determining the fundamental organization of children's behaviour. According to psychoanalytic theory, social values and controls are largely interiorized (made an integral part of the child's superego) on the basis of early parent-child interactions. The foundations of children's social attitudes and skills are obviously laid in the home. Patterns of dependence-independence, ascendance-submission, cooperation-competition, and conservativism-liberalism have their genesis in early parent-child interactions within the home. Affectional tendencies which are so important to psychological adjustment in adult life are dependent on the nature of parent-child relationship. The home is truly the greatest socializing agency in all contemporary cultured. In view of the importance of home experiences in the child's life, it is small wonder that Freud was able to trace most of man's psychological conflicts back to traumatic experiences during the first four or five years of life.

Parents are varied in their rearing practices and frequently unpredictable. Their interactions with children are often tinged with odd combinations of tradition, personal prejudice, emotional regard, and rule-of-thumb procedures. Few parents ever verbalize doubt as to their competence to guide the psychological growth of their children. Most parents cannot afford to doubt their abilities to rear children in the best possible manner. Self-doubts are too painful when one has such an emotionalized attitude towards his problems. However, it is clear that child rearing is fraught with self-doubt, insecurity, and psychological pain for the average parent. The evidence is all too apparent in parent's rationalizations and projections: "What was good enough for me is good enough for my children!" (This rationalization belies itself, since it is usually delivered in a highly emotional way). "The trouble with my kids is that the teacher don't lick 'em!" "My parents were always too strict with me. I'm going to go easy on my kids."

Three types of information about children are especially useful to teachers and parents. The first is knowledge of methods of studying children; the second is knowledge of the kind of behaviour which may be expected of children in each of the overlapping stages of development; the third is knowledge of how this behaviour is acquired and modified. Knowledge of methods of studying children is necessary because, although adults are continually observing and passing judgment on children in whom they are interested, such study in usually unscientific. Everyone who comes in contact with children studies them in a more or less incidental way.

The old coloured mummy, who when asked how she knew the water for the baby' bath was of the right temperature, said, "When de baby gets blue, ah know de water 'too cold; when he gets red, ah know it's too hot," was studying the child in her own way. Her method, however, was not a scientific one, and, as is commonly the case with "snap" judgements, frequently resulted in serious errors. One father said, "The boy is just plain lazy." Medical examination showed that the child was sick. Certain college authorities refused an applicant admittance to college "not college material," they said. A study of the past history of this student showed him to be exceptionally well-qualified for college work.

A physician suggested that a small boy afflicted with nervous twitchings, headache, and speech difficulty might be suffering from a brain tumour. Further study and treatment of the child proved that the cause of the symptoms was psychological. Additional evidence of the inadequacy of superficial observation in giving a true estimate of a child is indicated by people's failure to distinguish between intelligent and stupid children by merely looking at their pictures. One aim of this book, then, is to show parents and teachers how to study children more scientifically-how to make accurate, impersonal, systematic observations over a period of time, and to mental tests in studying the normal development or the special problems of a given child.

The only reliable source of information about a particular child is that obtained by studying the child himself. The second type of information which the book endeavours to give concerns the kind of behaviour to be expected from children of a given age. Such knowledge is very helpful in studying children, because we observe more accurately when we know what to look for. Knowing the characteristic commonly found in children of a given age is useful in directing attention along better controlled lines of observation. What, for example, can be expected of baby at birth? What motor ability, memory, play activities, reasoning, and imagination can be expected of an average five-year old? Strictly speaking, however, there is no such thing as an "average" or a "normal" child.

There are at present no adequate standards of child development. The picture of a "normal" child is still incomplete, but even an incomplete picture is useful for purposes of comparison. It helps the parent and teacher to see the extent to which the behaviour of an individual child differs from the reported behaviour of other children of the same age. Even though there are marked individual differences in infants, the younger the child, the more definitely can his behaviour be predicted. As he grows older and environment increasingly exerts its influence on him, the number of possible responses he may make becomes greater.

This increasing complexity of behaviour may be represented diagrammatically by an inverted triangle, the apex representing the child at birth, and the broadening sides representing later stages of development. At birth the kinds of reactions are relatively few. During the pre-school period the responses of a child of a given age become increasingly varied and less predictable. At adolescence the behaviour of the boy and girl is extremely complex. Knowledge of normal development would be the only thing necessary if children, like Topsy, "just growed." But they do not always grow in the way they should. They need guidance.

Therefore, a third type of knowledge is needed--knowledge of how children acquire their ways of acting, thinking, and feeling. By knowing how habits are formed, the parent and teacher will better able to guide a child's development, largely through controlling his physical and social environment. No further information would be needed if children built only good habits. But bad habits, like the poor, seem to be always with us. Scientific guidance from birth will reduce the number of bad habits in later childhood, but for many years to come teachers will find in their classes children with undesirable ways of behaving more or less firmly established. Since mothers are not omnipotent, omniscient, and omnipresent, undesirable responses will creep into their children's behaviour like weeds into a garden. Everyone associated with children has found himself in situations which have made him realize his need of more knowledge.

A child of three or four years says "I won't" or "No" to every request. What should the parent do? A child of five screams and kicks when required to do something he does not want to do. How should such a child be treated? A child in the first grade does everything he is told to do but nothing on his own initiative. How can the teacher help him to develop independence and self-reliance? An average child continually fails in his arithmetic. What can the teacher do about it? A fourth-grade child reads silently an average of one hundred words a minute.

Is this slow, medium, or rapid reading for his age? A child is very nervous and cries when taking tests of any kind. How may this tendency be overcome? A first-grade child will not sit still, but runs about the room continually. What can the teacher do with him? A third grade child is timid and seclusive. What treatment is demanded for the best development of such a child? Innumerable situations such as these continually arise in dealing with children. One aim of this book is to help the parent or teacher in recognizing some of the most common of these undesirable ways of behaving, in studying the possible causes, and in removing the causes and rebuilding bit by bit the desirable behaviour.

This work is remedial, but children as they are made it necessary. Children as they ought to be are the product of hereditary endowment and environment. To "increase in wisdom and stature" day by day, without lapses, without retardation, is the ideal of growth. To describe some of the known features of desirable development, to state some of the factors that make optimum development possible, and to suggest "first aid" for some common errors and accidents, are the three chief purposes of the following chapters. Each section will deal specifically with the characteristic behaviour, methods of study, and prevalent problems of one period of childhood.

The following periods will be discussed: the pre-natal period, birth, the first year of life, the pre-school period, the elementary period, and the high school period. These divisions have been recognized in many educational systems and so form convenient dividing points for describing the development of an individual. In reality, however, growth does not progress by separate stages but is continuous. Each period merges imperceptibly into the next and must be explained by what has gone before. Maturing is a continuous process. Each month of life is important and has its special opportunities and problems. Habits are being modified continuously.

Changes in environment require new accommodations on the part of the individual. Entering the kindergarten or first grade, beginning high school work, going away from home to college are new situations which demand of the child special new adjustments. The period of infancy and young childhood has the advantage of being the period in which many habits are initiated. "Well begun is half done." Habits are easier to form than to break. Habits, both good and bad, established in these first 'years tend to persist. Children seem not to outgrow their early experiences-especially vivid emotional crises-as they do their dresses and shoes. These experiences have been found to be retained and to influence adult behaviour.

The extreme view of the importance of the first years of life may be illustrated by a quotation from Alfred Adler, the Austrian psychiatrist. He is of the opinion that "'a child has formed and shaped his behaviour pattern at the end of his third year of life." Thereafter, Alder says, the child is not modified to any great extent by his environment, but makes his experience conform to his preconceived pattern. "He takes an experience and twists, turns, distorts, reshapes it until it fits into his pre-determined scheme of things." Although these statements probably give an exaggerated picture of the influence of the pre-school period on all phases of the child's development, there is no doubt about the importance of this period from a physical standpoint, and little doubt about its importance emotionally. Gesell states that "one-third of all the deaths of the nation occur below six years." Accidents, contagious diseases, and malnutrition are more prevalent at this time than in the school periods. Any physical defect grows worse more rapidly during the first five years than during any other period.

The significance of the pre-school period for the physical welfare and mental hygiene of the child, for education, for parents, for philanthropy, and for psychological research is well summarized by Arlitt. Because these early years are important and because fundamental principles can be explained best in connection with the less complex activities of the young child, a larger amount of space is devoted to this period than to the succeeding stages of development. Moreover, a larger amount of accurate knowledge is available with reference to the pre-school period than to any other. Although until recently the pre-school years were the most neglected phase of childhood in respect to scientific study, at the present time attention is focused on the young child to a greater extent than on the older child.

Tests, observation, and controlled experimentation should be applied to the school period with the same skill and assiduity that have been used in the pre-school period, in order to amass a similar body of detailed information concerning all phases of the life of individual children of the school age. It is a fact that a child's behaviour at adolescence is a natural and inevitable culmination of his previous development, and there is doubtless much truth in the idea of the infantile origin of conflicts and the persistence of attitudes acquired in early life; nevertheless the attitudes of adolescence are especially important in determining later development and deserve more emphasis than many psychologists and psychoanalysts have given them. No one phase of development is more important than any other.

The Baby at Birth

Certain questions arise concerning the newborn baby: What is his physical appearance? How much should he weight? What movements can he be expected to make? What does he see and feel and think?

Physical Characteristics

The baby' pulse is rapid-one hundred and thirty-six beats per minute as compared with sixty-eight to seventy-two beats of the average adult. His respiration is also more rapid than an adult', being sixty respirations per minute instead of eighteen. His bones lack firmness, for they are still in the making. One baby may weight three times as much as another at birth.

The majority of babies weight between six and nine pounds and are from fifteen to twenty-four inches long. Physicians sometimes divide babies at birth into two groups-under-fours and over-fours. Those weighing less than four pounds need very special care in every respect. A baby born during the seventh or eighth month instead of the ninth month usually has a deficiency of iron stored in his body. This handicap of the pale premature may be overcome to some extent by feeding him a half teaspoonful of spinach juice, sifted spinach, egg yolk, or other food rich in iron as early as possible. A fat baby likewise presents certain problems. Six or seven pounds is a desirable weight.

Physical Appearance

Anatole France describes the birth of Little Pierre as follows: "Meanwhile I set up such a yelling that they all though I was going to choke. I was red as a tomato and unanimously pronounced an ugly little creature. A newborn baby does not look mighty like a rose to anyone but a poet or his parents. To unprejudiced eyes he is a homely little creature, red and wrinkled. He has a relatively enormous head and abdomen, and relatively short legs. The baby' brain is approximately seven times as heavy as an adult's in proportion to the total weight of the body. An adult of the same proportions would be a fit subject for a freak show in a circus. The infant' eyes wander independently of each other and often cross.

The Activity of the Newborn

What may a mother expect her baby to do at birth? She should expect him to cry. In fact, crying occurs automatically with the first respiration. It is the most frequent sing that breathing has begun. Some babies have been reported to have sneezed themselves into the world. A few, bored from the beginning, start life with a yawn. Crying, sneezing, and yawning are responses which can be called forth at birth.

Breathing, circulation, and digestion are also processes ready to function. The pupil of the eye will grow larger or smaller in response to varying intensity of light.

The baby usually makes sucking movements, but not always. Sometimes it is difficult to induce the baby to take his first meal. The only baby that is perfectly still is a dead baby. From the time of birth, the baby is constantly moving in an aimless way-bringing the hands to the head, beating the bed coverings, making grimaces which sometimes seem like real smiles and sometimes are as grotesque as the expressions of gargoyles. He makes many kinds of jerky, kicking, random movements, which may be due to the rapid growth of nerve centres or to other internal stimuli. Even at birth a baby can turn its head far enough to permit free breathing. Babies do not smother themselves, as some old wives say. Suffocation may be due to thymus-gland trouble, but tales of accidental suffocation have no foundation in fact and should not frighten mothers.

If a baby is placed face down in pillow, he will turn the head so that he can breathe easily. In addition to the essential life activities and the manifold random movements, the baby at birth has a bag of special tricks. If a rod is placed in his hands, he will grasp it and support his entire weight hanging from it. Watson tested this reaction in infants and found that all but two per cent of the normal infants in the experiment could hang from a bar at least a fraction of a second. One held on as long as a minute. If the sole of the baby's foot is stroked, the great toe usually flies up and the other toes spread out like a fan or sometimes curl under.

This action, called the Babinski reflex, is normal for an infant but abnormal for an adult. Adults' toes bend down when the sole of the foot is tickled. Certain defence reactions are present at birth. If the inner side of one knee is pinched, the other foot is drawn up and begins to push at the hand that is pinching. If the baby's nose is held, his hands reach upward and strike at the thing that is causing the trouble. Cats, dogs, and other animals show these same defence reactions when they are similarly annoyed.

Physical Defects

Any marked deformity should be corrected as soon as possible. A club foot, for example, can be made normal if treated promptly, whereas if the defect is neglected the child will be lame for life. Blindness from Babies' Sore Eyes would practically never occur if a prophylactic were used in the eyes of every infant immediately after birth, and if every case of redness, swelling, and discharge from the eyes of infants were promptly and adequately treated. A bulletin of the National Committee for the Prevention of Blindness describes specifically the simple treatment of the eyes which should be given as a routine procedure immediately after birth.

Physical Care of the Baby

The first twenty-four hours of a baby' life are under the direction of the doctor or nurse rather than the mother. The first bath, the first feeding, and the first dressing are the work of an expert. The first garment placed on a newborn baby is the abdominal binder, which holds the navel dressing in place. It is worn only during the first few weeks. A knitted fabric of cotton and wool is very satisfactory for the binder because it expands and contracts with the abdomen, and so is neither too tight just after a meal nor too loose before.

The Baby's Thoughts

No matter how much like a serious thinker the baby looks, he is probably not having any "long, thoughts"-or even short ones. This "blest philosopher," as Words worth calls him, is conscious of masses of light and darkness about him, is startled by loud noises, resists hampering of his movements, and feels contented or uncomfortable according to his bodily condition. But he does not think about these things. None of the movements or feelings have yet acquired sufficient meaning to make them significant. William James describes the baby's mental state as a "big, blooming, buzzing confusion."

The Gestalt psychologists claim that "the first phenomena

are qualities or figures upon a ground"-a vague but real pattern. Vague impressions result in vague meanings; and without clear-cut meanings thinking is impossible. Meanings, and consequently thinking, develop gradually. Moreover, even if the baby could think, he would have little time for this activity, because he sleeps about twenty out of the twenty-four hours. Although the newborn baby's repertoire of physical, mental, and emotional reactions is limited, he has the capacity for building new movements and perfecting those he already has; for finding more meaning in the world about him; for making connections between what he sees and what he does; and for modifying his actions by thought.

The baby' Sensations

Pressure

One indication that the baby has some sense of pressure is the soothing effect produced by stroking or patting.

Sight

Tiedemann who is 1787 attempted scientific observation of babies, noted that immediately after birth infants turn their eyes to the light. Other observers have likewise noted that some babies turn toward a light as soon as they are born. Seeing, as we understand it, does not occur at birth. The mother's face, a bright pink rattle, and other objects are not yet distinguished by the baby. He has only a vague consciousness of light disturbed from time to time by bum of darkness. He turns toward light much as a plant does.

Taste

Most newborn babies are aware of strong tastes such as quinine, acid, sugar, and salt, during the first week, babies attempt tô get rid of bitter or sour substances placed in their mouths and make satisfied sucking movements in response to sweet and salty substances. They do not appear to distinguish mild flavours. Cod-liver oil, castor oil, and olive oil all seem alike to them. They take turnip juice as eagerly as orange juice.

Hearing

Hearing may be delayed several days, but the majority of babies after the first forty-eighth hours of life will squirm when a sound is made close to their ears. The Kuhlmann test places a definite response to sound at three months. Miss Shinn who observed and wrote the biography of her baby niece, reports the first sign of hearing on the third day when the baby started violently at the sound of paper being torn.

Thirst and Hunger

Thirst is present from the beginning and demands satisfaction more frequently than many mothers realize. A thirsty baby will cry as lustily as a hungry one. Hunger is not always present at birth, but is soon experienced.

Comfort and Discomfort

Lying in one position probably causes feelings of fatigue which are relieved when a cry brings someone to pick the baby up. Most babies at first cannot turn themselves over, and the careful nurse moves the baby occasionally from one side to another to relieve these feelings of fatigue. The baby experiences general feelings of comfort and discomfort-comfort when it is warm and fed and unhampered in its movements; discomfort when it is cold and hungry and restricted in some of its movements.

Temperature

Babies are also sensitive to cold and warmth at birth. Frequently they will stop crying when properly protected from the cold air of their new environment.

4

Basic Instincts Temperaments

The developmental period of the newborn infant, or neonate, is generally considered to include the first ten to fourteen days of postnatal life. According to medical terminology this period extends from the time of birth until the navel heals the latter occurring in most cases by approximately ten days of age. A substantial number of controlled observations and research studies have been conducted to determine the sensory, emotional, and mental development of the human infant during segment of the life span.

At the time of birth the human infant is helpless and would obviously perish if left to forage for himself. The newborn's most valuable asset is an unparalleled potentiality for continued growth and development. Although the higher order apes have fairly long periods of infancy, most infrahuman organisms are not dependent on their parents for such an extended period of time. Indeed, many organisms inferior to the mammal in phylogenetic evolution are abandoned by both parents at the time of conception. However, it is obvious that such organisms do not posses comparable potentialities for the extremely complex patterns of behaviour that are inherent in the human infant. One of the major purposes of child psychology is to investigate the various conditions under which these complex patterns of behaviour emerge. The study of any developmental process involves an historical perspective, a tracing of antecedents. In order to obtain a meaningful, interrelated continually of knowledge about the child's development it is necessary to investigate his earliest patterns of growth and behaviour. Since some of these behaviour patterns can be observed and identified in man's fetal and neonatal periods, scientific investigations during these early stages of human development contribute fundamental data of the science of human behaviour.

Furthermore, the description of the interrelationships in human behaviour is fundamentally advanced by controlled observations of the newborn infant. At this early stage of development, behaviour is less complex, environmental conditions can be controlled with greater ease, and twenty-four-hour observation is more feasible – all of which permit more exact investigations of psychological growth than are possible in later life when these comparatively simple conditions no longer exist.

Scientific studies conducted during the neonatal period have also provided data useful in the formulation of certain trends in psychological growth. An identification and precise description of developmental trends in startle pattern, optically determined nystagmus, and the like have made diagnosis and prognosis possible during this early period of human development. The employment of conditioned response procedures has also made it possible, for example, to diagnose impairments in visual acuity during early infancy; children with defective hearing can also be identified and corrective measures attempted.

Up to the present we have been concerned principally with cognition or knowing. We have tried to keep in mind, however, that its only value is for behaviour. We may, indeed, go still further, and declare that cognition itself is behaviour. It is a form of activity. The man who thinks is often working harder than the man, who is doing manual labour. Both processes require the expenditure of energy. And both lead to what we call fatigue when they are prolonged. In one case, it is chiefly the brain which is fatigued; in the other case, the muscle. We may say, then that not only do we learn by doing, but that learning is itself a form of doing. All the mental processes which we have been studying could not go on without an inner force pressing forward.

This force has been variously name some have called it will. But this word is used with varying signification by different psychologists. Some have called it attention. But this again is used in different senses. Perhaps the best word to use is conation. Conation, then, may be regarded as the most fundamental constituent of all conscious activity. Cognition only arises and develops in its services. Percepts and ideas are methods of grappling with given situations. They involve tendencies to go on with our life in certain directions. Or they may be considered as so many differentiated channels through which conation flows and which it has worn out for itself. Without them, of course, conation would be a poor thing. It would be nothing but a blind craving. It might be very powerful, but it could achieve little, because of its lack of organization.

It would be like the steam-power which has no delicately constructed machinery to set in motion. To achieve great things in industry we must have both motor power and machinery. One is of no account without the other. So with the human being, he must have conation, and that conation must be controlled and directed in certain ways. In the preceding chapters we have been considering the cognitive aspect of processes which are throughout animated by conation. We have, as it were, examined the machinery in action without paying much attention to the forces which are responsible for that activity. It now becomes necessary, therefore, to examine more closely the springs of that activity. We have seen that all mental activity involves corresponding nervous activity.

The foundation of the activity spending nervous activity. The foundation of the activity of the human body is a found of energy stored up in the nervous system, ever ready to be liberated when "touched off' by some stimulus. The impulses produced take varying courses according to the structure and organisation of the nervous system. Conation, therefore, depends largely on the state of the body. A healthy vigorous person is capable of more activity than an unhealthy and feeble one. But the vigour of a person' activity does not depend merely on his health and strength. A healthy boy may be very slow in cleaning a pair of boots, but very smart and energetic in a game of football. In other words, he responds more vigorously to certain stimuli than to others. Why is this? Why have already seen that the impulses produced by a given stimulus take varying courses according to the structure and organisation of the nervous system. But that structure and organisation can not only determine the course of an impulse but the magnitude of its effects. Just as a given individual may receive a warm welcome in one hour, with much consequent excitement and activity, but a very could one in another, scarcely any "fuss" being made of him, so a given stimulus may lead to very active responses in one individual, and to few if any in another.

A mother will often start out of her slumber at the feeblest cry from her baby, though she is not disturbed by much louder noises. Her nervous system is so organised that it responds in a particularly vigorous manner to sounds and other stimuli coming from this child. She was not born with these arrangements in her nervous system, but they have developed later in life, just as a tree brings forth flowers and fruit after some lengthy period of growth. They can therefore be called lengthy period of growth. They can therefore be called innate or congenital. If a woman had neither children nor other creatures to fondle, these special arrangements would be little utilised and would tend to die out for lack of use. Such a system of connections, together with the tendency which it involves to respond in a certain way to certain impulses, is called an instinct.

This particular instinct is called the parental instinct.

Human beings have a large number of instincts, though few are present ready-made at birth. We shall presently enumerate the more important instincts. Meanwhile, it will suffice to point out that a great deal of our behaviour--both that which involves more especially thinking and that which involves much bodily movement-is due to the instincts which we possess. We respond to certain stimuli and neglect others because "we are made that way." But this does not account for the whole of an individual's behaviour. Let us take another case. In a restaurant one night a waiter feel asleep. A number of young men shouted various names at him such as "Smith!" "Brown!" "Robinson!" But he responded to none of them. At length one of the party used another word. He spoke far less forcibly than in the case of the first names. But the moment he enunciated the word "Waiter!" The man sprang up as if shot. Now we cannot speak of a definite instinct in this case. Nobody is born a waiter. Yet the readiness of the responses point to a system of connections quite as strongly organised as an instinct.

In this case, however, they have been formed during the lifetime of the individual, through frequent repetition, as was explained in dealing with association. Such a system of connections with its tendency to produce behaviour of a certain kind in response to certain stimuli is called a habit. Now according to Professor James, "Ninety-nine hundredths or possibly nine hundred and ninety-nine thousandths of our activity is purely automatic and habitual, from our rising in the morning to our lying down each night. Our dressing and undressing, our eating and drinking, our greetings and partings, our hat-raising and giving way for ladies to precede, nay, even most of the forms of our common speech, are things of a type so fixed by repetition as a almost to be classed as reflex actions. To each sort of impression we have an automatic, ready-made response." This is probably a somewhat exaggerated statement. But even if it is only partly true, it emphasises the extreme importance of cultivating good habits and endeavouring to destroy bad habits in children. For youth is the time of plasticity.

The habits formed then are likely to remain, becoming stronger and stronger, throughout life. It is on such grounds as this that character has been called a bundle of habits. But the statement of Professor James seems to conflict with the statement lately made to the effect that "a great deal of our behaviour...is due to the instincts which we possess." How can the greater portion of our behaviour be ascribed in one placed to instinct, in another to habit? This can only be done if habit and instinct overlap in some way. And that is precisely what is the case. When we begin life, we have no habits.

This is obvious from our definition of habit. We have, it is true, few instincts. But many develop rapidly as time proceeds. Fear, anger, self-display, self-abasement, imitation, curiosity, play, and the tendency to handle and manipulate things soon show themselves. Now an instinctive action is called forth under certain circumstances. Thus a strange face may cause fear, interruption in what one is doing may arouse anger. Such circumstances are continually recurring, and the instinctive actions aroused by them are consequently repeated. But the repetition of any series of actions tends to fix that series; it becomes a habit. We seen, then, that our instincts themselves become habits. Viewing these habits from the point of view of their foundation, we may call them instincts. But since, when they become fixed, so much of their stability is due to repetition, we may still continue to call them habits. From one point of view they are instinctive, from the other habitual.

We may therefore use a term coined by Lloyd Morgan, and call them instinct-habits. It is thus that we can reconcile our own statement with that of Professor James. But these instinct-habits are not merely fixed forms of the congenital tendencies on which they have been founded. In the course of their development, the instincts are more or less profoundly modified by the particular nature of the experience through which the individual passes. In addition to this, other habits can be formed more or less independently of the instincts. Both kinds of change are largely due to the same causes-to the pleasure and pain experienced by the individual in the course of his responses. Pleasure and pain make us more selective in our activities; they consequently sharpen the intelligence; and this cooperates with them, both to produce various modifications and combinations in the instinct-habits and also to set on foot other habits. Those habits, however, which are largely based on strong and lasting instincts are usually the most powerful. And it is therefore important that we should make a survey of the instinctive elements out of which so much of our behaviour is elaborated. Mr. McDougall, one of the greatest authorities on this matter, divides what are usually called instincts into two classes -

- Instincts proper, and
- Innate tendencies.

According to him, what are properly to be called instincts are distinguished each of them by a special kind of emotion or excitement, and also by a characteristic form of movement. The movements for each of these instincts, including as they do facial expressions, have often been depicted by artists, and some of them are frequently produced artificially on the stage. Nobody has ventured to give a complete and final list of all the instincts. And no claim is here made either to exhaustiveness or to absolute correctness in enumerating the following :

INSTINCTS OF MAN

The Instinct of Repulsion

Like the last, this is an aversive tendency. Its corresponding emotion is disguise. In its primitive form, it involves the rejection from the mouth of noxious and evil--tasting substances, and the shuddering aversion from slimy and slippery things. In the course of development, however, ideational complexes as well as perceptual come to excite it. Thus the actions, speech, or general character of a man may cause our disgust. The teacher can make use of such facts in connection with the moral education of his pupils. Evil characters can be so shown up against the background of noble characters that the disgust of the children can be strongly aroused.

The Instinct of Night and Concealment

This instinct is more usually referred to by the name of its accompanying emotion, fear. Among the objects which often arouse it may be mentioned loud, uncanny noises, darkness, strange objects. All things which do us harm, causing pain, are liable to arouse fear, especially in cases where we are powerless to deal with them. It seems probable that both severe pain and the unfamiliar owe much of the influence which they exert to the co-operation of a more general and fundamental innate tendency-that of self-preservation. We speak of the object of fear as danger. Our remote ancestors must frequently have been overtaken and mauled by unfamiliar things and creatures.

The fact that loud noises and darkness give frequent occasions for fear must be explained largely by associations formed in the course of racial development. We must bear in mind that "our savage ancestors through innumerable generations were accustomed to meet with dangerous beasts in caverns, especially bears during the night and in the woods, and that thus an inseparable association between the perception of darkness of caverns and woods, and fear took place, and was inherited." At the same time it must be admitted that any inherited associations may be aided by new ones formed during the life-time of the individual. Thus the fear of some people in the presence of dogs has been traced to the fact that they were bitten in infancy. And sometimes they have no remembrance of the fact! More often, perhaps, associations involving definite recall are formed.

Thus, as Lock tells us, foolish maids talk about "goblins and sprights" as plopping the darkness, and so arouse fear which might otherwise never exist. Education endeavours both to rid the child of unnecessary fear and to make use of the instinct in other cases as an inhibitor of undesirable tendencies. It achieves the former object by making the child familiar with the cause of his dread in those cases where clear understanding demonstrates the harmlessness of the thing in question. And it uses fear in various forms of punishment and threatening. The child can escape the punishment by avoiding certain undesirable forms of behaviour. Needless to say, we only resort to the production of fear in extreme cases where nothing else can be done.

The Instinct of Pugnacity

The accompanying emotion is anger. There is no particular kind of object which excites this instinct. It is aroused by any object which causes or implies opposition to the free exercise of any other impulses. The tendency excited is one to break down opposition. Although parents and teachers find this instinct very troublesome when it conflicts with their designs, they should remember that it involves great conative force. The child who never gives trouble in this connection is usually a being of poor personality who will accomplish little in the world.

On the other hand, it is a matter of common knowledge that many boys who have given much trouble to their governors during childhood have achieved great success in after life. As the pugnacious child gets more self-control, the crude expressions of anger will disappear; the energy of the instinct tends to reinforce the impulse of the moment, whatever is may be, and so helps the individual to make greater efforts to overcome difficulties.

The Instinct of Curiosity

This is an appetitive tendency: its impulse is to approach and to examine more closely the object which excites it. The accompanying emotion is called wonder. The object must be unfamiliar. Not however, so unfamiliar that it causes fear. It must be partially familiar, partially unfamiliar. Sometimes the degree of unfamiliarity is such that an object excites fear and curiosity in rapid alternation. "Who has not seen a horse or other animal alternately approach in curiosity, and flee in fear from some such objects as an old coat upon the ground?"

When, however, an object is very unfamiliar, but not of a nature to arouse fear, it is usually ignored: we merely "gape" at it, and pass on. Curiosity is an instinct of which the teacher should make great use.

Skilful teachers of infants are continually causing the children to wonder what is coming next. And lesson from this. For the conditions of curiosity are precisely the conditions for effective cognition. We attend most keenly to objects which are partly familiar and partly unfamiliar. Our old ideas arise and enable us to grapple with what is new. The teacher should therefore see that his lesson is neither too old nor too new; he has to hit the right proportion between the two. The grading of lessons is both one of the most difficult and one of the most important of the teacher's functions.

The Parental Instinct

Its tender emotion, has already been referred to earlier in this chapter. It was there noted that this instinct is deferred to a comparatively late period of life. It shows itself, therefore, only in partial and incomplete forms in children. But something like it is induced by imitation. And if, as McDougall affirms, it is at the root of all tendencies which exhibit love and tenderness, such as generosity, gratitude, love, pity, benevolence, moral indignation, and even the passion for justice, it is important that the school atmosphere should be one of kindly consideration and sympathy, so that all the scholars may catch something of this spirit.

The Instinct of Acquisition

Takes various forms, and is hence variously named. It is sometimes called the sense of ownership: at other times, the collecting instinct. Both of these forms can be utilised by the teacher. When we consider a thing our own, we usually take more care of it than we should otherwise do. The children may be led to regard the class-room and its apparatus as their own, and thus to become keen on keeping everything at its best. Each individual may be given a particular reading-book of each kind in use, with his name such on by means of a label. He may thus be induced to take a special pride in his books. Obviously the instinct of self-display will also be helpful here. The collecting form of the instinct may be directed to the acquisition of specimens, pictures, stamps, and so forth.

It will thus initiate a valuable series of habits which may go far to increase the child's interest in various subjects of the curriculum, and thus materially aid the intellectual side of his education. The instinct may also be evoked with moderation in connection with memory, the child being induced to begin to save small sums and thus to form a habit of thrift. But, if it is concentrated almost entirely upon money and other valuables, the child being encouraged to hoard up every penny he obtains, it may lay the foundation of avarice, and even give rise to kleptomania.

The Gregarious Instinct

Prompts individuals to seek the society of their fellows. It is no doubt very strong in some cases, and may be cited as one of the motives which induce a child possessing it in a high degree to come to school. The separation of a child from his comrades, though indeed wounding his in other ways, involves some pain on account of the deprivation of fellowship which it necessitates. But the strength of this instinct varies greatly. There seems, indeed, to be an opposed instinct, which Professor James calls secretiveness. This is so highly developed in some cases that sociability seems almost impossible. Where this is the case, it is well to do all in one' power to increase the attractiveness of social communion. For there is no doubt that our best qualities can only be evoked through fellowship.

The Instinct of Self-abasement

This instinct is accompanied by the emotion of subjection. It shows itself "in a slinking crestfallen behaviour, a general diminution of muscular tone, slow restricted movements, a hanging down of the head, and sidelong glances." Such behaviour is evoked by the presence of some fellow-creature who is regarded as superior to oneself. The teacher is constantly making use of this instinct, though he may not be distinctly aware of it. He appears as a creature bigger, stronger, and wiser than the child, and the latter, in spite of self-assertive and other tendencies which manifest themselves from time to time, feels himself greatly inferior, and is disposed to subjection and obedience. And at a time when the child is unable to think and to choose wisely for himself, it is right that the teacher should make full use of the power thus conferred on him. A training-college student was once being interviewed with respect to her fitness for appointment, and it was noted that she had an excellent mark for discipline.

She was asked how she managed to obtain such strong control of her classes. Her reply-due probably in part to nervousness-was, "I don't know." She was however, indicating a fact of great importance. Her personality was such that children listened to her, and did what she told them "quite naturally." In other words, she had plenty of self-assertion, and this evoked a due amount of subjection in the children. Few teachers are able to control in this easy manner. Those students, however, who have little self-assertion, who find children continually in opposition to them, would do well to question seriously their fitness for the teaching profession. It is not meant that self-assertion is the only essential qualification of the teacher.

Intelligent preparation of lessons, so that the children are really interested, is even more important. The kindness and sympathy born of a lively personal interest in the children will effect a great deal. But even here, so far at any rate as the ordinary elementary schools are concerned, "the affection which is based upon a wholesome awe is that which the master should seek to inspire."

The Instinct of Self-assertion or Self-display

The accompanying emotion is elation. This is a social instinct: it presupposes spectators. In its higher forms it involves self-consciousness, and is known as pride. But it can be noted long before self-consciousness develops. Even the more intelligent of the lower animals show signs of it. "Perhaps among mammals the horse displays it most clearly. The muscles of all parts are strongly innervated, the creature holds himself erect, his neck is arched, his tail lifted, his motions become superfluously vigorous and extensive, he lifts his hoofs high in the air, as he parades before the eyes of his fellows.

The young child's showing-off before the admiring gaze of his elders and his repeated commands, "See me do this," "See how well I can do that," are expressions of the same tendency. This self-assertion is one of the most imperious demands of our nature, and it is a cause of much of our most persistent endeavour. We shall see that it is one of the factors in what is called emulation or rivalry. The teacher, therefore, should not check it brutally, but rather utilise it to lead the child to make efforts in desirable directions. It need only be checked when it conflicts with the development of other members of the community.

INNATE TENDENCIES

These are more general congenital tendencies which affect all our activities, including the instincts. They can thus become moulding and directing factors of great importance.

1. *Play*

In the past, many people looked upon the tendency to play as an unnecessary evil to be reduced to the smallest possible minimum. Now, however, it is recognised as an innate tendency which must be given full scope if normal development is to occur. Play is, of course, a form of recreation. It enables the individual to recover from the effects of work when he is not so fatigued as to require complete rest. And it is indulged in by the old as well as by the young. But to the very young child it is everything. And the early lessons in the infant schools appeal to it continually. As time goes on, however, the teacher gradually requires the children to give attention to many things to which they would never attend spontaneously. But, even when the more serious work is in progress, something of the spirit of play may still be aroused: the impulse to emulation or rivalry can be utilised. This impulse is often referred to as a distinct elementary instinct.

It more probably is a development of the tendency to play, incorporating elements from some of the other tendencies already mentioned. Thus it contains something of the instinct of self-display, and still more of the instinct of pugnacity. Professor James emphasises the element of imitation. He even goes so far as to say that emulation springs out of imitation. There is some truth is this. But imitation alone cannot account for it. We begin by imitating others. We go on to emulation of them. And in this the instincts of self-display and of pugnacity must be recognised as important factors. Many teachers fail to appreciate the extent to which this impulse can be used. It is admitted that rivalry is the soul of sport. But some think that it should be reduced to a minimum in work.

Professor James, however, declares that "nine-tenths of the work of the world is done by it." Though this may be an exaggerated statement, it serves to call attention to the extreme importance of emulation as a motive. Some teachers make the objection that, when competition becomes very keen, it leads to envy and hatred, and, further, that the boys who always get beaten must soon lose heart. But competitions need not always be between boy and boy. Section can be pitted against section, class against class. Much of the comparatively dull revision work which will always be necessary can be infused with new life if the element of competition is introduced.

The class can be divided into two sides, called Romans and Carthaginians, or by some other names. The results produced by the two sections can be compared. And permanent records can be kept. Opponents may be allowed at times to ply one another with questions. Lastly a boy should be induced to emulate himself. From time to time he should be led to compare his work of the present with that of the past, he should be praised for improvement, and incited to progress still more in the future. Where marks are systematically given, a summary can be prepared at regular intervals. And each boy, under the supervision of the teacher, can construct a "curve" indicating his comparative progress or retardation.

2. *Imitation*

Imitation is a most widespread tendency, not only throughout the race, but throughout the activities of any given individual. Its importance as a factor in education can scarcely be over-estimated. Our speech, our dress, our manners, our thoughts, and even our emotions are largely due to it. In these and other spheres a very large share of the habits we forms is due to the influence of imitation. If an English child is brought up in France he becomes a Frenchman. If he is reared in a middle-class family he becomes a bourgeois, if in a slum home, he is likely to become an Apache.

The exact amount we owe to heredity is in the present state of science problematical. But it is patent to all keen observers that imitation of the thoughts, feelings, and actions of those around us, especially during the plastic period of youth, is a most potent factor in education. It must be remembered, too, that we not only imitate our pastors and masters, but our fellows. Hence the justification of those parents who are at least as particular about the type of child in a certain school as about the type of teacher. We have used the word imitation in a very general sense.

(i) imitation of the emotions of those around us may be called sympathy;

(ii) imitation of thoughts may be called the giving way to suggestion and the propensity to it is called suggestibility;

(iii) imitation of actions has no special name and may be called imitation proper or merely imitation.

Sympathy

The primitive sympathy to which reference is here made includes none of the higher moral qualities usually connoted by the term. It is, indeed, an element of the higher forms. But it is not to be confused with them. It shows itself on the perceptual plane, and requires little ideation or imagery to account for it. It is well known that if one animal in a herd of wild beasts shows fear and rushes off in flight, the others may follows suit. This does not necessarily imply that they perceive the same things.

All that is necessary to account for it is that the instinct of flight and its emotion of fear are capable of being excited not only by certain unfamiliar objects, but by the perception of manifestations of the emotion in other members of the same species. Thus emotion is "catching." The sympathetic spread of emotion occurs in the same way amount children. We often call it the "sympathy of numbers." The "tone" of a class or school depends largely on the same thing. The intelligent teacher knows that if he can obtain the emotional attitude he desires from the majority of his pupils, the others are likely to be similarly affected. At the same time he is aware that a marked departure from this attitude on the part of one or two individuals, especially if those individuals have strong personalities, may spread to many of the others.

Accordingly he endeavours on the one hand to keep the majority in sympathy with him, and on the other to concentrate his influence on the one or two "dangerous" members of the class, so that they are unable to withstand the force of his stronger personality. Many young teachers fail to understand the true position. They imagine that by wholesale coercion they can force the whole class into the proper attitude. They fail to see that they are running the risk of evoking a spirit of angry rebellion, which may spread like wildfire through the whole class, and turn even the most well meaning boys into enemies of the teacher's authority.

Suggestion

The word "suggestion" is used with varying meanings, even within the realm of psychology. It is sometimes used to indicate the recall of something to mind. One thing tends to recall or "suggest" another which has been associated with it on a previous occasion. This is not the meaning to be given to the term in the present instance. Suggestion is here used to designate the process whereby one person is led to believe something, and often to act upon it, without any definite grounds for the belief, but merely on the statement, or under the influence, of some other person. We all have some suggestibility, i.e. an innate tendency to believe what we are told, or what is otherwise indicated to us by certain persons.

The degree of suggestibility varies from one individual to another and in the same individual at different times. Persons in whom the instinct of subjection is much stronger than that of self-assertion have usually great suggestibility. But most of us experience subjection when under the influence of certain persons or institutions. This kind of suggestion is called prestige suggestion. Connected with it is the fact that in many subjects our knowledge is deficient, or poorly organised, so that we are only too ready to accept the statement of some recognised authority.

Now children are normally in this position with respect to adults, especially with respect to those placed over them - their parents and teachers. And these have a right to use the suggestibility of the children in the interests of morality, impressing precepts and maxims upon their minds long before they can arrive at the stage when the reasons for these things can be understood. It is to be remembered, however, that the person who wishes to exert this power the children must be highly respected. The man of weak personality will do far less in this matter than the strong teacher; he may, indeed, produce an effect quite the reverse of what he intends. For there is such a thing as contra-suggestion.

When the boys do not feel the superiority of the teacher, their self-assuredness may take the form of believing and acting upon the direct contrary of his teaching. It is dangerous, therefore, to preach overmuch. For such reasons Mr. Keatinge advises the introduction of suggestions in an indirect fashion.

The boys will not be so much on the alert to withstand them when their minds are bent on studying the material containing them form another point of view. Thus when a boy is writing a moral maxim as an exercise in transcription, the "new ideas can be introduced so discreetly that no reaction is aroused, that sleeping dogs can be let lie, and the subject remain sublimely unconscious that he is being 'got at.'" While suggestion is a worthy instrument in cases like those specified, it should not be used in such subjects as science, history, geography, and arithmetic. Here the teacher's aim should be to induce the children to investigate and to come to conclusions for themselves, and an attitude of passive acceptance of all that their teacher tells them is fatal to progress in this respect.

Questions suggesting an answer of a certain kind should as a rule be sedulously avoided. Teachers who have a mind for experiment and who wish to assure themselves of the dangers indicated could produce startling results by suing suggestion in this way, and requiring the boys to write down their answers. Show the class, for instance, the portrait of a man without any hat on. Give only a few moments for the examination of it. Then remove it from observation and ask: "Had he a straw hat, a bowler hat, or a high hat?" The number of wrong answers will probably be much greater than would be the case if the question asked had been, "Had he a hat on or not?"

Imitation

We use this term, as already indicated, to signify the copying of the actions, manners, and general methods of procedure of other persons. It begins as a subconscious tendency. Thus the child automatically copies the speech of those around him, and most of us retain to the end of life the pronunciation which we heard in our infancy. Hence the need of a good speech atmosphere, both at home and at school. A higher form of imitation is that in which we definitely note the specific actions of others and then find ourselves imitating them. The idea of the action issues almost automatically in the corresponding movement. When the imitation is definitely deliberate, as when we decide to copy some model which we admire, the highest from is reached. Imitation is the means by which we acquire skill in many departments of activity.

In speech, gymnastics, writing, drawing, and general deportment, as well as in sports and playful activities, it is usually the predominant factor. The chief recommendation to make is that the models should be good, and should be clearly presented to the children. The teacher should bear in mind that his actions are being constantly watched, and that the necessity of setting a good example in all the details of his procedure is paramount.

3. *The Tendency to Seek Pleasure and to Avoid Pain*

The tendency to seek pleasure and to avoid pain is the most general and far-reaching of all innate tendencies. By some it has been called an instinct. But it is such a fundamental feature of all our activity that it should rather be regarded as a general law influencing all our mental life. As we have already indicate that a large part in developing many habits which are more or less independent of the instincts. For pleasure and pain initiate conation on their own account. Although we know nothing of the physical processes underlying them in the nervous system, we are certain of them as psychological facts and of their effects. Professor James puts the matter as follows: "If the mechanical activities in a cell, as they increase, give pleasure, they seem to increase all the more rapidly for that fact; if they give displeasure, the displeasure seems to damp the activities.

The psychic side of the phenomenon thus seems, somewhat, like the applause or hissing at a spectacle, to be an encouraging or adverse comment on what the machinery brings forth." Or, as Professor Stout says, "there is a constant tendency to persist in those movements and motor attitudes which yield satisfactory experiences, and to renew them when similar conditions recur; on the other hand, those movements and attitudes which yield unsatisfactory experiences tend to be discontinued at the time of their occurrence and to be suppressed on subsequent similar occasions. By the working of this Law of Subjective Selection, as it is called, relatively blind and undirected activities become gradually guided into definite tracts, each advance paving the way for further progress." The additional conation due to pleasure is called appetition; that conation which involves a ceasing or a turning away from activities which bring pain is called aversion.

This latter often involves not merely a ceasing from the activities which bring pain, but a positive struggle to get out of a disagreeable situation. It is important to note that there is often a remarkable reciprocal reaction between conation and feeling. As we have already seen, conation which is allowed free play produces pleasure. And the pleasure produced heightens the conation. When, on the other hand, a given conation is obstructed, it produces pain; and pain tends to damp the activity. The obstruction may increase the tendency for the moment. But, if that obstruction cannot be removed, the pain is also increased, and ultimately damps the activity. Of course all feeling is not produced in these ways.

Often pleasure or pain arises in the course of our activity quite independently of the tendency which is in operation. A young child may have a tendency to carry things to its mouth. A given thing may turn out to be "nice" or "nasty." In this case the pleasure or pain produced is not due to the furtherance or obstruction of the tendency, but to the nature of the experience produced by the tendency. But, in whatever way they are produced, pleasure and pain always arouse respectively appetition and aversion. Another, and perhaps a more appropriate, name for the law in question is the Law of Hedonic Selection, the word Hedonic indicating what determines the selection of certain activities. Now we are continually experiencing pleasure or pain. Consequently this law is always more or less in action.

Our appreciation of its activity, however, can be most definite in those cases where intense pleasure or pain occur and determine very marked changes in our activity. Thus the baby stretches out his hand to the candle flame and gets burnt. The pain determines a quick aversive movement, and probably stamps out for ever the tendency to touch flames. We call this learning by experience. At another time the baby may put his thumb into his mouth and suck it. This gives him pleasure, and he continues. Thus a habit is formed. But it is a bad habit. And his mother consequently endeavours to stamp it out. She may, for instance, put mustard on his thumb.

When now he puts his thumb in his mouth, he experiences pain. This checks the movements, and may thus destroy the habit. Now the punishments and rewards which we sometimes administer to children depend largely for their efficacy on the same law. And it might appear at first sight that we can get just the habits we require by a systematic use of them. But further examination will show that their efficacy is comparatively limited. With the baby, who approximates to a lower animal, we can indeed pursue a fairly mechanical system of rewards and punishments. We can arrange, for instance, that his tendency to suck his thumb is damped by the pain which occurs when mustard is placed upon it. He does not yet distinguish the fact that it is only the mustard which prevents him from getting the usual pleasure.

The experience is a whole in which he does not discriminate the parts. This whole is painful, and he gives it up. But if the habit has remained fixed till a later stage, our problem is much more difficult. For the child now sees clearly that the pain produced is not the result of sucking his thumb, but of the mustard which is placed upon it. We may continue to check him by insisting on mustard being kept on his thumb. But we may be merely preventing him from indulging a tendency which is increasing by the obstruction. If the child could get a few moments with his thumb clear of mustard, he might seize the opportunity to suck at it more greedily than ever.

We have innumerable instances of young people who have been repressed by harsh discipline during their school life, and who break out into evil courses when they are freed from control. Take now a case of reward. A young child lacks control in his excretory habits. When he shows some, he is rewarded by a piece of sugar, or by some other pleasant experience. This may not at first be definitely distinguished from the whole experience of which it forms the conclusion, and the pleasure derived definitely fixes clean habits. But if, at a later stage, similar means are employed to encourage kindness to his sister, they are now clearly distinguished as an end to which the kindness is only a means. It is, then, the tendency towards these rewards which is being developed, and various more or less disliked activities will be undertaken in order to obtain them.

If the rewards are discontinued, the other activities which it was intended to encourage may cease also. There is, of course, the possibility that these other activities may have gradually evoked some instinctive tendencies, which now support them. They may also have gained strength by reason of mere repetition, which, as we have seen, is an important determinant of habit. But if they run counter to any other tendencies of the child's nature, they are liable to be dropped when rewards are no longer forthcoming. It might appear to some readers that punishment and reward ought therefore to be discarded altogether. But this is not so. We have already seen that in the earliest stages they may be very effective. And even later, punishment, at any rate, cannot be dispensed with. It is often the only means of stopping a tendency which must be checked at all costs.

In the early stages of human life, the various instincts and innate tendencies show themselves in more or less separate and simple forms. But with the progress in intelligence, ideas increase in number and complexity and bring with them a corresponding complexity in the emotional life. One single object may evoke more than one instinct at the same time. Thus, at the sight of a snake or a toad, the child may show loathing, which seems to be a combination of fear and disgust; at the sight of a tall man riding a great horse, he may show admiration, which is probably a combination of wonder and subjection; at the sight of a troop of soldiers dashing along on horseback, he may show awe, which is admiration blended with fear.

In this way the instincts give rise to a large variety of complex emotional attitudes and tendencies. But, as experience continues, certain objects are continually recurring, being viewed from many sides and under varying circumstances. These objects become the centre of systems or masses of ideas, which are continually being added to and modified by further experience of the objects in question. In other words apperception is repeatedly taking place, our knowledge thus increasing in range and complexity. With this development on the cognitive side there is a corresponding increase in complexity and range on the emotional and conative side. We not only experience complex combinations of emotions, but we have different emotions in connection with the same object at different times according to changing circumstances. Further, since the object is again presented in similar circumstances of each kind, the various emotions and combinations of emotions are continually being re-excited in connection with the object and the ideas related to it.

In this way firm associations are formed between the object and its system of ideas on the one hand and a large number of emotions and tendencies on the other. Considerable modifications continue to take place with changing circumstances; but, on the whole, definite tendencies to act and feel in certain ways become fixed. Habits of feeling and acting are thus established; and the whole system of ideas, feelings, tendencies and habits may be called a sentiment. The "object" may be of any kind. In the more simple cases it is a concrete person or thing. But with further development classes of things may also become the centres of sentiments. And, finally, abstract things like justice and virtue may become the nuclei of these emotional and conative dispositions. Let us now take a simple example.

Suppose that a child is placed under a violent-tempered teacher, who is unsympathetic and indifferent to the child, and who is constantly threatening, scolding, and perhaps beating him. At first the child is thrown into a more or less simple state of fear at each violent act or speech of the teacher. But repetition soon creates a habit of fear, so that whenever the child sees the teacher, or even thinks of him, he becomes timorous, although there may be no present reason for fear. A simple sentiment such as this will readily become more complex both on its ideational and on its emotional and conative sides. Thus, as the child's knowledge of the teacher develops, his anger may be frequently evoked by what he is now able to judge as harsh punishments and restrictions. Disgust and the spirit of revenge may soon follow. These various dispositions to feel and act become more and more intimately connected with the object, which tends to excite them, sometimes several in combination, sometimes in turn, whenever it is presented, whether in reality or in idea.

The rudimentary sentiment of fear has developed into a full-blown sentiment of hatred of the teacher. It is obvious that similar sentiments may grow up about the ideas of other individuals or institutions. Thus some children develop an intense hatred of school, or of some particular branch of school activity. Sometimes this sentiment originates with the teacher, in the way already described, and spreads over to the subjects and to the institution in general; sometimes its origin is rather the way in which the subjects are taught, and the general organisation of the school, which is badly adapted to the child's nature. Let us now take an example of a different kind.

An act of kindness by the teacher to the child may arouse gratitude. This seems to be a combination of tender emotion and subjection. It is merely a complex emotion, and may occur only once. But if the teacher repeats his kindly acts, the gratitude of the child may become more or less habitual, constituting an emotional disposition always ready to be excited by the presence, or by the idea of, the teacher. Further, other instinctive tendencies may be aroused in connection with the object. The child's gratitude may lead him to bring the teacher flowers, or to offer him some service. He may take pride in doing these things, on account of his instinct of self-display being awakened, and thus a permanent disposition to seek the approbation of his teacher may develop.

Hip deep interest in his teacher may involve imitation of his acts where this is possible, sympathy with his emotions, and a high suggestibility to the ideas which he expresses. There may thus grow up in the child a complex sentiment, the various tendencies of which are towards, and in favour of, the teacher. This sentiment may be called love. Similar sentiments, modified by other instinctive elements and variously adapted to the different circumstances, may develop in connection with other objects, both personal and impersonal, concrete and abstract. Such sentiments receive various names according to the nature of the objects around which they grow. Love has already been mentioned. We use this word in speaking of persons, of activities, and sometimes of abstract things.

Thus we say that a person has a love of cricket, a love of justice, and so on. But another word which is often used, especially when subjects of study or investigation form the "objects," is the word interest. The work of the teacher with respect to many of the school subjects is to develop intellectual sentiments around them. There should gradually arise an interest in geography, a love of good literature, a desire to know more about history, and so on. The final test of a school's instruction is not merely the amount of knowledge which the children possess, but above all the interest which the pupils show in their work. As we have already seen, this interest is only possible with the increase of knowledge. Consequently, if interest has been developed, there will be much knowledge. But the great thing to look for is whether the children evince a tendency to go on with some of their work after leaving school.

The function of the elementary school is not to cram as much knowledge as possible into the child's mind, but, while giving some knowledge, to create an appetite for more. The school should prepare the children for making a good use of their leisure as well as for beginning to learn some trade or profession. And in doing this the school is not really impractical. For those who employ their leisure profitably will be all the better as workmen. This building up of a "many-sided interest" depends largely on the way in which the teacher sets about his work. It can only be done successfully if he takes account of the instinctive tendencies and emotions which the children possess on coming to school, if he appeals to these in the first place, gradually refining and organising them by the matter which he selects, by his methods of presenting it, and, above all, by his own enthusiasm for it, which will, to a large extent, communicate itself by sympathy to the children.

A teacher, for instance, who is not a lover of literature himself will scarcely develop much of the literary sentiment in his pupils. The teacher must not expect the higher forms of interest before the lower forms have had their day. He must remember that the young child is largely a creature of sporadic emotions and tendencies. But the same primitive tendencies which determine knee attention to such crude tales as "The Three Bears," "Jack the Giant--killer," and "Cinderella" will, if carefully nurtured, refined, and organised, bear fruit finally in sentiments which will bring with them keen appreciation of "Hamlet," "The Merchant of Venice," and "The Mill on the Floss."

The same tendencies which induce the child to work hard at his clay-modeling, his paper-cutting, and his drawing will, with proper development, give rise to interest in machine drawing, in scientific experiment, and in architectural planning and design. All that has just been elaborated may be summed up by the statement that interest determines attention. Attention is the direction of cognitive activity to one object rather than to another. And this direction depends largely on the conative forces which are at work. When these conative forces have been organised into a complex system of tendencies and habits, the interest may be called a sentiment. And that is usually the case when the child has made some steps forward in a subjects. Observe, however, that the new matter presented must be within the intellectual grasp of the pupil.

Looked at from the cognitive side an interest in a subject includes a system of ideas which has been developed; and the new matter presented must be capable of comprehension in the light of what is already known. Suppose that a teacher develops an interest in geography by a carefully graded and suitable series of lessons up to a certain point. Suppose, then, that he begins to give further lessons which cannot be grasped on the basis of the knowledge which has already been acquired.

The boys may begin to attend to such lessons with great keenness, due to the interest they already have. But the intellectual conditions of apperception not being present, no progress can be made. The boys will not only be unable to go on attending, but their failure will go far to kill their interest. The checking of any activity is painful; and pain, as we have seen, gives, rise to aversion. To get continued attention to any lesson, therefore, we must fulfill two great requirements:

- What we present must be capable of being apperceived or understood by the pupils; and
- It must be interesting to them, i.e. it must appeal to their emotions and tendencies, innate or acquired. We have just seen that the second condition is insufficient without the first. But the first is just as incapable of securing attention without the second. Many people can understand easily enough what a prosy lecturer is repeating, but they are not interested, and they consequently fail to attend. "It is true that to find a book interesting we must have sufficient knowledge to understand it; but it is not true that we find interesting everything we have sufficient knowledge to understand." As well as being able to understand we must be anxious or desirous to do so. But, it may be pointed out, we often find people attending to things which are not interesting.

"What more deadly uninteresting object can there be than a railroad time-table?" asks Professor James. Yet people are found attending to it every day. Are, then, the principles we have laid down invalid? Attention in such cases is still determined by interest, though that interest is not in the object as such. But attention to the object in question is a necessary step in the course of a more comprehensive activity which is interesting. We have no interest in a railroad time'-table as such, and we should never attend to it for its own sake.

But if it is necessary to know the time of a train in order to proceed on a journey, we consult the otherwise uninteresting time-table with eagerness. We can either say that the time-table is still uninteresting in itself, but is attended to for the sake of our interesting journey, or we can say that the time-table becomes interesting because of its connection with our journey. It matters little which form of language we use, so long as we are quite clear as to our meaning. Professor James prefers the latter; for he goes on to say: "Yet where will you find a more interesting object if you are going on a journey, and by its means can find your train?" And he frames the general statement as follows: "Any object not interesting in itself may become interesting through becoming associated with an object in which an interest already exists.

The two associated objects grow, as it were, together: the interesting portion sheds its quality over the whole; and thus things not interesting in their own right borrow an interest which become as real and as strong as that of any natively interesting thing." Such interest is often called derived interest, and the attention which it involves is sometimes spoken of as voluntary attention. Now there are various degrees of "derivation." In the case already cited, the object in which a derived interest is taken is most intimately connected with the interest or purpose which controls the whole business in hand. Further, attention to that object is only necessary for a few moments. It is, then, a very small episode in the career of the parent interest. Consequently it is not noticed as a necessary evil; it is swallowed up, as it were, in the interesting business of making a journey. But often the object to which attention must be paid if our interest is to work itself out is of greater complexity and demands a large amount of distasteful activity.

In such cases, it is not swallowed up by the interesting whole of which it forms a distasteful part. And there may be a real struggle between aversion from the distasteful business and the desire to proceed with our business. But even here the interest in going through with the matter may be strong enough to win the day. The following is a case quoted from Professor Ribot:-"A child refuses to read; he is incapable of keeping his mind fixed on the letters, which have no attraction for him; but he looks with avidity upon the pictures contained in the book. What do they mean?' He asks. The father replies: When you can read, the book will tell you.' After several colloquies like this the child resigns himself and falls to work, first slackly, then the habit grows, and finally he shows an ardour which has to restrained.

This is a case of the genesis of voluntary attention. An artificial and indirect desire has to be grafted on a natural and direct one. Reading has no immediate attractiveness, but it has a borrowed one, and that is enough. The child is caught is the wheel work, the first step is made. This is perhaps an optimistic account. It presupposes a very strong parent interest, one which will hold on its course continuously through much uncongenital material- a rare thing with young children. It represents, however, the kind of thing which the teacher should attempt. He should, of course, begin by inducing voluntary attention to objects which are closely connected with some of the primitive interests of the children and which do not involve very much effort or a very long period of concentration.

Gradually, however, he can lead the children to take longer excursions through fields which are not attractive in themselves. Here, however, he will sometimes find that attention slackens, either because, the parent interest is not strong enough, or because the unattractive field is too broad or barren, or because some other attraction is soliciting the attention of the child. The teacher is often himself to blame for such unfortunate occurrences. He may have failed to appreciate the forces for and against him.

But, sometimes, though he is clearly aware of these forces, he deems it necessary to require the children to make the effort in question. They will have to make such efforts in later life, and they must be gradually accustomed to them as they grow up. Habits of attention have to be acquired. In such cases, the teacher must arouse some other forces or conation in order to secure the victory. For as we have already ordered to secure the victory. For as we have already noted, some interest or tendency is always necessary. The difference between the various educationists is largely a difference as to what interest or tendency. Where the tendency or interest, with which the intrinsically uninteresting object is most intimately connected, lacks the requisite force, more external interests or motives have sometimes to be aroused.

Reward and punishment, praise and blame, have their place here, especially in the early stages of the child's life. If, however, reward and punishment, praise and blame, are largely relied on throughout the child's whole education, his efforts and attention will come to depend on these. But when he goes out into the world, the regularity of these stimuli will diminish. The habits of making efforts may persist to some extent. But the loss of the motive power will soon be felt. The great object of the educator, however, is to bring up the child that when the time comes for him to be given his freedom, he may behave well on his own initiative. How necessary, therefore, it is to accustom the child gradually to think and act independently of such stimuli as definite rewards and punishments! But what is to take the place of rewards and punishments, praise and blame, when a parent interest fails before a dreary task, and when the habits of concentration are insufficient to carry the business through? We have repeatedly said that there must always be an interest.

Where is it to be found in the present instance? There is

one interest or sentiment which comes to dominate all the others. For its "object" is ever more or less present with us, and is the starting-point of some of our strongest instinctive tendencies. It is the interest in ourselves. We may refer to it as the self-regarding sentiment. In the early stages it is very crude and fragmentary. And the instincts which are connected with it are the egoistic or self-centred ones, such as those of pugnacity, of self-assertion, of acquisition, and of feeding. But, as time goes on, other instincts are aroused and incorporated in the sentiment. Thus the gregarious instinct will lead the child into the society of others, and by some of these his instinct of self--abasement with its corresponding emotion of subjection will be aroused. Sympathy, imitation, and suggestion, both separately and as elements of the religious sentiment, will also play a part. Meanwhile the self-regarding sentiment is developing on its cognitive side.

In learning of and from others, the child comes to know himself more comprehensively. He recognises himself as a unit intimately related with, and depending for his welfare upon, other units, many of which are vastly more powerful than himself, and the whole of which constitutes a most important part of his total environment. It goes without saying that these thoughts are not clear and definite in his mind. Only philosophers state them in this abstract way. It remains true, however, that in developing his social consciousness the child is at the same time developing his self-consciousness. Now if the self-regarding sentiment can be made to include a full recognition of one's duties to others, together with adequate tendencies in harmony therewith, it will become the most potent factor in good behaviour. Many agencies may help on this process. Religion is often the most important.

But the young infant cannot understand this; and other means are necessary in early life. Among these may be mentioned rewards and punishments. These very means which are gradually to be discarded are often useful in developing the instrument which is to take their place. There is little doubt that they have often been abused. But the modem reaction against the unbending authority of the past has in some cases overshot the mark. We have been so often bidden to respect the natural tendencies of the child that there is now a real danger is some quarters of their being allowed to grow up at random, like weeds in a garden. But without the strong intervention of authority, some of the child's natural tendencies would, under modern conditions of life, have little chance of being aroused.

It must be remembered that fear and submission are just as natural as anger and self-display. And if the self-regarding sentiment, which will later in life be the great arbiter in deciding on the most important questions of behaviour, is not gradually transformed from a more or less complete absorption is self to a comprehensive and well-balanced consideration of self and one's obligations to others, the conduct of the future will not be of a highly moral kind. True self-respect, which is to be the ruling sentiment, must include respect of others. It therefore involves not merely self-assertion, but a due amount of self-abasement. "The main condition of the incorporation of this disposition in the self-regarding sentiment is the exercise of authority over the child by his elders.

At first this authority necessarily demonstrates its superior power by means of physical force, later by means of rewards and punishments. On each occasion that the exercise of personal authority over the child makes him aware of a superior and inflexible power to which he must submit, his negative self-feeling is evoked; then his idea of self in relation to that person becomes habitually accompanied and suffused by this emotion in however slight a degree, and he habitually assumes towards that person the attitude of submission.

Thus the disposition of this emotion becomes incorporated in the self-regarding sentiment. Children, of course, differ very much with respect to the relative strength of their instincts. Some possess such a nicely balanced system of instincts, the altruistic tendencies being in due proportion to the egoistic, that their behaviour works out largely in harmony with the needs of society. With the majority, however, this is not the case, and special educational treatment is necessary. This treatment often has to include rewards and punishments. But these means should never be abused. As the child grows more sensitive, praise and blame can be used with marked effect. Many teachers neglect these milder means. Praise especially, however, can be made a most potent instrument of progress, particularly in cases where the teacher is highly respected by the children. Another means of developing a higher form of self-regarding sentiment is by definite instruction.

Moral instruction has often been condemned on the ground that it appeals only to cognition. It is pointed out that many men know what they ought to do, but fail to act accordingly. But we have repeatedly insisted that instruction should not be divorced from behaviour. It is quite true that mere knowledge of one's duty is of little value without the right tendencies and habits. But if such tendencies have already been developed, by religious teaching and by the other means referred to, further instruction with respect to duty will both strengthen and guide them.

The ideas aroused, whether by story or precept, are of little value considered solely on their intellectual side. They must arouse emotions and impulses to action. But if these have already been partially developed in the ways already mentioned, moral instruction may bear considerable fruit. In this field, as well as in all other fields of knowledge, we cannot arrange for the child to find out everything for himself in the course of his individual experience. We enlarge his views of himself and of his relations to the world by telling him more than he could ever discover if confined to the limits of his own life. It is this intimate connection between knowledge and tendencies, which gives rise to what are called ideals, purposes, aspirations, and ambitions.

In the early stages of human life, and throughout the whole of the lives of the lower animals, conation arise and run their course with little thought accompanying them. But in the case of the human being the sporadic conation of early life are gradually modified and directed to definite ends, which the individual foresees, i.e. of which he has ideas. There gradually grows up a more or less clear understanding of the whole business of life. We not only push forward, but we know whither we are tending. In other words, we acquire ideals, purposes, or aspirations. Looked at from the conative side, these are tendencies or impulses accompanied by emotion. Looked at from the cognitive side, they are merely ideas of the ends towards which we are tending.

But in practice they are not to be separated into these aspects. And if this is so, we can improve them not only by cultivating the emotions, tendencies, and habits which constitute their motive power, but also by developing their intellectual side through what is called moral instruction. This moral instruction can take various form. In some schools definite lessons are devoted to it. With the younger children these lessons would take the form of short stories vividly told, without overinsistence on the moral implied. But in all schools, whether special lessons are assigned to moral instruction or not, the ideals embodied in religion, in literature, in the fine arts, in government and other human institutions should be brought home to the boys, so that their minds are opened to the greater sphere, of which their own personal environment is only a part or aspect.

In this way the self-regarding sentiment comes to incorporate within itself a rich system of ideals or purposes which are harmoniously systematised, so that behaviour gradually changes from being a mere succession of isolated responses to this or that stimulus to an interconnected series of acts forming an orderly sequence. And when one partial purpose or interest is on the point of being overcome by aversion from the unpleasantness of the task which arises in its course, the whole system of aspirations can be evoked to support it.

This highest type of self-determined effort is usually known as volition. And the attention which is paid to the intrinsically unattractive material can be called volitional attention. This is the highest form of voluntary attention. But like all other forms of attention, it still involves interest. The interest in this case, however, is partially derived from another factor. In the lower types of voluntary attention already described, attention to an unattractive object is determined by interest in something with which that object is more or less closely connected. In the volitional type, the parent interest in question is not strong enough by itself to overcome the aversion from the unattractive object, and has to be supplemented by interest derived from a still higher source-the self-regarding sentiment, or, to use more ordinary language, the determination to do our duty at all costs. It is such acts as these, whether they involve chiefly the direction of attention or the performing of some concrete act, which may be called self-control. Our highest aspirations are called in to control the lower propensities when these are in danger of gaining the victory over more ideal impulses. It is obvious that habit is a most important factor here.

If the child can be frequently led to revive thoughts of himself and of his nobler aspirations at times of temptation, he will acquire a habit of self-control. Such a habit will tide him over many difficulties in which he would cut a sorry figure if left to the mercy of momentary inclinations. Further, the work of volition will become easier. For the moral life is not necessarily a series of severe conflicts. Habit not only strengthens the sentiment of duty, but it fixes the general line of procedure. It cannot, of course, provide for all the varieties of conduct which are necessary in a, complex society. We can never hope to live the highest type of life by mere habit. But it can render the self-regarding sentiment so strong and certain in its action that there are few if any conflicts. In this way the self comes to rule supreme over conduct, the individual is raised above moral conflict; he attains character in the fullest sense, and a completely generalised will, and exhibits to the world that finest flower of moral growth, serenity.

His struggles are no longer moral conflicts, but are intellectual efforts to discover what is most worth doing, what is most right for his to do. Character, then, is the source of our conduct. It is the sum of all the tendencies which an individual possesses. It is innate tendencies which the individual possesses on coming into the world, or which develop as time progresses. But these become modified by the physical and social environment of the individual, giving rise to more or less fixed dispositions to act in certain ways in relation to certain objects. Character has, therefore, been often called a bundle of habits. But it is more than this. For habits are mechanical reactions to certain definite situations, whereas human life is never a series of repetitions of exactly the same situations. There must, therefore, be a power behind the habits which secures modifications of conduct as different circumstances arise.

A youth may have formed an excellent set of home and school habits, but if these are all his moral stock in-trade, he may fail miserably when he enters upon the freer life of college or of the world of business. Life is at all points too complex an affair to be worked by machinery. Character, then, retains much of the instinctive and emotional basis which is the starting-point of the habits, which helps to sustain them, and which is itself reinforced and more firmly established by them. It includes the organisation of these tendencies, with their emotions, into sentiments; above, all, the organisation of that great ruling sentiment which we have called the self-regarding sentiment, but which when truly moralised, is usually known as devotion to duty. And since, under such conditions as we have described, the tendencies are towards right conduct, pleasure is found therein-that pleasure which is due to the harmonious working of a system of impulses which all obtain their due amount of satisfaction. As Aristotle says, "A man is not good at all unless he takes pleasure in noble deeds." No one would call a man just who did not take pleasure in doing justice, nor generous who took no pleasure in generosity, and so on.

In other words, the moral life is one of true happiness. And in educating children towards it, we are making them not merely more useful to the community, but a permanent source of satisfaction to themselves. The teacher must not expect moral action of a high type from very young children, who have a very vague consciousness of themselves and of their relations to others. In the early stages he must be satisfied with the lower types of voluntary attention. Nevertheless the volitional type will gradually show itself. At first it will be of a very rudimentary character, scarcely distinguishable from the other types. As examples of the development of elementary violations, with the more or less rudimentary states of the self-regarding sentiment therein involved, we may take the following cases:--

(i) Another boy, who has seldom been late, and perhaps never punished, may be in similar circumstances. But he may be trying for a reward card for punctual and regular attendance, and the idea of this may be sufficient to reinforce the warning of the school bell. In this case the self-regarding sentiment is a little more complex. The idea of the reward card may involve the consciousness of himself as a person to be approved. But in both these cases the consciousness of self is of a very rudimentary description.

(ii) But with the highest type of boy, there may arise cases in which he is not directly dependent on some definite approval or disapproval. He begins to be the spectator in the gallery to himself. He says to himself, "I ought to be ashamed of myself idling here when my duty is to get to school. This higher from of self-consciousness is rare. But it is to be found.

(iii) Another boy might be a member of a class in which a strong corporate spirit exists, and which hopes to distinguish itself as the most punctual in the school. The idea of its loss of prestige, of the disgust of his comrades at his failure to keep up the reputation of the class, may arise in his mind and overcome all other considerations.

This is quite a high type of volition for a young boy.

(iv) Suppose a child, who has been punished for arriving at school late without excuse, is watching some men at work in the road when he suddenly hears the school bell. He has some interest in getting to school early. But it is not sufficiently strong to cause him to tear himself away. If, however, he suddenly decides, I don't want to be punished, so I'll be off, he may be considered to have performed an elementary volition.

(v) As praise and blame acquire more power over a boy, owing to his developing self-consciousness, we find many cases of volition of a distinctly higher order. Thus both boys instanced in the last examples might be overcome by the extremely curious nature of the operations they are watching. But a third boy might reflect: Father will be so sorry when he hears I have been late. And if he is very susceptible to the praise and blame of his father, he may make a great effort and be off.

When such a stage as this last has been reached, the child is already beginning the higher life.

If he has access to good literature, and still more important, if he grows up among people of high moral purpose, he may finally rise to such strength of character that he becomes a permanent law unto himself, and is able to decide for the right amid temptations of the severest kind. Now in the task of forming character, the educator is not always thinking of the complex whole which he is endeavouring to shape. He has frequently to deal with the individual tendencies and habits which go to make that whole. In particular, he has often to face the task of repressing evil tendencies and habits. Punishment is the most ready instrument.

But all other means should be tried before recourse is had to this drastic and dangerous remedy. Let us, them briefly consider some of these other means. In the first place, a tendency or habit is likely to die out on account of lack of exercise. If we can avoid the circumstances which excite it, we are giving it a chance to disappear. This may be called the method of disuses. Thus a boy may be given to envy. If we can prevent him from being overshadowed and supplanted by others, we are giving him an opportunity to rid himself of this bad quality. We are pursuing the same method when we prevent copying by such careful arrangements that there is not temptation to it. So with lying, laziness, and many other bad tendencies.

A good organisation of the work so that each boy finds plenty to do, and does it, will close up many loopholes which would otherwise allow evil tendencies to creep in. But the converse of the principle just stated is also true. An instinct which is frequently exercised becomes firmly grounded in habit. And this fact will be of great use in developing the good tendencies. But it has a still wider application. For, while we have a large number of instincts, we have only a certain amount of conative energy. If this is continually being drawn off into certain channels, it cannot take other courses. Hence the development of good tendencies tends to suppress the bad. This may be called the method of substitution. The more, therefore, we can fill the minds of the boys with healthy interests, the less chance is there for the evil to prosper. A special case of this last method is that in which one tendency is more or less incompatible with another.

For instance, envy could be opposed by esprit de corps. A boy could be so consumed with the desire to see the reputation of his school augmented that he would be delighted with the achievements of his comrades, even though they threw his own into the shade. Our duty, then, is to watch for budding instincts of a promising kind, to foster them, and to lead them into channels in which they will develop into useful habits. To the teacher who is inclined to view the innate tendencies which he finds in the child with absolute despair, it may be pointed out that no instinct can be considered absolutely bad in itself. One and the same instinct, according to the field in which it is employed, may be the germ of good or of bad habits.

We have already seen in the last chapter how the instinct of acquisition may lead on the one hand to useful habits of collecting and of thrift, and on the other, to bad habits of stealing and other forms of unjust dealing. As another example, let us take the tendency to bully, found in some boys of striking personality and strong physique. This tendency is compounded largely of self-asserting and pugnacity. But from giving rise to bad habits it can sometimes be turned into useful channels. Thus the boy may be made a monitor with some right to control his fellows and some duties towards them. The tendencies in question will thus become transformed into habits which are beneficent both to their possessor and to the community in which he is placed.

This may be called the method of diversion. We have already noted the importance of imitation as a factor in the production of conduct. If the teacher is highly respected, his example will have a powerful influence. But the example of the other boys is also a powerful factor. For developing a systematic coordination in other boys to achieve the harmony in the class as well as in the society. For we have seen that suggestion is a powerful force with young children. But we must remember that there is danger of contra suggestion if much direct preaching be done, especially in the case of older children and with a teacher of weak personality. It is necessary here to point out that no given method is infallible.

The inordinate strength of an evil tendency, the impossibility of controlling all the circumstances, and many other conditions, render it hazardous to predict success in any particular case. And we sometimes have to fall back on punishment. Punishment, then, is often a necessary evil. Sometimes there are plenty of good tendencies, but they are overwhelmed by some evil tendency which cannot be removed by any other method than brutal extinction. Take the following example. Frank, when he was of six, had for a while been away from home, and on his return suffered severely from head.

There was no managing him in the nursery. For a fortnight life with him was endured by the nurse and the other children; it is difficult to find a word strong enough to describe the pitch of his lawlessness and even rudeness. Frank was properly whipped. The whole atmosphere of the house was different afterwards; it was as if the child had before been possessed by a devil, now angels came and dwelt in him! At home it was the last whipping he needed for more than a year. "Punishment had produced an effect which, from the outside, looked like moral conversion." Moral conversion it cannot be. Pain cannot turn the child from an enjoyment of wrong-doing to a love of right. What had happened was that the better instincts of his nature-better instincts which were undoubtedly there-did not show themselves in action, because other and bad instincts blocked their path. In some cases the discipline of consequences may be resorted to.

In other words, the child may sometimes be punished by allowing him to suffer the obvious results of his actions. Thus a child who fails to get ready for a walk may be left at home; or a boy who has broken something may 'be required to pay for it. This kind of punishment often saves friction, the child recognising its justice. But it cannot always be used. In some cases the punishment would be too great, in others too small. One boy who neglects to put on his overcoat contracts pneumonia and dies; another does not even catch cold. We cannot leave all to nature. Authority must often step in with its more artificial punishments. Lest any teacher, however, should construe this advocacy of punishment into a general permit for indiscriminate resort to it, let us hasten to add that neglect of the child's more specialised tendencies is an irreparable error.

Out of the child's instincts it is possible to develop a number of sentiments which will become the stimulating and directing forces of behaviour on comparatively high planes. But if we continue to resort to punishment and reward throughout the child's school career, we shall make the Law of Hedonic Selection the ruling principle of his life. Many of his other instincts will die out for lack of exercise. Darwin, late in his career, regretted that he had lost all interest in literature. He found it impossible to revive any desire for the reading of works of imagination. His inordinate pursuit of science had prevented the growth of his literary sentiment.

This may not be considered as greatly to be regretted in the case of Darwin. For his dominant interest was a highly useful one. But with the more ordinary human beings, there is no such lofty interest. If we fail, during their school life, to make something of the comparatively feeble tendencies which they possess for higher things, we turn them out with no ennobling interests, but with the general tendency to seek pleasure and avoid pain and some lower instincts as their chief motives.

5

GROWTH, DEVELOPMENT AND MATURATION

With reasonably adequate nutrition and care the infant grows in height and weight until he reaches a mature level of physical development. This type of growth is apparent to almost everybody. The mother says, "My boy is growing so fast that I can hardly keep him in clothing." Schools make provisions for this growth process by graduating the size of seats as children increase in age. There is, however, another general type of maturing that occurs simultaneously with growth which is not so readily observable. This growth process affects the infant's and child's behaviour in a more direct way than any other developmental function. With advancing age during infancy and childhood there is a corresponding increase in the gross magnitude and organizational complexity of the central nervous system. Microscopic study of the brains of deceased infants of different ages demonstrates the growth changes that have taken place in the central nervous system.

The maturation of neural tissues sets certain limits for children's behaviour.. No amount of parental coaching is sufficient to enable the three-month-old infant to talk in sentences. Neural development is too limited at this age for such complex behaviour. It is extremely important in the rearing and education of children to know what these maturational limits are for many different kinds of behaviour. Knowledge of these maturational limits by parents and teachers makes it more possible for them to provide the most appropriate learning situations for children - situations that are neither too difficult nor too easy.

It should be noted that maturation of neural tissues as necessary but not a sufficient condition for the appearance of certain types of behaviour. Between two and three years of age the child who grows up in a more or less normal environment usually learns to talk in short sentences. The maturation of the central nervous system plus numerous language experiences make this behaviour possible. If the child is deprived of a language environment this behaviour will not appear. For example, the congenitally deaf or hear-deaf child will not learn to talk until certain steps are taken to provide him a language environment through amplified speech sounds or tactual stimuli.

What is Maturation?

Maturation, as a scientific concept, has been used for many years by geneticists to designate the process of development during which a germ cell becomes mature - that is, the process by means of which the chromosomes of the immature germ cell are decreased in number by one-half. The term was borrowed and made popular in child psychology largely through the efforts of Gesell, who wrote in an early publication: "Growth is a process so intricate and so sensitive that there must be powerful stabilizing factors, intrinsic, rather than extrinsic, which preserve the balance of the total pattern and the direction of the growth trend. Maturation is, in a sense, a name for this regulatory mechanism". At a later date McGeoch defined the concept in terms of behaviour change: "Maturation... includes any change with age in the conditions of learning which depends primarily upon organic growth factors rather than upon prior practice or experience". In other words, "maturation" is a name for the growth process during which a structure or a function is more and more becoming adult, that is "mature".

These definitions stress different aspects of the maturational process, but are essentially similar in their emphasis on organically internal growth processes that are primarily, or momentarily, independent of environmental factors external to the organism. It seems unprofitable to attempt a clear cut differentiation between maturation and experience as they influence behaviour in most situations. However, despite unavoidable overlapping, the concept of maturation is an important one in that it can be used to designate certain variables influencing psychological development and behaviour over which man has little or on control at the present time.

Before proceeding to the subject of the present chapter I wish to say a word upon physical education. A comparatively independent branch of Professor Bain's theory no doubt it is, although acquaintance with the condition of bodily health would be a matter of no small importance, even were intellectual training our only concern. But for parents, private tutors, and the heads of school-houses, knowledge of how to promote the physical growth and vigour of the young is indispensable. Too many continental writers on education have followed Professor Bain in ignoring the claims of the body and its intimate connection with the mind. And the result is that, while their class work and discipline are admirable, it has lately been found that in some schools a third of the scholars suffer from headaches, due mainly to long school-hours and too much home preparation, which has to be done chiefly, of course, at nights.

Not a little harm has, I suspect, been caused by the over-statement we often hear, change of work is as good as play. It is no such thing. Good no doubt it is, and better than entire idleness in many cases, but play is work for children, that is to say, it is active occupation; and change to this form of work they require at pretty frequent intervals, if their other work is to have any zest in it. A healthy child three years old runs perhaps two or three miles in the course of the day, but would be seriously tired if it had to run a quarter of a mile at once.

Children are soon exhausted and soon refreshed. And we have to remember that their brains, like the rest of their bodies, have a double work to do where the work of the adult brain is only single; the child's brain has both to act and to grow. Nay, it has to grow in two respects, both necessitating frequent relaxation or entailing certain injury.

It has to grow in bulk and it has to grow in complexity of structure. Beside sufficient but not excessive exercise, the chief condition of growth in bulk is well-nourished and well--aerated blood; and with this condition long confinement is incompatible. The chief condition of the other and higher growth is due to rest after exercise to enable the new nervous connections to perfect themselves. The brain is not a delicate organ in the sense of being easily hurt by work, and even hard work; but it is extremely delicated in this sense, that all forcing and excessive strain deteriorate it in strength and still more perhaps in quality; it is, in this respect, like a good watch which will serve you your life-time with care, but is almost sure to snap somewhere if you over wind it.

Parents and headmasters and mistresses must have a real acquaintance, though it need not be profound, with the physiological laws on which bodily growth and vigour depend before the rising generation can be secured against the educational abomination of desolation, as Professor Huxley calls it, that brain-forcing which is now too much in vogue in secondary schools. Without this, the foolish public is just as likely, if it should ever become alarmed, to err to an equal extent in the opposite extreme and refuse to children the mental quickening their brains require. But, besides these, there is a much more intimate connection that is commonly supposed between moral health and bodily health.

It is not meant that soundness of body is alone sufficient to ensure generosity and purity of heart, but that active exercise is a check to many temptations which are only too powerfully abetted by sluggish limbs and hysterical nerves, while many play has not only light as air each limb, each thought as clear as day, but most likely has too an abounding good nature and cheerfulness which provoke and strengthen friendly feeling.

For a long time it has been the custom to represent the mind as a complex of faculties-faculties of sense, of memory, of imagination, of judgment, of reasoning, of emotion, of volition, and so forth indefinite. But this terminology, though it has its conveniences, and is besides one we can hardly discard in ordinary conversation, has nevertheless been the occasion of frequent errors and will lead us also astray, if we do not make clear to ourselves what we understand by it. In the body we know there are definite organs, having definite functions the heart to propel the blood, the liver to purify it, the lungs to oxygenate it, and so forth. And, when careful and long-continued observation had disclosed the fact that in the brain we have an organ holding a most intimate relation to the mind, so that for example a well-developed and well-nourished brain was concomitant with excellence and vigour of mind, or intoxication or disease or the brain with delirium or aberration of mind, then, on the strength of this fact and in conformity with the faculty theory, it was confidently and reasonably concluded that within the brain itself would be found in one part the organ of memory, in another the organ of imagination, in another the organ of volition, and so on.

Time would fail me to tell of all the attempts, extending over half a century, to find organs for supposed faculties and faculties for supposed organs. Meanwhile, the opinion has steadily gained ground that the so-called faculties are but psychological abstractions, names due at first to a faulty classification of facts, the real explanation of which they served at length to hide. To the question, how does a man move about? I answer, rightly, by means of his legs. But to the question, how does he remember? There is only the semblance of information in the answer: By means of his memory. Legs are a reality, and only one among several possible instruments of locomotion: fish swim and birds fly. Yet memory is not in this sense a reality, as will be apparent directly from a parallel case. Professor Huxley, it is said, is a masterly expositor of science.

How does he expound science so ably? By means of his admirable faculty for exposition it is clear that there is here no advance. What is the moral? Let us see what the physicists did in a similar perplexity. A needle moves towards a magnet placed near it, or the needle is dissolved in sulphuric acid. How? Owing to the magnetism of the magnet and the solubility of the needle was the sort of explanation first offered and accepted-an explanation which carries us no further than giving a name to the phenomena or actions to be explained. And during this stage everything was regarded as the seat of, or as endowed with, a multiplicity of powers and properties by which its actions and reactions were supposed to be determined.

But the explanation which the physicist now gives, or seeks to give, consists in showing what was the arrangement of the body concerned

(1) at the beginning,
(2) at the end of the action in question, and
(3) the quantity of energy it has lost or gained in the passage from the one arrangement to the other-facts, that is, which can in all cases be represented by a certain configuration in space and by reference to some given quantity of matter moving through a given distance in a given time. The unity of the physical world was in danger of being lost sight of amid the multitude of forces and powers: the unity of mind is still in similar danger. Can we, to avoid this, substitute for the reference to host a faculties, current in the old psychology, any conceptions as definite as matter and motion, so as really to explain the facts only named before? It would be too bold to say 'yes' and I do not like saying no. Look for a moment at what has befallen the phrenologists.

The progress of physiology has at length placed it beyond reasonable doubt that there are no organs in the brain at all having any sort of analogy with mental faculties. In the brain and its continuation, the spinal cord, we have millions of microscopic cells which are the terminations of nerve fibres, coming from all parts of the body, and other cells again forming centres for a network of connections between those first cells, and connected again in turn in like manner with cells higher still, and so on. The nerves reaching the brain and spinal cord from the rest of the body are of two kinds, and two kinds only; those which start from moving or active parts like muscles and those which start from sensitive parts like the skin, the eye or the ear.

Under normal circumstances, the latter nerves are stimulated or set into action by some change produced by the external world on the sensitive surface in which they terminate-say of the tips of the fingers, or the retina of the eye. The effect of this change then travels up the nerve to the brain: hence these are called centripetal or in going nerves. Under normal circumstances, again, the other kind of nerve is stimulated by a change taking place in the brain cells. The effect of this change travels down the nerve, and, by exciting the muscle to move, produces some change in the external world: hence these are called centrifugal or outgoing nerves.

The cell in which an ingoing nerve terminates is connected with some cell in which an outgoing nerve begins, so that the excitation which reaches the first passes on and arouses the second; and thus the action of the external world on the body is followed by a reaction of the body upon the external world. When one bird hops on to trap, the trap reacts, and the bird is caught: when another hops into a crocodile's mouth, the mouth closes and he is caught too: what springs and wires accomplished in the one case, nerves, nerve-cells and muscles accomplish in the other. And, as by a more elaborate contrivance of springs and wires a more elaborate trap could be produced, so, by a more complicated connection between nerve-cells or centres, more elaborate reactions to the action of the external world become possible.

This, then, is all that physiology certainly finds in a brain: neither more nor less than a vastly complex mechanism of exceeding delicacy, whose function is to co-ordinate and adapt the reactions of the body to the actions of the external world, a mechanism which is more complex

(1) the more ways there are in which the external world can affect the body,

(2) the more ways there are in which the body can react by moving, and

(3) the more ways there are in which possible actions and reactions may be combined.

Thus, by way of illustration, an animal that has eyes and ears has a more complex brain than one that has eyes only; an animal that has both arms and legs than one that has arms only; an animal that moves either arms or legs after the stimulation of either eyes or ears than one that can only move its legs when its ears are stimulated and its arms when its eyes are. Concomitantly with the brain-changes described, there are certain mind-changes: to centripetal stimulations correspond sensations, hence the centripetal nerves and their cells are often, though not accurately, called sensory: to centrifugal stimulations correspond the exertion of movement, for which reason these nerves and their cells are called motor. When definite portions of the brain are destroyed by injury or disease, hearing cases, though the ear and its nerves remain intact; when other definite portions are destroyed, sight cases.

With the destruction of together parts, again, the power to move the right hand is lost, of yet other portions the power to move the left, and so on. Further, the loss of particular parts renders particular coordinated movements, such as walking anatomically regarded, furnishes us with equivalents to nothing in mind but sensations and movements, and complexes of sensations and movements. And, now, instead of studying others' brains, for we cannot see our own, let us turn to our own minds, which none but ourselves can see. What have we here? Nothing but sensations and movements or complexes of these, the physical equivalents of which we find to constitute the whole structure of brain? Nothing, I believe, except the mind which is conscious of having all these, together with the pleasure or pain it receives from them. I do not expect you at once to accede to this: I hope, nevertheless, to do something to make good my analysis as we go along.

But the first thing is to get it into better shape: Prior even to this, however, I want to digress for a moment to obviate and objection that may occur to someone-an objection with which I entirely sympathize. You may say with not unnatural aversion: Are, then, our noblest thoughts and aspirations nothing but complexes of sensations and movements, the concomitants in some mysterious way of material changes in the brain? No, the reality of your thoughts and emotions-so far as reality stands for meaning and worth-lies in these as they are when you think them and feel them, just as the reality of Nature lies in the living from and face of Nature, not in the decompositions, whether logical or material, which aid our curiosity when we try to know not it but about it.

A child disappointment is sure to seize us if we imagine that the reality is what we have reached by our analysis and dissection, instead of being what we have left behind. We seek to know about the parts of Nature that we may the better appreciate and understand the whole. In this spirit, then, let us resume our analysis of mind. The simplest state of mind we need consider at the outset would be some such as the following: There comes before you the perfume of a rose; you are pleased and either stopped to enjoy it more or you pluck the rose. Here then are

(i) an object presented and attended to,

(ii) the feeling it produces in you, the subject attending to it, and

(iii) the action which following upon the pleasure.

But, here, note that this action is only possible by attending to it while you do it. There are here, then, two sorts of things attended to; and in this case, at all events, they are not obviously different from sensations and movements. Suppose, however, you have just read the scene in King Fohn where his nephew is to have his eyes put out. Here there is strictly speaking no sensation, but the scene as you picture it is made up of what still remains of past sensations, and if you had the misfortune to have been born blind much of.the scene would be numbering. Neither is there here, perhaps, any movement, unless your feeling of pain at the horrible scene should find vent in words or facial expression. Yet, at any rate, there are the beginnings of movements, as you imagine yourself raising an alarm, or attempting a rescue. Or, suppose you reflect awhile on the saying: "Virtue is its own reward."

Such a state of mind is enormously complex, as you will at once realize if you imagine yourself expounding the maxim to a boy of twelve. Virtue stands for virtuous acts, or for a life of such, and this has finally to be pictured out in detail by means of what the boy has himself seen and done in the past. It would be tedious to multiply illustration further. Try, if you choose, for yourselves and see if you do not find that the material of all that can be presented to our minds is reducible to sensations and movements, just as the material of all the vast variety of substances on the earth is reducible to some one or more of the chemical elements. The greatest part of our work is, it is clear, in both cases, to study the compounds. The inquiry of chief interest in psychology is, then, that concerning the formation of complex ideas out of simple ones, of perceptions out of sensations, of thoughts out of perceptions.

It is easy to take to pieces, but putting together again is a very different matter. Locke, who was very successful at the first process, the analysis, failed completely at the second, the synthesis. Let us, then, take care, and advance only a step at a time. First, what is requisite in order that two or more sensations and movements should form a complex? There is no sort of psychical cement or psychical attraction, so far as we know, or can at present conceive. The one condition for forming a psychical compound is contiguity. This is why when hearing the voice of a friend there is at once present to our mind his appearance as well. But this connection is not as close as it might be because it is sometimes broken.

We hear our friend's voice without seeing him, or see him when he does not speak. On the other hand, some of the complexes formed never have their elements in this way presented apart, or, if presented apart at first, become after a time so closely conjoined that we cannot be introspection separate them. In these cases the complexity only admits of course, of indirect proof and the fact of it is apt to be overlooked. Most persons, for example, would regard the sight of a coloured surface as an elementary fact, since we have seen no uncoloured surface and no non-extended colour.

This is one source of the inability of adults to understand the difficulties children have in apprehending what to their teachers seem absolutely simple and self-evident. Next, let us ask in what ways the needful contiguity is brought about. For the present, we need only to note two which are of fundamental importance. In many cases, sensations are presented to us over and over again grouped in the same way. Thus, we have the whiteness, softness and coldness of snow; the colour, taste and fragrance of an orange; the brightness and warmth of a fire, and so on. In this way, groups or complexes of sensations are formed, independently of the mind or subject to whom the sensations belong, independently, that is, so far as the character of the group is concerned.

But in the case of movement it is to a large extent otherwise. When sensations occasion us pleasure, we move either to express our pleasure or to secure its continuance; when sensations occasion us pain, we make movements expressive of pain or on purpose to be rid of it. Such movements, being contiguous with the sensations, become associated with those sensations and will together give rise to a new and more complex state of mind. Thus, to repeat my former instance, the perfume of a rose leads to the act of plucking it, the means whereby the scent of many former roses was more fully enjoyed. Similarly, the dog that has been thrashed cowers or runs away at the sight of the wipe from the smart of which his legs or his humble demeanour delivered him before.

These, then, are the two sources by which the material of our experience is brought together and formed into complexes or united wholes: first, independently of us, the external world, and secondly, independently of the external world, ourselves, i.e. our interest in our own feeling of pleasure and pain, which determines our movements or reactions to it. Owing to a certain constancy in these two factors, complexes originally formed are united for the most part more closely by repetition. Day after day, we have presented to us together the same arrangements of the world about us; day after day, the same pleasures and pains lead to the same movements to secure or avoid the causes of them. And, thus, out of what is originally much such a chaos as the world resolved into its chemical elements would be there arises, by this process of combination and recombination, what we call our experience, the contents of our mind.

It is by carefully forms that we must hope to obtain real explanations of those mental phenomena to which the theory of faculties does but give names. This, of course, we cannot attempt, except in a few cases, within the limits of these lectures. But now let me briefly summarize, and in one or two points, supplement this meagre sketch of the general nature of mind. We have in what we call mind

(i) a subject or self, whether it knows itself or not, which is conscious of objects or ideas and

(ii) the ideas or objects of which it is conscious, using the terms, idea and object in a very wide sense. Such mental objects in their simplest, crudest, form are -

(a) sensory objects or

(b) motor objects, or, in more familiar language, sensations and movements. We can only be definitely conscious of, that is to say, attend to, a few of these at a time. Those to which we attend together, whether sensory or motor objects, or partly the one and partly the other, thereby tend to form a new whole or

complex idea. And, when other objects succeed to the first place in our attention-the place which is usually either given to or seized by newcomers-this complex idea or mind-object does not dissolve and disappear utterly, like a snowflake on a river. It is only crowded out into a dim or dark background, which we may call the region of sub-consciousness, that is to say, the region of all but unconsciousness.

From this region, it can again emerge, not resolved into its components, but the same complex object as before, though fainter in intensity, and, so far, securing less attention. Once more in the forefront of consciousness its elements are more closely combined; moreover, at any time when thus revived it may enter into the composition of another object of consciousness more complex still; and so, step by step, the mind is said to grow. We may, now, perhaps, proceed to consider this growth in more dental. The actual beginning of consciousness is as indescribable as the beginning of life. Even the earlier stages of consciousness can only be inferred from a study of the later by interpreting the external behaviour of infancy in analogy with the external behaviour of the later stages.

But among the materials of consciousness, the sensory and motor objects presented to the young soul, when attention first awakens, we may safely reckon all the varieties of sights, sounds, touches, tastes, smells, for which it has organs and opportunities and all the movements it limbs by any chance may execute. We may go further, and, instead of supposing the entire formation of this mental chaos into a mental cosmos to depend on the child' own activity, may reasonably suppose that it starts with certain lines of association, at least, prepared beforehand and vaguely indicated.

To grant this is to grant the doctrine of psychical heredity, the doctrine, that is, that those connections which were slowly established between some cells and others in the brains of its ancestors in the course of, and in consequence of, their experience, are already more or less completely preformed in the child's brain before its experience begins-so far preformed that a minimum of experience, in its case, suffices to perfect the connection, say, between certain sensation and a certain movement, which in the case of its forefathers was only perfected after the lapse of years, perhaps of centuries.

It is to this inherited difference of organization, and consequent difference of mental possibilities, that we must often refer the varying rapidity with which different minds unfold in particular directions, and the varying interest they take in different pursuits. In view of facts like these-which I regret I cannot here consider more fully-one may be pardoned for doubting whether the same means will be equally adapted in all cases to secure the same end: whether what will best train one mind and disposition will best train another and different mind and disposition. People in the western counties travel eastwards to go to London, but those in the eastern counties would have an expensive and fatiguing journey if they did the same.

It is not, then, enough for parents and teachers to have distinctly before them an educational ideal; it is hardly less important that they should understand the individuality, as we say, of their pupils. Even a horse breaker cannot dispense with such knowledge: much more is it impossible to be a good educator without the tact and insight to understand one's pupils.

This perhaps is one of the points as to which it is true that a good teacher is born into many lives besides their own, enjoy seeing others ride hobbies they would never mount themselves: broad in their tastes and broader still in their sympathies, to whom everybody tells his good news and not a few confess their faults or bring their difficulties! These are the men and women, when you can find them, to choose for schoolmasters and schoolmistresses. But there is much truth in the old rhyme: "Evil is wrought by want of thought as well as want of heart. No institutions are so conservative as educational institutions a fact for which it is not hard to find reasons.

After the revival of learning the idea of training had dawned on but two or three minds, and the circle of useful knowledge was so small that it was natural to set all alike to tread the same weary round. And so the tradition has become established which is continually treating minds the most diverse after the same antiquated fashion. To many teachers, it never occurs to ask what intellectual training will be best for this pupil and for that: so far as moral training goes, that must, indeed, be a very perfunctory and clumsy teacher who treats all alike. No doubt it requires some experience to make the most of clever but odd children, and the practical difficulties must often be considerable. Still, spite of all, in discussing the theory of education we ought to take account of the mischief done by trying to pull and the minds in a school to one shape just as the country barber polls their hair.

If anyone should doubt that the mischief is great let him read the results of an inquiry of this point made by Sir Francis Galton and tabulated in his English Men of Science, their Nature and Nurture. But it is primarily with what is common to the growth of all minds that we have now to do and here also there is room for some weighty practical reflections. Let us, however, first see something of the growth itself. Though the organized experience of its ancestors may enormously accelerate the infant's earliest progress in knowledge, yet we shall not be far wrong in supposing it to advance by gradual steps even here.

Its great defect at the outset is inability to concentrate attention. For want of this, it is some time before even the first step can be taken towards the simplest combination of the material constantly provided for it by its senses and its own spontaneous or instinctive movements. The 'massive' sensations of organic life, the sensations and movements connected with breathing, pulses, digestion, the feeling of being well or ill- to all of which we adults are oblivious, except when they are very pronounced because our interests carry our attention elsewhere- these organic sensations probably form for some time the staple elements of the infant consciousness. Amid such a mass, the light and transient impressions of the higher senses fail at first to afford any pleasure, and so fail to call forth any interest, comparable to the solid satisfaction of a vigorous digestion and a glowing pulse: the young hopeful vegetates triumphantly.

After a while, however, the preliminaries and essentials of a meal come, by reason of their contiguity in time to the meal itself, to secure some attention and to be known by themselves: to the spoon belongs the merit of first enticing the baby mind into the regions of objective knowledge. Soon the fortunate moments become more and more frequent in which a moving light, the jingle of a rattle, or the magic pinches which nurses administer and carry it still further in the same direction. Its consciousness is no longer that of a large oyster in nebulous wholes, faces and moving objects stand out vaguely from the general blur, and everybody is agreed that baby begins to notice.

But how very obscure and ill-defined these earliest complexes or perceptions are brought home to us most strikingly by comparing infantile movements with our own. There is no reason to suppose that the ability to perform any definite movements lags far behind the ability to form definite perceptions. A baby expresses his pleasure by the most various antics, in the course of which many movements that will afterwards be propulsive occur by chance; but it is long before anyone can be performed apart from the rest.

The child at first can do nothing without doing everything. As the physiologists would put it, there is too much radiation and too little restriction. Every excitation arouses the whole brain instead of discharging itself along definite tracks, like a downpour of rain on some land new risen from the bed of the sea and on which the weather has still to trace out a network of streams and rivers. As the one process takes time, so does the other, though both seem very much matters of course to the unreflecting observer, when the development is complete. Now, the great means of advancing this parceling out of experience into parts, of making groups of definite objects and acts out of an indefinite maze of sensations and movements, or to use Herbert Spencer's favourite phrase, of progressing from the homogeneous to the heterogeneous, is Interest.

The uniformity of Nature-the regular recurrence of sweet and white in sugar, of meows and scratches when puss is picked up by the tail-does much to suggest which two and two to put together. But ages may elapse before we take the hint, unless as in the above instances we are interested. And, for my own part, I doubt not that ages did elapse before the creature mind appreciated and appropriated even the most elementary lessons which an infinite patience had planned for it. Would that those who carryon Nature's work had more of Nature' patience! Interest in sensations it is, as we have seen that determines movements, and on movements in connection with sensations a very large part of our knowledge depends. What we learn by means of our eyes and our hands would be reduced almost to nil if we were prevented from moving them. Interest also works by concentrating attention upon some objects to the exclusion of others. And here, again, its connection with movement is apparent, though this time it is by checking movements that are begun, the continuance of which would draw off attention.

In these two ways the infant individualizes objects, and separates, among the mass that is presented to it together, those things that belong together. The bucket that lies on the floor is distinguished from the floor on which it lies, and the clatter of a rattle from the many other sounds heard simultaneously. But, beyond this narrow region of its experience, or rather these isolated patches, into which its formative activity has introduced the beginnings of order, the primal indistinctness and confusion reins, and will reign, till interest furnishes the budding intelligence with a motive to enter and assimilate. This interest is, as we have seen, determined by pleasure and pain.

But what determines these; what is there common to, all that pleases us? If I answer doing what we please, it may perhaps be thought that this is as good as no answer at all. Yet it is much truer than at first sight it seems, that all pleasure involves doing, involves activity. Even the apparently passive pleasure of watching a display of fireworks or hearing the waves break upon the stones requires activity and involves fatigue; so that, if your eyes or ears were already exhausted or you were yourself generally weary, these things would please no longer. And when everything about us is too indifferent and monotonous to engage or retain our attention, we long for occupation and change or fall asleep for want of it.

In saying that the activity concerned in pleasure is doing what we please, I mean all such activity as well engage in spontaneously, our energies being fresh, and either waiting or seeking the opportunity for action. Such is the position of healthy children let loose from school. During the quiet and constraint of the morning's lessons their muscles have been rested and refreshed and now find vent in wild shouts and play. Of such sort is the activity of a child for the first three or four years of life.

All that it does because it is fresh and ready for the work: one advance secured, it has an interest in the next, to which it was before indifferent. It does not attempt to bite till its teeth begin to work their way through its gums, nor to articulate till it has learnt to babble, nor to walk till it can crawl. And so, during only what it is ready to do, and, therefore, has an interest in doing, advancing under the prompting of its own growing powers, it advances with enormous rapidity. In two or three years it has learnt without trouble or fatigue a vast number of complicated movements, is practically acquainted with space, knows the properties of numerous objects and above all has acquired an intelligent command of language.

This is probably a godlier array of acquisitions than any it will have to show after ten years of school. No doubt, in all this it is helped by heredity; very naturally, our inherited experience is realized and put to use as soon as it can be useful. But this does not affect the practical lessons to be drawn from the suggested study of infancy, nay it adds to them. The child has not yet exhausted the organized heritage of his ancestors; there is a natural order of mental development and the process is still the same, from the more general and simple separations and combinations of the elements of its experience to the more complex. And, when we see how surely and thoroughly the tiny scholar advances in knowledge while this method is of necessity followed, we must allow the desirability of abiding by it still, when Nature's training begins to slacken and to need supplementing by other means.

The younger the pupil is the more imperative is it for the teacher to adopt what Brain cells the psychological sequence of subjects, to direct growth that is incipient; but to avoid all forcing and the foolish haste that tries to cram with ready-prepared material, as if the time required for mastery and assimilation were time lost. During infancy, i.e. till the seventh year or later, the mind is mainly occupied, in the way described, in mastering the rudiments of perception and movement and so much of language as this involves. What it has thus accomplished remains its permanent possession, and can be lived over again in fainter forms without the repetition of the original experience. Still more, it can be recombined in other forms independently of external presentation or actual movement, that is to say, the young child can imagine what it does not see and has not seen; but only by the aid of pictures or narratives.

Imagination is as yet to a very small extent constructive: children before seven or eight have little fancy and less thought. Picture-books, nursery-rhymes and fairy-tales, if they call for no combinations of ideas more complex than those which the child has already formed and the elements of which it has experienced, and if they promote only good nature, kindly feeling, and dislike of wrong, are admirable adjuncts of toy hammers, bricks, spades and buckets. But they should be only adjuncts: a child is receiving higher education when engaged in play of the latter kind or in ripping up and smashing the handsomely finished toys, with which unphilosophic grandmothers love to adorn their Christmas-trees.

When a little child is so quiet that his mother or nurse suspects mischief, he is probably making most strides towards being a man of independent judgment and character. When he is tired of entertaining himself, then bring out the pictures, or, still better, draw new ones before his eyes. And if you tell him a tale, tell him an old one rather than always something new. For if the tale is a good one and will help to make him a man, the impressions must be deepened if they are to be fixed. Besides, everlasting novelty will tend to produce a vapid and wandering mind. All this implies an amount of individual attention which no school-teacher could afford to give, but then is it not clear that schools for children under nine or ten are only good where home education is impossible?

The Kindergarten system, in the hands of one who understands it, produces admirable results, but it is apt to be too mechanical and formal. There does not seem room for the individuality of a child, to which all the free play possible should be given in the earliest years: afterwards it can more effectively take care of itself and will be less easily repressed. The chief danger with the Kindergarten is that its rules and method should be known and applied, or rather misapplied, by persons who have either forgotten or never understood its principles. I fear there is truth in an observation of Dr. Fitch'-that there is many an untrained teacher who gets "sixpenny book about Froebel's gifts, buys a box of cubes and some coloured strips of paper, sets the children to build bricks and weave little mats, and then says that she has adopted the Kindergarten system.

The difference between the trained and untrained teacher is, that the one thinks that the mere adoption of the gifts and mechanical exercises devised by Froebel is all that is necessary in the system; the other, by getting hold of the principles which underlie the method, is in a position to devise new and appropriate methods for herself-methods and exercises probably much better adapted to the needs of English children than Froebel's, which were meant mainly for the children of

German peasants. The fundamental idea of Froebel, that of life as a unity, manifesting itself in various ways, a whole that becomes more complex by gradual development but never ceases to be a whole, has important bearings upon education at every stage, applies not only to infancy, but to childhood and youth as well. Let me briefly illustrate. We understand what we make chairs and dolls and steam engines, and can at any time take them to pieces and put them together again.

But things that live and grow that have never been in pieces, and that cannot be taken to pieces without for ever being destroyed-such as a plant, an animal, and mind, a nation,-are harder far to understand. We are forced to take them to pieces in imagination; mentally to analyse them and give a separate name to different organs and functions and stages of the one individual life. Where, however, are the leaves and branches and roots of the oak in the acorn? Where are the gay plumage-the keen sight of the kingfisher in the egg? At what moment does the child's imagination begin; when has he first a conscience or reason? Such, I take it, were the reflections which worked in Froebel' mind. To call attention to a complete scheme of education based on these ideas of the unity of life and its gradual development and organization by pamphlets, books and newspaper articles, was his main occupation for thirty years before he even started a Kindergarten.

And, in fact, but for the lamentable circumstance that his own schooling had been of the scantiest description, and that he was, therefore, debatted by his ignorance of classics from finding a place in the secondary schools of his country, we might never have heard of the Kindergarten at all. The leading principle in Froebel's educational scheme which led him to see the man in the child at play, and led him to believe that by guiding the child's play it was possible to train his mind, is nothing more or less than a great biological truth applied. And most assuredly if it be true, and if it has been fruitful, so far as infantile education goes, it is true, it is worth applying a great deal further.

The child's mind, like its body, grows gradually, and the future vigour of both depends on the right food and the right exercise being applied. What is right at one time is wrong at another; it is wrong to give meat to babes or milk to men; it is wrong to teach the babe to walk before it can crawl. For the mind, too, every branch of knowledge is good in season and wrong out of season. The question is, What is the natural order, what is the psychological sequence of subjects? And, again, what will each subject do, what is its educational value? A child's body cannot make bone out of starchy food, like rice and sago, though it may make fat: and useful information and sound moral precepts will not save it from intellectual and moral rickets, though they may convert it into a splendid prig. No, while I believe that modem school-teachers are really beginning seriously to ponder these vital questions and even to think that some knowledge of the laws concerning the nature and development of mind might help them, yet at the best it must be long before such a thoroughgoing reform as I imagine Froebel contemplated can be actually brought about.

The practical difficulties in the way are manifold; the difficulty of even seeing the truth is great. First of all, it requires a good deal of faith to put information in the second place and education in the first, to have patience to let the child' mind grow. But, leaving this aside, it is hard, I repeat, to see that what the man wants most is not what the child wants most. The mature man, bearing the heat and burden of the day, finds himself stayed or thwarted-if a merchant perhaps because he cannot read Spanish; or if a manufacturer, because he cannot use some dare he likes without rotting the fabric-in a word, he wants knowledge. Not so the boy: what he wants first of all is exercise.

If I were to say he wants play, that would be misunderstood, and yet it would be true in a sense, and the sense in which Froebel saw it and applied it. What the boy wants is to *try* his powers: gymnastic for his muscles and gymnastic for his mind. If you can impart the knowledge that will be useful by and by while training his mind, so much the better every way. He will not like his work the less for seeing that it will be useful. Quite the contrary. If, when you teach arithmetic, for example, you put him to find out from the data you give him how many square miles there are in his parish or how many people to the square mile; if you put him to apply his *geometry* in pegging out a tennis-court or finding the height of the church-spire, so much the better: he will like his lesson all the more. Yet he will be interested in the results not because they are useful, but because he has found them out by himself.

By the seventh year, or thereabouts, the period of childhood may be said to have commenced. The characteristics of infancy do not all at once disappear; there is still interest enough in sensations and movements. But the novelty has diminished; old experiences are continually recurring and many are now so familiar that their charm has gone. To tear up paper boxes, and to roll cotton bobbins over the floor have ceased to be matters of absorbing interest for half an hour, because they have ceased to have anything new to disclose. A fresh trait is now apparent. Having secured the great mass of the raw material of experience and shaped it into the simplest forms, the child now begins to build up these simpler forms into others more complex: having converted the clay into bricks, its interest is, in large measure, transferred to the random heaps of these; and it begins to erect with them the outer walls of the temple of knowledge.

In other words, the vast store of concrete perceptions gathered in the busy, happy days gone by now begins to engage the attention, on which the external world, less an unknown fairyland than before, makes smaller claims. The activity which was lately employed in building up perceptions and intuitions is now busy discovering a further order among these. In respect of this further order, even perceptions and intuitions are material, just as bricks are material when our end is to build a wall, though to the brick maker they were the forms into which he moulded what would else have remained shapeless clay.

This new intellectual activity the beginnings of which characterize childhood is thinking, or, more precisely, conceiving. But just as in combining sensations into perceptions the material was given to the subject attending to them, so again here. The material for conception is furnished by what is often termed the faculty of imagination or of representation. By this we must not understand any new activity of the conscious subject or thinking mind; for, in some mode or other, representation takes place whether we will or no. Representations are given to us just as their originals were; and, so far, the only activity concerned is that of attending to or receiving them. You can no more hinder a train of ideas passing through your mind than you can hinder a succession of sights and sounds being presented to your senses, as you walk along the street.

The more you are interested in the one, the less you will attend to the other, though both are there through all your waking life. As we saw in the last lecture, the impressions which the child receives and combines today, though crowded out of consciousness, are not crowded out of existence. It is a general law in psychology that the more intense impressions tend to draw off attention from weaker ones. It is also a general law that even when the same impression is continually presented, its intensity tends to become less and less. Semper idems entire and idem residues are the words in which Hobbes formulated this law: it is almost all one not feel at all and always to feel alike.

For example, the miller sleeps so long as his wheel continues in motion, but wakes up when it stands still; the occupant of the pew falls asleep during the delivery of a monotonous sermon, but wakes so soon as it ends. When, however, the external stimulation ceases, the intensity of the impression very rapidly declines. By the action, then, of these two laws it is that the occupants of the stage of consciousness at anyone moment are presently driven off; and are kept off so long as there are new arrivals of interest to take their place. But the moment this interest slackens, or the way is clear, the old impressions begin to revive, as we see perhaps best of all in our dreams. And, when they first appeared we called them presentations, we may call them representations on their return.

But we cannot execute those movements in the case of representations which we were led to make in the case of the original presentations, for you cannot pluck a remembered rose nor shake hands once more with a departed friend, however vividly both are represented to your mind. On this account, the representations have been termed mental residual, what the mind has secured and made its own from the changing world without. They constitute, in distinction from the external world which we control only by actual movement, an internal world, which we are said to control by thought. What we mean by this control we shall see more clearly by and by. Let us first become a little better acquainted with this new world, which has grown up between the infant would and that external world to which all its first interest was given.

Though called into existence, in good part, by the child's own activity, yet it did not own its existence entirely to this: it has therefore, as I have said, laws of its own. Representations or ideas will arise in his consciousness neither arranged in a logical order nor arranged so as to afford him most entertainment, but the order in which one will succeed another will depend solely upon certain quasi-mechanical relations between

(i) the intensity of each representation, and
(ii) its compatibility with those which have already entered within the threshold of consciousness from the vague realm beyond.

Left to themselves representations go dancing through each other like the pictures in a dissolving view. How bizarre and meaningless are the products of such interaction of representations, when uncontrolled, we see in our dreams. Yet this interaction among representations admits of control in two ways; and first by suggestion. When words are spoken the representations associated with these words. if there are nay, at once arise in consciousness, and others incompatible with them are excluded. It is in this way that, as we have seen, infants may be entertained by means of their imagination, that is to say, by means of the mechanism of representations just described. In the same way substantially, presentations may awaken or suggest connected representations, when there is a sufficient store of these, and the mind is sufficiently disengaged from the present impressions themselves. Some school-teachers, in withdrawing attention from the world of Nature to the world of letters; act upon the tacit assumption that mental growth is independent of converse with the external world. Besides the forms of control by suggestion, the train of representations can be directly controlled by attention.

It is this direct control by attention which we call thought in the wider sense i.e., active imagination and logical thinking. Intellectual advance in childhood is made by means of all three. By the aid, then, of language, by the suggestions of the world without, and by its own reflexion and fancy, the child is enabled to work up its representations into new and coherent wholes. At the outset, it stands as helpless in the presence of this new world of representations as it was at first in the presence of the world of sense and movement; and, as its progress in reducing this to order, in advancing from isolated and unrelated sensations and motions to definite perceptions and acts, was largely accelerated by the labours of those who had lived before it, so we shall find it to be here. What heredity did in the one case, language does in the other.

Save for this, as instances like that of Kaspar Hauser and other children of the woods show, the most gifted mind would never rise much above the level of a brute. Language is the chief instrument by which the residual of perceptions and actions instead of remaining a waste of such stuff as dreams are made of become elaborated into conceptions and ideas. Yet language in the first instance does but fix and make permanent combinations among ideas which the mind has formed without it. Language aids thought, it does not dispense with it. With this preamble, we may leave language out of account for a time, and observe the bare process of thinking without it. Strictly speaking, that juvenile romancing and castle-building, which even the most prosaic persons must recall with delight, is a species of thought-a fact which may, perhaps, obtain for it more indulgence than it sometimes receives. For these early feats of imagination are so much more coherent than dreams as to show plainly that the naturally random succession of ideas has been controlled; indeed, if we observe ourselves carefully-if any will confess to a weakness for reverie-we can detect ourselves actively shaping and selecting our characters and scenery.

And, no doubt, children do the same. Here, again, then, we have practical applications thick upon us. All further progress, not merely intellectual but moral, depends on the elaboration of representations; and their successful elaboration depends, caeteris paribus, on their mobility, in other words, on a quick and lively imagination. Without this, I do not say merely that literature, geography and history must be appealingly dull, but even what are regarded as the triumphs of pure thought, the higher principles of science and philosophy, will be unattainable. Without it, too, human sympathy could not be expressed, and all fine feeling would be impossible. It is a natural mistake to suppose that because an extravagant and ungoverned imagination is antagonistic to the reasonable in thought and action, therefore, he is 'best off in both who has least imagination.

There is another way of saving your neck besides starving your steed, and that is to learn how to manage him. A quick and lively imagination is as indispensable as quickness or fineness of sight and hearing; and, like these, can only be improved by exercise. Nature, accordingly, does well in inciting the young to a ready command of the materials of this inner world. It must be allowed, however, that such flights of fancy as children indulge do little more than insure this command. Thought in the narrower sense it is not. If you ask me to say in a word what thought is, you must not expect a definition on which you might stake your life. Roughly speaking, at all events, and more exactly than it seems at first sight, thought may be defined as seeking the identical or similar among ideas that are partially different; or, again, as bringing together and uniting ideas that agree together.

For example, when a child, familiar with bats, birds and butterflies, reflects that they all fly by means of wings and recognizes them as in this respect alike, he has been thinking: and if he connects this thought with a movement, as by flapping his arms and jumping into the air, he will have fixed his thought by the aid of a sign: flapping his arms and jumping in the air will now be for him a symbolic representation of all the variety of bats, birds and butterflies he has seen or will see. Of course, unless he is dumb, he will hardly adopt such an unwieldy symbol; language will save him trouble by suggesting a much simpler movement, that of pronouncing the word wing-fliers. Not, however, that any such symbol is essential to a single act of thought so simple; but it can hardly be dispensed with, if the ideas brought together are to remain united.

If, now, the child compares wing-fliers with arrows and with kites, and recognizes that even these widely different objects agree in being things that fly, this new ground of agreement between things before disconnected, whereby further classification of his experiences is possible, will be a new thought. And, in this way, he may proceed in other directions recognizing first those things that have most in common and thus forming small classes, which he may combine again, so far as they are similar, into larger classes; and so on continually. At the risk of being tedious, I must dwell on this matter somewhat more in detail.

What I want above everything to impress is the paramount importance of the educator keeping close to the order of mental development. The mind can only grow by degrees; it cannot comprehend the agreement, or form a conception combining facts of a more general kind, till it has first combined facts more concrete and less general, whose more obvious points of identity are sooner evident. Just so often as it is forced to skip these earlier steps, just so often will confusion be the result. The psychological character of such confusion we must defer to another lecture. I only desire now, in this general survey, to lay stress on the necessity of giving time for each stage in the mental development being consolidated in its turn. To hurry over foundations because they are out of sight is to produce a structure like Nebuchadnezzar's image: a head of fine gold on feet of dirty clay.

The more lofty the structure we intend, the more needful is it that it should have good understanding. Now, in thinking there are two difficulties:

(i) we can only attend to a few things or ideas at once;
(ii) it is harder to recognize identity the more it is overlay with diversity.

On both accounts, therefore, it is plain that real thinking can only advance gradually, and, indeed, very gradually. Having learnt to perceive the quality of roundness in its hoop, a child will identify the same form in a wheel notwithstanding its spokes, then in a plate and a penny, although so much less in size, then in a bun, though the form is here less perfect, and the matter too interesting for much attention to more form; and thus, at length, the conception of roundness becomes clear, and by means of this the differences of round objects fallout of sight, the multiplicity becomes a unity. When similar groups of three cornered things and square things have been formed, the young thinker may, by and by, rise to the more general conception of shape, a conception which it could by no possibility have reached directly.

For now the lower concepts, round, three-cornered, square etc. stand out by themselves as single objects to which, so soon as the child's mind is familiar with them, he can attend as easily as he could to a hoop, a plate, a penny, before: and as the differences in colour, size, material and what not, do not enter into these higher complexes, round, three cornered, square etc., the points in which they resemble each other-occupation of space and the possession of bounding lines-are recognized, and thus the general conception of figure or shape is attained. When the materials for the formation of a concept are sufficiently prepared in the child's mind to make the recognition of their points of agreement possible, he is sure to experience pleasure when he is led to see the identity even by direct suggestion, in which case the child is said to understand.

And his pleasure will be greater still when the resemblance is the result of a comparison he has himself instituted, which case more properly deserves to be called thought. Left to themselves, however, most children, at all events, will make but slow progress, partly for want of the aid of language, partly for want of the necessary juxtaposition of the material. But, though they need help, they should not be helped too much. They may seem to get on faster when everything is well done for them, but the permanent efficiency of their minds will be less. Their bodies never grow so fast as when by some accident they are confined for a time to their beds, when though they might have been less in stature they would have been more robust if they had to support their own weight.

The most careful and comprehensible teaching, widely as it differs from stocking the memory with words and phrases, does not come up to the ideal of mental training: it imparts sound instruction but it does not do all that can be done to give sinews to the mind. Rousseau's observations on this point are excellent. Our unlucky facility in cheating ourselves with words that we do not understand begins, he says, earlier than we suppose; and, accordingly, he suggests that a child' vocabulary should be kept as limited as possible, lest it should have more words than concepts for the words to symbolize; its nurse is to be strictly forbidden to din useless words into its ears. The more we depend for the attainment of our end on the child's activity, the more imperatively necessary is it, however, to secure his interest.

Not much good will come of irksome thinking: the mind set down to an un-congenital task will expand about as much as a sea-anemone would in vinegar. What, then, is the nature of intellectual interest? The pleasures of memory, the pleasures of hope the pleasures of imagination have long been favourite themes, but I am not at this moment aware of anyone who has attempted to sing the pleasure of thinking. Yet thinking has its pleasures, and pleasures too which children, if wisely handled, keenly enjoy. One of its pleasures arises from what Professor Bain is fond of calling "the flash of identification between things never before regarded as alike"; in other words, the pleasure of novelty, a pleasure which, as I have said, is much enhanced, when the discovery has been our own. I place of the novelty at first supplied by new perceptions comes the novelty of finding new bonds of connection among these to keep up the interest in knowledge.

How real this pleasure is evidenced by the classic instance of Archimedes which has given the word 'Eureka' a place in the English dictionary. And the admiration people are never tried of expressing as often as they contemplate Newton's inimitable discovery of universal gravitation is further proof of the pleasing wonderment all minds feel in the detection of unexpected likeness, in finding the one in the many. A more familiar illustration of the same thing we seen in sallies of wit, the gist of which also lies in the surprise of an unsuspected resemblance. On this account, Jean Paul Richter warmly recommends that children should be encouraged to be witty and he even kept a book with the title" Anthology of my Scholars," in which he recorded every successful stroke of wit his pupils had made, not omitting jokes directed against himself. Some of these were very clever, although nobody that I know of has followed Jean Paul's example. Perhaps, however, the most important evidence of the pleasure of intellectual exercise for our purpose is that manifested by children who succeed in the problems one sets them: in addition to the fairly intellectual pleasure of simplification, there is the pleasure of power.

On this point I will digress for a moment to make a practical remark which a little tact ought to impress on every teacher, but which none the less the habit of regarding mainly absolute results leads many to overlook. With the schoolteacher the standing rule should be: Never let your pupils suffer a defeat, if only because defeat demoralizes. Of course, like most prescriptions, this fails sometimes, and is moreover to be taken with a grain of salt: sometimes, for example, overweening confidence needs to be checked, sometimes temporary defeat ensures more lasting victory in the end. But, whoever has often contrasted the brightness and liveliness of children who succeed with the downcast and puzzled looks of those who can make no way must be convinced that the one class have gained, and the other lost, interest in their subject or confidence in themselves, or both. The inclination of the mind, says Locke in a passage in his Journal, is as the palate to the stomach: that seldom digests well or adds much strength to the body that nauseates the palate and is not recommended by it.

The persistence of such mental disgust is amazing, as most of us perhaps can testify, and I am satisfied that many a lifelong dislike and incapacity for a subject has been due to an inauspicious beginning. The Jesuits, many of you know, had a practice which would astonish some modem schoolteachers: they kept a register of marks indicating each scholar's proficiency-and the boys who got least marks got least work. The plan was really a most philosophical one: where all try, work should be adapted to capacity and then all alike taste the pleasure of success, and so, to adopt Locke's simile, soon increase their appetite for work. At the entrance upon any sort of knowledge, as Locke has elsewhere said, when everything of itself is difficult, the great use and skill of a teacher is to make all as easy as he can. But, returning from this digression to the nature of intellectual interest, there is still an aspect more important than the pleasure of the flash of identification and the pleasure of success: I mean the pleasure of satisfied curiosity. Wonder, it is said, is the parent of knowledge.

Of this emotion children for the most part show no lack, before they go to school at all events; then, perhaps, the need of imbibing what they are not expected to understand cures them of their thirst for knowledge. The curiosity of the child is to be distinguished from the interest the infant finds, in acquainting itself with the sensible properties of all it can *see* and touch. Curiosity implies a consciousness of ignorance on some definite point and a desire for enlightenment. Even a further distinction is possible, that which the Germans sometimes express by the words Neugier and Wissbegier: curiosity to know, for example, how a given story will end and curiosity to know, say, how it is that the moon does not shine every night, as the sun shines every day, or why ladies keep on their bonnets in church while gentlemen take their hats off.

It is this latter curiosity that is of interest to us, because it is a powerful motive to intellectual activity. And here, for the first time, we come upon an activity determined by a definite want, an intellectual hunger. This curiosity is characteristic of a somewhat later period of childhood than that in which the formation of concepts begins. Not that children never ask troublesome and puzzling questions much earlier than this; but, for the most part, the relations of things are indifferent to them until they have progressed far enough in the process of conceiving to be able to think about the things themselves. Then thought awakens the desire for knowledge. And this necessitates a new return to the world without what is wanted now are propositions not concepts; propositions stating the reasons or causes or purposes of the events and arrangements perceived, the how and why of what happens. Now, I do not say that education is to consist merely injudiciously aiding the child to satisfy this craving in the irregular fashion in which it will naturally arise: though this is no small matter, and many have been the men of eminence who have attributed their success to sympathetic aid to thought thus casually rendered.

But this alone is rather supplying material for growth than directing the growth itself. All I wish to insist on is that you cannot advantageously begin to train a child in a branch of knowledge about the subject-matter of which he has at the time no curiosity and in which his interest cannot, or cannot yet, be awakened. If the subject is one he must learn, because of its utility, well and good: learning must here be a duty: but the full fruits of intellectual training can only be secured from work that is a pleasure. There is no branch of knowledge which cannot be made an efficient instrument of intellectual culture in the hands of a sufficiently able teacher and for those who desire to master it. One cannot have lived much among men without seeing that powers which have been developed in one case by the study of classics have been developed in others by the study of mathematics. Not, however, that this makes one-sided study desirable: far from it, as these men are the first to admit.

Where nothing better can be done, as the less of two evils, the pupil might receive his chief intellectual training when his activity can be most counted on, even though it is one-sided. Yet there is hardly any limit to the variety of interest that may be called into activity in most children of average capacity, if their curiosity is wisely directed at the outset. This, however, requires an amount of care and attention that can only be given at home and is one more argument for home education at first. The secret of securing interest in varied forms of knowledge is to secure a variety of concepts: there can be no desire for knowledge where there has been no thought about the things to be known. The condition of all-round culture is all-round training from the first: training for all the sense, a stock of perceptions as wide and varied as the world can give; then, the discovery of resemblances among the innumerable particulars and the first steps towards classification; and then, so soon as the concept or class-notion has been formed, the acquisition of a name by which the materials brought together may be held together and a new advance made possible.

The need is for laying the foundation all round, and for making possible regular advance. It is customary with architects in their specifications to direct that all the walls of a building shall be raised to the same height together: the builder may not carry up a side wall as high as the eaves and let the front wall remain built no higher than the plinth or, perhaps, without even the foundations cleared. It is unnatural when you have been working with your trowel as high as the chimney tops to descend once more to the ground; moreover, if you do, the new wall cannot now without great pains and trouble be bonded into the old, and even should this be accomplished after a fashion, the result will only be that either the new wall or the old will crack. The reason why so many have now to lament the one-sidedness of their intellectual interests is either that they were allowed or caused to advance when children in one direction, instead of advancing in all pari passu.

With many parents and teachers in the present day, one-sidedness, instead of being discouraged, is deliberately fostered. Because the man who can do one thing well is the one the world wants and pays honours, therefore they at once direct all the child's energies into that channel in which he seems most likely to attain pre-eminence, just as gardeners do when they leave only the biggest pear on a tree, hoping with this one, when monstrous grown, to win a prize. Now, though this procedure secures certain obvious advantages to society, and so to the individual whose fitness for special functions makes him valuable, yet the disadvantages to him as a man, and not as a money-maker or a marvel, are even more obvious, and we may, therefore, be sure that the gain even to the world is not a real gain. But, again, one-sidedness in the child is often the consequence of one-sidedness in parents or teacher. This is strikingly illustrated in that interesting book to which I have already referred, Galton's English Men of Science.

We cannot suppose that an innate taste for science is more general among Scotch children than English, but in Scotland the university programme and the general method of teaching are much more suited to men of a scientific bent of mind than those in England. Accordingly, Galton found the cases in which scientific tastes were traced to teachers to be ten times more numerous among his Scotch correspondents than among his English. If children are left to grow up without observing large classes of facts that are really under their eyes and without acquiring even the names of such as they notice for themselves, one-sidedness is as inevitable as blindness would be if their eyes were always bandaged. But I have been a great deal more discursive than I had meant to be or ought to have been. Besides beginning to think and awakening to a desire for thought-knowledge or truths, the material of science, childhood advances upon infancy in two other respects, in forming a clear perception of time and a distinct consciousness of being a self or person, with a memory of what it has lived through in the past and an expectation of great things to be done in the future.

Yet this sense of personality is primarily important in connection with moral training and may be deferred for the present. In youth, as distinct from childhood, i.e. in the period beginning about the fifteenth year, the intellectual advance calls for little special remark. Concepts of a more abstract kind are possible, and the danger, not insignificant even in childhood, of acquiring words loosely without doing the work of thinking, which the word should but fix, is now greater than ever. For the concepts learnt later are concepts formed by the comparison of other concepts, so that the symbols of the one may be used as equivalent in certain cases for the symbols of the others by an imitative knack, without the real significance of any being known. Terms like house and cow you cannot remain long in the dark about. But terms such as nation, law, force, may be easily used without any clear knowledge of their meaning, still more terms like nature, justice, life.

The isolated truths concerning the causes and connections of things become in youth the material for a higher order of elaboration; inference and systematic thinking begin, and the cogency of argument is distinctly felt. It is very remarkable how late this form of mental activity sometimes appears. Children can often be brought to see the meaning of each step in an argument, the conclusion as well as the rest, yet a little cross-examination will disclose the fact that they do not assent to the conclusion because they assent to the premisses, but because they see its truth in a particular instance or take it on authority. On this ground, I should myself incline to defer the teaching even of Euclid until such time as there is clear evidence that the scholar can reason, that is to say, see the truth of one proposition to follow from the truth of a series of others. Meantime, much geometric knowledge of a valuable kind educationally could be acquired by direct intuition: if, indeed, Euclid should not be superseded by modern geometric altogether. Feeling for proof, a sense of logical cogency, is of all things one that the educator should spare no pains to develop; but he will do this best by waiting till the feeling arises. Rousseau was in this respect, wiser than Locke, in urging, contrary to Locke's advice, that to reason with children, before they reason themselves, is to make them disputatious, not logical. The most important characteristics of youth pertain, however, to the moral rather than the intellectual side of mind.

It is not so much shaping their minds as shaping their characters that is the great business now. Childhood is reasonable, though it does not reason, and is easily led; but youth, though it reasons, nay, partly because it reasons, for reason suggests superiority to authority, is turbulent and troublesome: in manhood sweet reasonableness returns. The proverbial maxims of most people recognize this fact: school-teachers, who only know the lawless youth and not the man master of himself, are apt to forget it. But for the present we must defer the consideration of this point. I propose returning to this and cognate matters later on. And now I have said all that the limitations of these lectures will allow me to say about the general nature and growth of mind, and I have insisted sufficiently, at every opportunity, upon the necessity of always keeping this fact of growth in view. There is nothing in the mind that was not first in the senses, said a scholastic philosopher. Nothing, added Leibniz, but the mind itself.

The additional clause must be allowed. But this mind itself stands for nothing but the subject who attends and feels; what it attends to, both in thought and action, have come into the mind through the senses, including therein bodily movements. My thoughts are mine, my acts are mine; but only because I have combined them out of material which was not mine but only given to me. This mind by itself is, as Kant well said, the poorest of all concepts; what has worth is the mind's contents, the fruits of the talents entrusted to its use. To despise these, because in their crudest form they are mere sensations and movements, if folly, and yet a folly which psychology has not so far succeeded in scaring away. Nevertheless, these words of Professor Bain are 'hardly overstated: If we did not originally feel the difference between light and dark, black and white, red and yellow, there would be no visible scenes for us to remember: with the amplest endowment of retentiveness, the outer world could not enter into our recollection; the blank of sensation is a blank of memory. Yet further.

The minuteness or delicacy of the feeling of difference is the measure of the variety and multitude of our primary impressions, and, therefore, of our stored-up recollections. He that feels his remembrance of sounds bounded by these; he that feels a hundred sensible differences has his ideas or recollections of sounds multiplied in the same proportion. The retentive power works up to the heights of the discriminative power; it can do no more........ this is the deepest foundation of disparity of intellectual character, as well as of variety in liking of pursuits.

Stage of Child Development

Why is it that what children want seems silly to grown-ups, and what grown-ups want seems silly to children?

Such was the question asked by a grill of ten. The answer to it is that children are swayed by comparatively crude and simple innate tendencies, whereas in adults these tendencies have been modified and organised into a complex system of sentiments which involve richer intelligence and which give rise to wants of very different kinds. The teacher, however, must not regard the cruder impulses and desires of children as silly.

He must rather recognise in them natural forces which by modification and development will become the springs of the higher forms of behaviour. And he must recognise, further, that the process of modification and development goes on gradually, so that what appeals to a child at one age will not appeal to him at a later stage. An exact knowledge, therefore, of the stage of development-with respect to both intelligence and tendencies-which the child reaches at each age of its career is of supreme importance. Much casual information, gained by more or less unscientific child-study, has been collected by various industrious individuals.

But reliable scientific data are now beginning to be recorded, though a great deal still remains to be done in this field. Since the body is closely related to the mind, it is important to know something of the way in which the human organism develops. Growth both in height and weight does not take place uniformly. There are spurts and arrests. Arrests occur at about 6, 11, and 18 in the case of boys, a little earlier in the case of girls. The greatest spurt is at puberty. Since girls usually undergo this change earlier than boys, they gain rapidly on the boys for a time. Although at most ages they are lighter and shorter than the boys, they usually show distinct superiority in both respects at the ages of 14 and 15. Now whether there is a very close correspondence between mental growth and bodily growth is at present uncertain.

There seems, at any rate, to be a general correspondence. It is certain, for instance, that there is an arrest in mental development about the age of 11, and further that there is rapid mental development at the time of puberty. The teacher should, therefore, abstain from making great exactions at the former age, but he can look for marked advances when he knows that puberty has arrived. Observations on the continent seem to indicate that the first marked arrest in physical growth is due to the great change which going to school involves. We have noted that the arrest occurs at about 6, and this is usually the age at which children are obliged to begin school on the continent.

It is probable that the sudden change from the comparative freedom of home life to the more restricted life, with respect both to thought and movement, which even the most modem schools involve makes too great a demand on the child, so that he suffers both mentally and physically. The rate of mortality has been found to increase during the first school year. It is possible that these serious consequences can be to a large extent avoided by the improvement of school conditions.

For where the school conditions are most unfavourable retardation is greatest. School conditions can be improved both on the hygienic and on the paedological side. With respect to hygienic conditions, the amount of space per child, the efficiency of ventilation, the regulation of heat, and the provision for frequent movement from place to place are most important. These matters, of course, are also important in the home, in which the child spends even more time than in school. Careful measurements of children in Glasgow showed that on the average boys from one-roomed homes were 11.7 lb. lighter and 4.7 inches shorter than boys from four-roomed homes, while girls from one-roomed homes were 14 lb. lighter and 5.3 inches shorter than girls from four-roomed homes.

The teacher can do little to improve the hygienic conditions of the homes of his scholars. But the alarming results of poor conditions in the home should impress him with the necessity of making the school life as healthy as possible. With regard to the pedagogical conditions of the school, the most general statement to be made is that they should be much less rigid than is usually the case. A great deal has already been done in our infant schools in this respect. The influence of Froebel, who emphasised the need of allowing spontaneous self-activity on the part of the children has done much to revolutionise the character of the school life of young English children.

But more remains to be done. And madame Montessori, a great Italian educationist, has developed a system of education for younger children which we should do well to imitate in many respects. To quote from a recent account of her schools, Dotoressa Montessori has always protested against the assumption that good order and immobility are interchangeable terms. She is no advocate of lax discipline; but she holds that we must revise our conception of discipline, especially when we are dealing with young children, for whom bodily exercise and freedom of movement are among the first conditions of healthy and happy life.

A repressive system of education, which compels children to do what they do not want to do, and holds in check their healthy and natural activities, has made repressive discipline a necessity if any semblance of progress is to be made. The function of discipline, in a school of conventional type, is to shut down and sit upon the safety-valve of naughtiness, a safety-valve which the children's spontaneous energies, when wantonly repressed, instinctively try to use. In a school in which the energies of the children are constantly and happily employed, that safety-valve has never to be used, and the need of repressive discipline ceases to be felt.

In a Montessori school each child is given the maximum of freedom that is compatible with his not hurting or incommoding others; and so long as he is busily and suitable employed he is not likely to hurt or incommode others, or to make himself a nuisance to the school as a whole. Weakly children suffer more retardation on entrance into school than strong ones. The teacher, however, with his thoughts bent on producing results is often inclined to concentrate his efforts upon these pupils. His desire also to secure a good percentage of attendance makes him view with disfavour and irritation any attempt on the part of the parents to coddle the child by allowing him to stay at home when he does not feel anxious to go to school.

But the parent's point of view is often the right one, though frequently it is not until the doctor reinforces it by his authority that the teacher is disposed to give way. If we are to smooth the transition from home to school, we must be prepared to exercise great elasticity in our requirements during the early stages, and especially with weakly children. Mr. Winch has demonstrated, after careful investigation, that early entrance to school is not advantageous to intellectual progress. When children were tested at the age of 7-8, it was found that those who had been at school since the age of 3 produced results which were no better than those of the children who did not commence school before 5. Early entrance to school, then, is of no advantage even with respect to progress in the school subjects.

With respect to general intellectual progress, it is probably harmful. For it tends, as we have seen, to produce retardation in bodily growth; and, although the correspondence between physical excellence and intellectual ability cannot be demonstrated at all point and in every individual case, it has been found that on the average this correspondence is very marked. The brighter children as a whole are bigger than the duller ones. In early education, therefore, whatever else we do, we should make certain that the child leads a life of healthy bodily activity. Coming now to the intellectual nature of the child, we may state at the outset that the normal child possesses in some degree all the powers which the adult enjoys. To take the highest of all the intellectual powers, it has sometimes been stated that reasoning does not occur till comparatively late in childhood.

But the intelligent use of such words as because and why by young children is clear indication that they realise that interconnectedness of ideas whereby steps are made from one concrete fact to another. A little boy of two-and-a half was playing at being a baker. His father, not knowing this, entered the room, and asked him for a kiss. I'm a baker, he replied. His father persisted, asking him: Well! Why won't you give me a kiss? He answered quite clearly, because bakers don't give kisses. His ideational system concerned with bakers represented these men as too dignified for such homely lapses as kissing. In the field of perception, it is found that the child cannot distinguish such small differences as the adult. With respect to colour, tone and weight, for instance, differences which are easily recognised by adults are totally ignored by children.

It has been calculated that for a difference to be just noticeable to a child of six, it must be three times that which could just be recognised by a child of twelve. After the age of 12 there is little if any progress in ordinary perceptions unless special training occurs. It is uncertain whether this perceptual imperfection of children is due chiefly to lack of development in the organs of sense or whether it is the higher cortical processes which are at fault. It is, however, clear that much perceptual activity is necessary in order to exercise the parts concerned and thus to promote their full development.

This is secured by the early observation lessons. A further marked difference between the perception of the young child and that of the adult is that the former is usually unable to perceive several things together. The child tends to fixate one thing and to ignore the others. Thus when children of six were asked to compare the distances between points, it was often found impossible to get them to do it, because their attention remained fixed now on one point now on another. The same thing is noticed in the observation of pictures. Young children notice one object after another, but often fail to put all the objects together to form a complex whole. And when they are allowed, as they should be, to draw anything they like, they often put in very carefully certain things to which they have given attention, and leave out or only roughly indicate many others which adults would consider of greater importance.

Often, too, there is no idea of proportion between the parts. Thus a house is drawn with a great keyhole as its prominent feature. Or a lady with a row of very large buttons as her chief characteristic. In dealing with perception in the early chapters we noticed that it is never a mere reception of sensations. There is always a subjective reaction. On account of associations formed in the past, revivals of traces of past experience occur, and change the mere sensing into the cognition of some object.

Sometimes there traces introduce error into our perceptions. Unsuitable traces are revised and overwhelm the actual sensations, making us think we perceive an object which is not the one before us. This is often called an illusion. Children are more subjected to this error than adults. Their discrimination of the actual sensations is so poor that these are more likely to awaken unsuitable traces, and to be overwhelmed by them. A child, for instance, cognised a vase of ferns as a pot of green feathers. We adults seldom make such mistakes because

(i) the subjective factors are controlled by more clearly discriminated sensations, and

(ii) because the objects cognised have been perceived many times before, with such multifarious and clear sensations that the revivals of them now called up on account of the past processes of association are in harmony with the objective factors of sensation.

The need of continual and concentrated observation by children is, therefore, very great. They must be allowed to handle and actively deal with the objects to be perceived, so that they get a variety of sensations which supplement one another. We have seen that perception very early becomes illuminated by ideas. In other words, it is not mere perception but apperception or observation. The instance of the child cognising the vase of ferns, although an erroneous observation, is a case in point. And all the other instances quoted are also cases of observation. It is important to consider the observation of the child from the point of view of the kind of ideas he usually employs.

The very young child, left to himself, uses chiefly particular and generic ideas. He merely enumerates objects or persons. At about 8, actions are commonly noted. This involves a step in the direction of abstraction. From 9 to 10 spatial, temporal, and casual relations receive more attention. After this the various qualities of objects are more and more referred to. It is claimed by some that these stages are so marked as to enable a normal child's age to be determined with fair accuracy by the replies he gives in observing a picture. Correctness of observation shows considerable progress with advance in years. At 7, every third element of positive statement is false.

At 14, only every fifth statement is wrong. This, of course, is on the average. Most mistakes arise with respect to the number of objects. Teachers, then, must expect to receive incorrect answers. They must not be disappointed or irritated by the mistakes of the children, but must cheerfully proceed to correct them, or, better still, to get the children to correct themselves by further observation. The mistakes with respect to number seek to be connected with the fact that children cannot grasp several objects together. Some educationists are of opinion that we should delay our teaching of number. There is no doubt that much effort is wasted when we try to teach something for which the development of the child is not yet adequate. The errors of young children in observation are no doubt large due to their lack of sensory discrimination, wrong ideas being called up to overwhelm the actual sensations.

But the great suggestibility of young children is another important factor. They are extremely susceptible to influences determined by the form of question or by any other indication that they are expected to give a certain answer. No very reliable information is at present forthcoming with respect to the correlation between suggestibility and age. Teachers should in all observation lessons exercise great care to avoid questions which suggest either right or wrong answers.

Questions of the former type are perhaps the more common. The children are led swiftly along, echoing the observations of the teacher, but doing very little real observation themselves.

But many conscientious teachers are prone to inveigling children into erroneous observations and then rounding on them for their errors. This is discouraging to the children. By all means let us encourage independence of observation. But all means let us encourage independence of observation. But let us remember that the powers of children are very limited, that they are readily susceptible to attempts to lead them astray in any direction, and that discouragement is as harmful to independence as undue assistance. The pupil may, through wrong treatment on the part of parent or teacher... suddenly become remiss and his efforts, mainly in a particular subject alone, falloff; the relations between the pupil and the teacher undergo a change, they lose confidence in each other, the pupil loses confidence in himself, and his work in all subjects suffers. We see, then, that ideas develop very early in the child's mind, and that these determine to a large extent what he observes.

As Meumann puts it, the old tenet, The development of the child proceeds from perception to ideation, is as a general statement incorrect; it is only a partial view of intellectual development; the latter proceeds to a far greater extent from idea to perception, since the ideas controlling the process of apperception determine what is perceived and by them the gradual consequent progress of perception is stimulated. But these ideas are not mere ideas.

They are the cognitive aspects of tendencies or conation. They are the cognitive aspects of tendencies or conation. The wholes thus constituted may be called interests. Meumann often prefers to use the term will. He writes, for instance: The child sees that to which his will to see is directed not that which is brought before his senses, and the purpose to see is further guided by general ideas of what is to be seen. If we are to get the child to observe well, we must bring before him objects and pictures which are not only suitable to his stage of intelligence but which appeal to his interests. It becomes, therefore, very important to know what are the normal child's interests at the various stages of his development. Unless we appeal to these we shall not get a large share of the child's attention. According to Herbert Spencer, the child recapitulates in himself the whole course of development of the race.

It is pointed out that he certainly does so on the bodily side, starting as he does from a single cell and developing through stages similar to those of the lower animals and of primitive man until at last he becomes a human being of modern type. It is assumed, therefore, that his mental development takes a similar course, Thus Herbert Spencer writes: The education of the child must accord both in mode and arrangement with the education of mankind considered historically. In other words, the genesis of knowledge in the individual must follow the same course as the genesis of knowledge in the race. If this is true, the child at different ages will have interests corresponding to those of our remote ancestors at different stages.

And we shall require to feed those interests with suitable material. Thus one writer, beginning with the child at the age of six, prescribes the following as the chief interests for each successive year:

(i) Hunter's life.

(ii) Nomadic life; grazing is a new occupation of man; lower animal life enters into the service of man.

(iii) Agricultural life.

(iv) Development of retail trade and small industries.

(v) Development of wholesale trade; foreign commerce and great industries; growth of great cities.

But it is not sufficient merely to state that the child's interests develop in this order. Only by observing the child can we determine with certainty what are his interests. When we do this, we see that there is indeed an element of truth in the stages sketched out; but that there is far from being a complete correspondence between the development of interests in the child and in the race. In so far as the interests of the race have gradually developed from absorption in the concrete wholes of perceptual activity, through stages in which more and more hidden qualities and relations have come to light, and have finally attained to consideration of things from many abstract point of view, we may agree that they furnish a rough outline of the general course of child development.

But a strict adherence to the historical stages of culture as a guide to curriculum is not possible. Let the stages of a national culture be represented by the letters of the alphabet, starting with A as the earliest stage, and let it be supposed that a child, whose individual development has brought him to the stage F, is living in the actual stage R of his nation's culture. Now, the child being a rational, creature, the reaction of R upon F is inevitable; the child of stage F can, in the circumstances supposed, no more escape the influence of R than he can elude his own shadow in bright sunshine.

The fact is unfortunate for the theory; for what is likely to become of instruction adapted to stage F for a child surrounded by R? He is no mere duplicate of then men of his race who lived in period F; his stage ought, in truth, to be indicated not by that letter, but by F + x, a stage which, it is assumed, has never been reached before. Or, to put the matter in another way, we may say that the present advanced state of civilisation is the product of the collective efforts of millions and millions of human beings, each doing a tiny share which is now preserved as a starting-point for others-in language, in buildings, in implements and machines, in social organisation and customs.

It is absurd to imagine that any given child could recapitulate in his own life even a small fraction of this advance. But, being born in the midst of all this civilization, he grows up with it as his constant environment, and he quickly becomes familiar with thousands of things, each of which has cost years, if not centuries, of development in the life of the human race. The really illuminating category, then, under which to describe the child's activities, and one which includes them all on an equal basis, is that of present function. Their backward reference to the life of a remote ancestry is of far less moment to the educator than the fact that they are essentially the manifestation of a developing psycho-physical organism, and that in some way they make possible the activities of later stages and in the end condition the adequate performance of the functions of maturity.

From this standpoint it becomes of even greater importance than before to know accurately from a study of children themselves just what we can call functions and activities of an immature mind. We may roughly divide the period of childhood into three stages .

(i) First period of childhood, from 2½ to about 6 or 7;

(ii) Second period of childhood, from 6 or 7 to 9;

(iii) Pre-adolescent period of childhood, from 9 to puberty.

The interest of the first period are almost entirely centred in play. Physical activity is the most absorbing interest. The objects with which the child deals are not attended to so much for their own sake as for the activities which they render possible. But as imagery arises in the child's mind, he is easily diverted to activity in which this is involved. For, it must be remembered, his images are probably more vivid, and consequently less distinguishable from percepts than those of the adult. Often the imaginative activity is combined with the perceptual. Astride of a stick a child considers himself to be riding a horse. Seated in a chair he is driving a coach.

A few bricks make up for him a train. We adults are inclined to look with contempt at the poverty of these inventions. But to the child they are probably rich with reality. Imitation, of course, plays an important part at this period. The activities of the adults around him provide the child with a wealth of imagery with which he continually plays, needing often only the slender support from the concrete of actual perception. And since his concrete environment is not sufficient, even when thus economically employed, to support his budding imagination, he will delight in the greater freedom which myth, fable, and fairy tale open up to him. And here again, those adults who have lost the keen relish of fiction are inclined to doubt the utility of it.

But these exercises in imagination are probably defining and refining ideational machinery which will be of great service later on. Curiosity is rampant during this period. At first it is satisfied by further manipulation and contemplation of concrete objects. The child will take a watch, and handle it, hearing its tick and regarding it again and again. But as ideas and images develop, questions are poured forth. Why, What, How, are continually on the child's lips, unless he is suppressed or ignored. And he is satisfied with the crudest of explanations.

For his ideas will often carry him no further. And it would be foolish to attempt anything more elaborate. The inability of the child, at this time, to grasp and be interested in any very large wholes is seen in the fact that children of six and seven, in telling what they wish to become when grown up, always name some prominent detail in the adult activity of their immediate environment, never the occupation as such. For instance, a little girl who really wishes to become a housekeeper will say rather that she wishes to wash dishes or sweep. A boy, instead of saying the wishes to become a blacksmith, will say he wants to shoe horses. We may say, if we wish, that this is due to the inability to make abstractions at this age.

This is no doubt true, but the point is that it is the striking detail, and not its setting, that is of interest. Above all, we must note the fluidity of the child's mind at this period. No interest with him lasts long at a time. He will turn readily from one thing to another. We must not, therefore, expect from him concentrated attention of long duration. In the second period there is no sudden change. Play, curiosity, imagination, and imitation still play a large part in the child's life. But there gradually arises greater ability to concentrate attention for comparatively long stretches of time.

There is, thus, a beginning of interest in details. But this is generally in close connection with physical activity. The child becomes keen on acquiring skill. He is ready to imitate all kinds of activity, so long as he is confident of success. But he is usually unwilling to attempt even simple things unless he feels that he can do them. Further, he has now an eye on the results of his operations. The child's range of ideas widens rapidly during this period. He takes an interest in the broader environment of which his daily world is only a part. He listens with keenness to descriptions of the people of other lands, and eagerly scrutinises any pictures or objects relating to them. Striking biographies and stirring events are extremely attractive to him, and continue to be so even beyond this period. Games are largely individual, though competitive, during the early part of this period.

Imitation still plays a large part. But children at this age have usually insufficient powers of adaptation and of perseverance to carry on group games with much success. Running games are popular with both sexes; in the case of boys they are very much liked, and continue to be so, but with girls they are not so much esteemed and decline rapidly in attractiveness. This seems to be a period of bewilderment and maladjustment. There is evidence of uncertainty in the midst of the new demands made upon the child. Whereas in the first period a very large proportion of boys unhesitatingly choose the occupation of their fathers as their ambition, a much smaller number now do so. Moreover, nearly a half of them gives no reason for their choice of occupation, whereas both before and after this period there is much more decision.

In these matters, however there is further evidence of a widening field of interest and knowledge. Girls want to be teachers or dressmakers. Not a few boys want to be soldiers. But whereas it was the drum and the uniform which attracted them in the first period, they have now some idea of patriotism. In the pre-adolescent period there are marked changes. Social tendencies develop strongly, and group or co-operative games are extremely attractive. There is, of course, competition in these, but it is rather between group and group than between individuals. This is the age when esprit de corps can be highly developed.

The boy is willing to sacrifice his own glorification to that of the group of which he is a member. Much use of these tendencies can be made in the way of stimulating the boys in their work. This development of the social consciousness brings with it great susceptibility to the influence of others. And it is to be noted that evil influence has now as great a chance as good ones. Perhaps, indeed, they have more chance. For that attitude of rebellion against restraint which is so marked a characteristic of adolescence is beginning to show itself. Since this is the period when permanent sentiments begin to arise, it is extremely important to watch over the lines on which the boy or girl is being directed. A prominent characteristic of this period is that of making collections.

The instinct of collecting is also to be noticed in the earlier periods. But in these it is more or less sporadic, and there is little perseverance. Now, however, boys will persist for week and months in getting together specimens of various kinds. Stamps, picture postcards, and cigarette pictures are among the most common things collected. But the instinct in question may be utilised for many other purposes. Leaves, flowers, pictures illustrating history or geography lessons, quotations from favourite authors, shells, fossils, and many other things can be collected and arranged by the children, who in so doing will both increase their knowledge of their environment and develop interests of an elevating description. An interest in puzzles seems to be a special characteristic of this period.

Some regard this as an evidence of mental freedom, a breaking away from the narrow limits of childhood. Interest in mechanical puzzles seems to develop first. But this is soon followed by keenness in the geometrical arithmetical, and language varieties. For, with the growth of ideas, there develops the impulse to use them-in other words, to reason. Reasoning in the truest sense of the term-the use of abstract ideas in the solution of problems-the use of abstract ideas in the solution of problems-make rapid strides during this period. Few teachers seem to take advantage of these facts.

The problems set in school are too often uninteresting tasks taken from books and lists of dull examples. If only some of these could be modified and so presented that they really appeal to the pupils as puzzles, much more interest would be taken in them, and greater perseverance evinced in working them out. Imitation is still a prominent feature during this period. Indeed, the collecting and puzzle interests just referred to are in many cases aroused to their full pitch on account of imitation of others. The imitation of this period, however, begins to show a more generalising tendency.

The child of eight imitates specific acts. Older children, and especially adolescents, get behind the specific act to the attitude or emotional tendency prompting it. This is one of the great factors in the susceptibility to the influence of others, especially of teachers and friends, which we have noted as a characteristic of this period. This susceptibility goes on increasing after puberty, culminating in boys at about 16 and in girls at about 14.

6

HEREDITY AND ENVIRONMENT

Only the basic principles of heredity and those facts that are important in guarding against the perpetuation of undesirable traits and physical conditions in offspring merit discussion here. Our knowledge of the subject has come from the researches of human heredity begun by Galton, and researches in plant and animal breeding initiated by Mendel, an Austrian monk.

Complexities of Heredity

We can only marvel at the miracle Nature displays in heredity. From each mating of sex cells, all of which look alike when viewed with the microscope, Nature produces an individual different in characteristics can be arranged spatially in the tiny germ cell unless we can assume that these characteristics are produced by the infinite varieties in molecular pattern which are possible in the highly complex chromatin substances.

The elaborate mechanism of inheritance is in no way better illustrated than in the nearly complete similarity of identical twins, who result from the separation of the embryo into two equal halves at an early stage, and therefore receive identical hereditary factors. Fraternal or unlike twins are produced from separate eggs, each of which is fertilized by a separate sperm cell. Genes act in many instances as enzymes which control biochemical activity. The genes of man have not been counted but are multitudinous. Infinitesimal in size, the genes have packed in them all of the potentials and all of the limitations of heredity. The chemical organization of the gene is such that it is not affected by ordinary changes in man's environment.

When a gene, from causes as yet unknown, does change its structure or is elected from the chromosome, a mutation is said to have occurred. Mutations, during the maturing of plant and animal cells, may be increased by heat, cold, x-rays, and radium. Mutations often produce some typical hereditary defects; occasionally they introduce a useful variation. Loss of a gene is usually lethal. Two terms commonly used in genetic parlance are locus. We do not yet understand all about genes. In some instances Mendel's concept of dominant and recessive characters can be followed in man's hereditary mechanism, but few human characteristics have their base in a single gene.

The majority of man's characteristics are the result of a complex interaction of a considerable number of genes and genetic environments. Certain concepts have been developed which help us to understand more of these interesting influences. Variation in penetrance is used to explain why a trait usually dominant fails to be expressive in a given circumstance. It has been postulated that when penetrance is imperfect some element in the gene's environment has prevented the gene from expressing its potential. A common instance of varied expressively is encountered in variation of lobster-claw fingers. This condition may vary from a thumb opposing a single huge fused finger to hands which are only slightly deformed. And yet progeny of the latter may have children showing the former. A further modification of Mendelian concepts is the finding of multigene action.

From two to as many as forty-eight genes may cooperate to produce a particular characteristic. Many characteristics which very by small steps are conditioned by multiple cooperating genes. It is thought that characteristics such as musical ability, personality traits, colour in Negro-white crosses, body build, and mental ability are determined in this way. Some inherited traits do not appear in every generation though they are transmitted through these generations. An interesting illustration is furnished by Osborn. Dr. Osborn recounts: An instance of a minor hereditary deviation from normal is a stiff finger defect in which one or two of the joints of the fingers are solidly fused so that they have no motion.

A man who played a minor role in history had these stiff fingers. He was John Talbot, First Early of Shrewsbury, who fought against Joan of Arc. John appears in Shakespeare. He met death in battle in 1453, and tradition had it that he fell from his horse and broke his thigh. Then a French battle-axe split his skull. His body was brought back to England and buried in Shrewsbury Cathedral. In 1914 a descendant of John Talbot in the fourteenth generation was in charge of repairs of the cathedral which made it necessary to remove John's remains. His skeleton could be identified by three marks: the split skull, the broken thighbone, and fused joints of two fingers in each hand-exactly like the fingers of his descendant five centuries later who had charge of the proceedings.

Mendelian Inheritance

Mendel's law enunciated the principle that paired unit factor characteristics in the male and female parents do not blend in the offspring, but the units of heredity, or genes, remain distinct in the germ cells of the offspring, recombining in future generations according to probability and chance. This law may be illustrated from animal heredity. Among guinea pigs the crossing of a black strain with a white strain produces in the first generation only black offspring; but if these pigs are bred among themselves, the resulting offsprings are in the ratio of approximately three black pigs to one white. Black coat is a dominant characteristic and white coat a recessive characteristic.

We can understand these results if we assume that the black guinea pig possesses a factor in the germ cell for black colour and that the colour factor is lacking in the white pig. Black coat and white coat are alternative characteristics. If a black-pigment-producing substance is present in either of the two germ cells that go to make up a new individual, that animal will be black, i.e., black is dominant. If none of the genes of the reproductive cells contain such a substance, no black pigment can develop and the animal is white. It may help us to understand the law better if we consider the explanation afforded by the belief that the chromosomes are bearers of the hereditary characteristics.

The reader who has studied elementary biology will recall that the chromatin, or deeply staining substance of the cell nucleus, arranges itself into short threads called chromosomes whenever there is a cell division. Each chromosome splits lengthwise. The number of these chromosomes is thus constant for any species of animal. The number in each of the body cells is twice that in the mature sex cell. In other words, the final maturation processes of sex-cell development allow a separation of the chromosomes into two sets or groups, so that there may be two kinds of sperms and two kinds of ova so far as the inheritance or non-inheritance of anyone characteristic is concerned. The number of chromosomes in man is forty eight in the body cells; twenty-four in the sex cells; forty- eight in the fertilized egg.

Sex-Linked Characters

Apparently, the causative factors of certain other characteristics are located in the pair of chromosomes which determine sex or, more exactly, in the tip of chromatin carried by the X-chromosome but lacking in the V-chromosome. Such unit characters are sex-.linked. Remembering the nature of the sperm cells previously described, we see that a dominant sex-linked character in a many may be transmitted to his daughter but not to his son. If it were a recessive character, it could not appear in any of the children, provided the mother was normal in this respect. Recessive sex-linked characteristics, when transmitted by the mother, would be apparent only in the sons.

A recessive characteristic appears in the male when the X-chromosome carries the recessive character; it appears in the female only when both X-chromosomes carry the recessive character. Colour blindness is an example of this kind of inheritance.

How Sex in the Offspring is Determined

All pairs of chromosomes in the body cells of animals, with the exception of one pair, are similar in appearance. These are the so-called sex chromosomes, the X--chromosome and the V-chromosome. The body cells of the female contain two X-chromosomes, and the body cells of the male contain one X-chromosome and one Y-chromosome. Each germ cell contains one chromosome from each pair. Obviously the ova will all be alike. The sperms, on the other hand, will be of two types. Half of them will contain the X-chromosome and half of them will contain the V-chromosome. The sex of the offspring depends upon whether the sperm cell which fertilizes the egg contains the X-chromosome or the V-chromosome.

Mentality and Heredity

Mental ability is without doubt inherited, since there is a high correlation between the mentality of fathers and sons, and between the mentality of brothers. There is also a high correlation between the mental abilities of husbands and wives. This helps to raise the father and son correlation. The question of environment enters here, since children of the most brilliant parents usually have the best surroundings. In mentality, as well as in physical stature, size, and some other characteristics, the offspring of widely different parents appear to be intermediate between the two.

It would seem, as pointed out earlier, that the quality of question is produced by many or multiple unit factors. If the father possessed twenty factors for mental ability and the mother ten, the offspring would be most likely to receive about fifteen and would, therefore, be intermediate in condition, thus giving the appearance of blending inheritance. Apparently there are good strains of human stock. Dr. Woods has shown that the first thirty persons selected for the Hall of Fame averaged one near relative of distinction apiece. One out of four of the persons listed in standard biographical dictionaries has a near relative of distinction. In the great group of Americans who are not listed in a biographical dictionary, only one person in five hundred is closely related to a man of distinction. Statistics in the builders of America by Ellsworth Huntington, Yale social scientist, and Leo F.

Whiting, Eugenist, show that for every twenty clergymen one clergyman's son is listed in Who's Who, whereas the proportion for other professions is 46 to 1; for skilled labour, 1,600 to 1; for unskilled labour, 48, 000 to 1. The children of clergymen have the advantage, of course, of growing up in homes where the standards of education and morals are high. We have the story of the family of the illustrious Jonathan Edwards which shows innumerable examples of the highest intellectual and moral worth among its descendants. On the other hand, there is the story of the Jukes family, investigated by Dugdale, and concerning which we find the following statistics: In five generations of the descendants of a worthless fisherman there were 1,200 persons; the history of 1,040 of these persons is partly known or well known.

About 300 died in infancy; of those remaining 7 were murderers, 60 were habitual thieves, 130 were convicted criminals, 140 were physically wrecked by their own diseases and wickedness, more than half of the women were prostitutes, and 310 were professional paupers living in almshouses a total of 2,300 years. Not one of these persons had a common school education and only 20 learned a trade, 10 of whom learned it in a state prison. Here it is not easy to separate heredity and environment or to estimate the cost of this family to society.

Inherited Abnormalities and Diseases

Any listing of hereditary abnormalities is provisional. The following list of inherited characteristics is taken from Preface to Eugenics by Frederick Osborn, published by harper and brothers, with the permission of the author and publisher. Not all of the characteristics of Dr. Osborn's list are included below but those that are included are quoted exactly. The majority of these characteristics are rare. Most of the characteristics in the list are little affected by environment.

Some Dominant Hereditary Defects

- Sudden allergic swelling of mucous membranes. Quincke's or Bannister's disease.
- Short-limbed dwarfism.
- Recurrent periods of fast heartbeat. Tachycardia.
- Small fold of skin at the inner angle of the eye connecting the upper and lower lids. Mongolian fold.
- Incoordination of muscular movements, indistinct speech, and dullness caused by degeneration of certain parts of the cerebellum. Starts in early adult life and causes early death.
- Imperfect development or absence of teeth.
- Large thirst and excretion of large quantities of pale urine.
- Excessive body hair.
- Bluish enamel, soft dentine, and rapid wearing down of the crowns of the teeth.
- Shaking palsy. Progressive trembling and a tendency to change from a walk into a run. Parkinson's disease.
- Colourless spots in the skin.
- Drooping eyelids caused by partial paralysis of the muscles.
- Progressive deafness beginning in early maturity.
- Degeneration of various parts of the brain, accompanied by loss of memory, fits of weeping, craving for sweets, defective speech, and continuous movements of the hands. A disease of middle life.
- Tooth enamel very thin or absent. Teeth usually become brown.
- Alternate coloured and colourless rings in hair; pepper and salt hair.

Some Recessive Defects

- Decrease of function of the adrenal gland, producing bronzed skin, progressive anaemia, low blood pressure, and digestive disturbances.
- Many types of mental defect or low-grade mentality.
- Urine becomes nearly black when standing, due to oxidation of alcapton in it.
- Absence of all pigment from the skin.
- Colour blindness, red-green. Sex-linked.
- Chronic inflammation of the joints with progressive deformity. Beauvais disease.
- Cleft palate. A fissure in the roof of the mouth
- Idiocy, progressive blindness, and death in infancy. Tay-Sachs disease.
- Incoordination of muscular action. Also dominant.
- Sight is better by night or in twilight than by daylight. Sex-linked.
- Progressive mental disease characterized by incoordination of muscles, disturbance of vision, and convulsions.
- Abnormal tendency to bleed due to a failure of coagulation of the blood. Sex-linked.
- Small skull and feeble-mindedness.
- Loss of the use of muscles, beginning at puberty or before. and progressing until patient is helpless within a few years. Death occurs in early maturity. Sex-linked.
- Inability to use the excess sugar in the body due to absence of the hormone insulin. Big environmental factor.
- Recurrent spells of twitching of the muscles of the arms and legs and incoordination of muscles.
- A chronic skin disease characterized by epidermal flakes resembling the scales of a fish. Also dominant.
- Creeping paralysis. Sex-linked.

Marriage between near relatives is usually not advisable because some hidden hereditary family weakness in both persons may appear in the offspring. If both parties are free from hereditary defects, such a union is not to be feared.

Heredity and Conduct

One may say that from the standpoint of the race, the germ cell is of greater importance than the individual. A person is like the father because he is descended from the same line of similar germ cells. The children of soldiers who are mutilated in war will be as normal as others; the physical condition of the parent will not be transmitted to the child. An injury to the germ cells is much more serious than an injury to the body tissues of the individual. We cannot change the hereditary characteristics embodied in germ cells, but we should remember that these cells are a living part of the body and that they are subject to some of the same influences that injure other tissues.

We would expect to find the greatest vitality in those cells of a normal and healthy body. Certain poisons, which are distributed through the circulation, can reach these cells, and a poison that is capable of serious injury to the growing or adult organism may thus be expected to extend in its influences to the sex cell. Lead is such a poison. When there is serious lead poisoning in either the father or the mother, many of the babies are stillborn, and those who do live often have inferior vitality. Syphilis produces a poison that has most harmful effects, especially upon the nervous system of children. One may ask whether the importance of heredity does not end the parental obligation to exercise proper control over his temper. The answer is that faulty mental hygiene will injuriously affect the environment of the children. If the parent is a confirmed neurasthenic, he is almost sure to impair the mental health of his children.

Feeble-mindedness

Four measures have been proposed for controlling the propagation of defectives:

(i) Education,

(ii) Legislation,
(iii) Segregation, and
(iv) Surgery.

No one of these measures is fully satisfactory. Education of the general public may make society more alert to the problem. Laws limiting the marriage of feeble-minded persons have been enacted in many states. Segregation is an ideal procedure whenever it can be applied, but it is hopeless to attempt to secure all the afflicted and to place them in segregation hospitals. Surgery has been performed to sever the vas deferens in the male or the Fallopian tube in the female. Thus prosecution is prevented. No sacrifice of sexual activity or capacity results. Twenty-seven states already have carefully written eugenic sterilization laws.

The principle of compulsory sterilization was approved by the Supreme Court of the United States in 1927 by a decision in which Justice Oliver Wendell Holmes remarked. Three generations of imbeciles are enough. These laws provide for expert unbiased medical investigation, usually with the written consent of the nearest relatives, to make sure that sterilization is applied only to cases of hereditary feeble-mindedness or mental disease. Over 51,000 sterilizations have been performed in this country. Relatives of patients, physicians, and social workers approve the plan because they have observed that sterilization is a protection, not a punishment, and that it enables many patients to return to their homes and live normal lives. The long-range importance of sterilization is readily seen.

Evidence indicates that families furnishing children to state homes for the feeble-minded multiply about twice as fast as the rest of the population. From this group too come criminals and inmates of reform schools. Experts estimate that it would be possible to decrease feeble-mindedness 36 per cent in one generation by means of sterilization. One state reports that sterilization is already providing an estimated annual saving of $2,000,000 in the cost of caring for its feeble-minded and insane in institutions.

Eugenics

In choosing a life partner young people today are giving more consideration to sound chromosomes for their children. Eugenics has come to mean improvement of the genetic constitution of the race. It comes from the Greek word Eugenes-being well born. Dysgenic means detrimental to the hereditary constitution of the race. If the race is to achieve maximum efficiency and happiness, more attention must be given to increasing the reproduction of our fit stock and decreasing the reproduction of our defective stock. Care must be taken that our way of life does not favour propagation of the least fit instead of the most fit. There is need for persons with better comprehension, broader vision, more stamina, more capacity, and willingness to serve unselfishly.

We have need to increase the number of children reared by parents who are well qualified biologically and culturally. Of course, we will not lose sight of the fact that environment plays a major role with heredity in shaping people.

How mutable, or changeable, is human nature? This question is implicited in any study of the influence of heredity, or biological inheritance, on growth and behaviour. Anyone who believes that only a minor portion of an organism's capacities and pattern of response are inherited must also believe that the organism can be moulded in large part by its surroundings-its environment. Subscribers to this view are called environmentalists. To paraphrase a distinguished exponent of environmentalism, John B. Watson, Give me a dozen children and full control of the environment, and I will make them what I wish-atomic scientists, commissars, professors, or beatniks.

If this assertion is correct, human nature is indeed changeable and future generations of mankind can be made to differ in basic character from the present generation. Yet the hereditarian insists that man is what he is, and that no amount of manipulation of the environment, unless it is accompanied by some form of selective breeding, can change him significantly. Only recently the science of genetics-the study of heredity-received a setback in the U.S.S.R. The Soviets felt that a felt that a belief in genetics implied that human character was determined, in part, by biological inheritance; to that extent, human nature was immutable. Legislating out of existence one set of views about the nature of the world, the Soviets supported another, which holds that changes in the environment of an organism alter the genetic characteristics transmitted to the organism's offspring.

This belief, known to the Western world long ago as Lamarckianism, was accepted in the West as a means of explaining variation among offspring, but was fairly well disproved by the 1920's. As a scientific theory it has little to recommend it, although it is most useful as a scientific rationalization for those who believe they can change the basic character of mankind. Yet even now, soviet scientists are attempting to restore Soviet genetics to a Western point of view. The belief espoused by the Soviets in the inheritance of acquired characteristics may seem, at first sight, an optimistic one. It holds that any efforts at self-improvement live on in one's offspring.

But Herman Muller, America's Noble Prize-winning geneticist, suggested that this concept might not be as optimistic as it first seemed. If it were true, he noted, then individuals in a backward environment-an environment that allowed little growth in intellect or development of potentialities-should become genetically inferior. As Muller pointed out, this is not so. It certainly is not true, for example, of Chinese peasants. Assuming the same form of breeding in two differing environments, individuals from environments that have been depressed for generations display, as a group, when placed in an adequate setting, the same level of abilities as any other group.

Those who stress that heredity-as defined in Western culture-is the significant determinant of human capacities would maintain that just as a fine environment cannot make men into angels so a degraded one cannot make them like beasts. These, then, are the issues involved in the study of heredity and environment as they affect human nature. Although a lengthy discussion of the mechanisms of heredity may belong, more appropriately, in a course in genetics, the foregoing philosophical considerations are clearly a part of child psychology. How they are regarded determines to a considerable degree the way the child is viewed.

Inherited Similarities

Most psychological research into the influence of heredity has been directed toward determining its role in producing differences among humans. But the overwhelming significance of heredity is not really in this area; rather it is in the area of achieving similarities between individuals. Humanness is the result of a number of genetically determined characteristics which, interacting with one another, produce that portion of behaviour that is not common with other species. La Barre argued that the characteristics that made humans unique, except for resemblance to other higher primates, were bipedal locomotion, stereoptic vision, hands, and a fairly high capacity for learning. When man, heir of four limbs, uses only two of them for walking, his clever primate hands are then finally freed from use in any kind of locomotion whatever.

They can now be used for purely exploratory grasping. The advantages of this are not to be underestimated. Emancipated hands are not enough: many dinosaurs had them, but they lacked sufficient brains. Intelligence is not enough: elephants have a great deal of intelligence behind their trunks, but they do not have stereoscopic sight; the prehensile-tailed monkeys are intelligent too, and they have stereoscopic vision as well, but they do not ordinarily see their tails. Stereoscopic eyes are not enough either: for the intelligent, tree-living apes have them, with colour vision and the yellow spot in the retina to boot. It is the combination that counts. Man has paired grasping organs, fully in his field of vision and wholly freed from locomotor duties, in a stereoscopic-sighted, big-brained mammal-and these add up to the answer. Anaxagoras claimed that man had brains because he had hands, but Aristotle argued that man had hands because he had brains.

When the implications of these statements are better understood and the dust of battle has settled a bit, modem anthropologists are inclined to give the decision to Anaxagoras rather than to Aristotle. But hands, brains, and eyes are a case, really, of hens-and-eggs causality; nor did it all begin, strictly speaking, with man. For in all primate evolution they influence each other mutually and develop progressively together; and the ability to monkey with things that man got from his primate ancestors is still one of the keystones of human nature. Certainly such hands and eyes and brains put an animal into closer object-relationship with reality and enlarge the animal ego in the technical sense of increasing awareness and testing of reality. Very literally, such animal as man has more contacts with reality.

Through producing a better understanding of the environment, this primate trait, curiosity, has so much value for survival that natural selection has made it a human characteristic inherited in much the same manner as the opposable thumb. The existence of the curiosity drive and the need it may arouse for stimulation probably produces fundamental differences in learning between primates and non-primates. This is shown, for example, in the work of Harlow and others who have found that primates attack problems involving manipulation, such as unlocking doors and solving problems, without any special reward.

If such a reward is introduced, the primate does less well in these tasks. Yet there seems to be little doubt that intrinsic reward hastens learning. Since all responses that satisfy curiosity care rewarding to primates, it seems reasonable to believe that the primate will learn a wide variety of behaviours, some of which will have survival value. In contrast, the learning of non-primates seems largely restricted to techniques to reduce such drives as hunger and thirst. Through an interplay of environment and biological inheritance, the primate-and especially man has developed physical characteristics that enable an active, manipulative approach to the environment. As a consequence, genetically determined structure and behaviour produce a basic similarity among all men. Within this similarity heredity helps to establish variations, or individual differences.

The Hereditary Process

The mechanisms of heredity are essentially the same for all species of plants and animals, although they may be more easily investigated in an ear of com or the fruit fly than in humans. What is discovered about hereditary transmission in one species can apply, with few qualifications, to all others. Among humans a sperm cell of the male penetrates the ovum of the female and thus fertilizes the ovum. Each normal male and female cell has 46 chromosomes. As a result of cell division, any single sperm or ovum contains approximately half the number of chromosomes of its parent cell-usually one-half of 46, or 23.

In the fertilized egg known as a zygote the chromosomes of sperm and ovum combine to give the fertile egg 23 pairs of chromosomes; this restores the normal complement of 46 with half inherited from each parent. Each of these chromosomes is composed, in turn, of many genes. The sperm and the ovum are germ cells. Their substance, the chains of genes formed into chromosomes, is called germ plasm, which is quite distinct from the plasm of the body, called somatoplasm. Through the germ plasm parents transmit their genes to their children. The offspring in turn pass of these genes to their progeny.

In a sense, germ plasm, transmitting characteristics as it does across generations and generally unaltered by environmental influences, is immortal. Genetic inheritance determines in large part, the physical structure and behavioural potentialities of human organisms. The exception occurs in the case of mutations caused by factors in the environment. These mutations sudden change in the gene structure which result from X-ray, cosmic ray, or fallout irradiation, or from exposure to mustard gas. What any individual is genetically determined largely by chance. Half of his genes come from the one sperm cell, among millions of possible sperm cells that penetrates one of the hundreds of egg cells produced by a female during her reproductive life.

Each parent contributes one member of each pair of the many thousands of pairs of genes that affect human inheritance. Each sperm cell and each egg cell differs in the genes it contains from all other sperm and egg cells produced by the same individual. By the random combination of the genes from a particular sperm with the genes of a particular ovum, a human is formed. This human is unique from other humans and yet like fellow men in many respects. Every individual, as we now know, contains thousands of genes. In some cases one gene is dominant and another is recessive. Those who receive one of each kind from their parents manifest the dominant characteristic, but stand even chance of passing along the recessive gene to their offspring. Since genes are acquired from parents, it is very likely that individuals are more like their parents genetically and, hence, in observable characteristics than like people in general.

However, many characteristics, which are recessive in both of one's parents and therefore not visible, may turn up in the individual. This is one reason why children do not always resemble their parents as closely as might be expected. Although some characteristics are determined by a single pair of genes, many more characteristics result from the interactive effect of a large number of gene pairs. Suppose that intellectual ability was determined by nine pairs of genes, which is likely to be less than the actual number. Suppose further that thee could be only two possible genes in each pair-one that disposed toward brightness and the other toward dullness. Now suppose that the genes disposing toward brightness were dominant in two particular parents, whereas those disposing toward dullness were recessive. Since brightness is dominant in this case any of the nine pairs of genes containing one or both bright genes would dispose the offspring toward being intelligent.

Inheritance of Individual Differences

All humans differ from one another. How much of these differences may be imputed to heredity? Although this is not an entirely valid question, since heredity and environment interact, some answers to it can tell something about the relative contribution of each to human variability. The idea that abilities are inherited certainly is not new. Long before there was a science of behaviour, the belief in the inheritance of traits formed the basis for class distinction. The knight, no matter how impoverished, could not many the merchant's daughter, no matter how substantial the dowry.

During the late Middle Ages people believed that there were vast differences between the nobility and the merchant class and between the merchant class 'and the peasantry. Those in superior positions considered themselves, somehow, transcendentally different, and held that this superiority was transmitted to their progeny. Even though such ideas, like subsequent notions of racial purity, rested on value judgments about the relative worth of individuals and on rather dubious genetic principles, they do indicate that man has long believed in heredity as a determinant of personality. The first scientific study of the inheritance of ability was undertaken by Sir Francis Galton in English Men of Science.

A cousin of Darwin and a member of the brilliant but eccentric Darwin-Wedgewood-Galton family, Sir Francis may have been drawn to this area of research by his ponderings over his extensive family and its rich contribution to English science and industry. His discovery that a relatively small number of English families produced most of England's scientists suggested to him that genius was inherited. The difficulty in interpreting his work is the same one encountered in unconnected since his time. Some English families certainly produced many scientific geniuses-but can this be attributed to heredity? The child of a genius may inherit genius or, just as likely, may acquire it through association with a dedicated, brilliant parent-or both.

This same contamination of heredity by environment pervades several recent studies which nevertheless have some bearing on the inheritance of individual differences. The United States has an open class society. Individuals of great ability may rise and those of slight ability may descend in occupational level. Although there is considerable variation in ability within any social class, IQ differences are still found to exist among members of various classes when large samples of individuals are measured in each. If intelligence were inherited, these differences, though attenuated, should also appear in the children of these individuals. Individual differences do exist.

Although superior environment in upper occupational levels may play a part in producing them, the similarity in the size of the gaps over a 20-year span during which class distinctions have markedly decreased suggests that heredity figures strongly. Many studies have measured family resemblances in intelligence. The closer resemblance in intelligence between identical than fraternal twins is of particular interest, because pairs of fraternal twins should be expected to share the same environment just about as much as do pairs of identical twins. However, this closer resemblance between identical than between fraternal twins in intelligence-test scores has also been demonstrated in several more recent studies. Jost and Sontag presented evidence on the inheritance of autonomic nervous-system responsiveness.

The autonomic nervous system is basically a network of nerves which regulates the body's involuntary functions, such as digestion or breathing. Jost and Sontag based their findings on measurements of heart and respiratory patterns, electrical skin response, pulse, and other indicators of autonomic performance. Differences in autonomic performance, they found, were less for identical twins than for siblings and less for siblings than for persons not related to each other. Since emotionality is controlled by autonomic functions, their findings detected some inheritance of this characteristic.

Freedman and Keller compared sets of identical and fraternal twins. Occasionally the suggestion has been made that identical twins show a greater resemblance than do fraternal twins because the former are treated more alike. Using the Mental and Motor Scales of the Bayley Infant Behaviour Profile, Freedman and keller compared twins within the first year of life when the effects of differential treatment between types of twins could be expected to be minimal, if not nonexistent.

The differences in scores were found to be significantly smaller between members of identical twins as compared with members of fraternal twins. This closer resemblance at such an early age supports the notion that hereditary influences have been at work. The foregoing studies all shed some light on the inheritance of characteristics. However, except for the Freedman and Keller investigation, these studies, like Sir Francis Galton's experiments in the last century, do not provide adequate controls for testing similarity of the environment. Other experimental procedures are needed if one wishes to identify more accurately the relative contributions of heredity and environment.

Three kinds of procedures employed to accomplish this task have been selective breeding, studies of identical twins, and investigations of adopted children. What evidence about human characteristics has been produced by each of these three approaches? Most research by psychologists into the role of heredity has concentrated on the influence of heredity and environment on scores in intelligence tests. This is partly the result of an historical accident. Soon after the turn of the century psychologists had developed an adequate test of intelligence, but there is still no comparable measure of personality. Moreover, an older generation of psychologists believed that intelligence was a central factor in personality. By knowing the intelligence of an individual, they held, one could also know many other things about him-his honesty, his leadership ability his values. Today's psychologists are much less certain that a high IQ automatically makes an individual trustworthy, loyal, obedient, God fearing, and kind.

Thus, studies of intelligence seem to have less bearing on personality structure than they once had. And although psychologists should like to know more about hereditary influences on personality characteristics, this is an area in which they are least knowledgeable.

Identical-Twin Studies

This single approach is perhaps the best available technique for evaluating the effect of heredity on human capacities. Genetically, identical twins are exactly alike. They result from the division of a fertilized egg after it has been penetrated by a single sperm; this division produces two individuals identical in heredity. By separating identical twins and raising them in quite disparate environments, and by holding heredity constant while varying the environment, the relative influences of each became discernible. The group of twins discussed most intensively were those studied by Newman, Freeman, and Holzinger.

These men investigated 50 sets of fraternal twins, a like number of sets of identical twins raised together, and 19 sets of identical twins raised apart from one another. The 19 pairs of identical twins raised separately are of present concern. Some rather startling resemblances were discovered among them. For example, consider these findings about Ed and Fred. The most interesting feature of this story is the remarkable parallelism in the lives of these twins in spite of the fact that they lived without knowledge of each other's existence for twenty-five years. They were both reared as only children by childless foster-parents, both being led to understand that they were own children. Though they lived a thousand miles apart, they had about the same educational experience, and both found employment as repair men in branches of the same great telephone company.

They were married in the same year and each had a baby son. Each owned a fox terrier dog named Trixie. According to their statements, both of them from early boyhood were obsessed with the idea that they had a brother who died and often stated this to their playmates. The story of their discovery of each other's existence is almost stranger that fiction. When Ed was of twenty-two he was accosted by a jovial fellow who had just come from a distant city to work at Ed's department. Hello, Fred! How's tricks? He inquired. Ed explained that he was not Fred and denied that he knew the newcomer, but the latter was hard to convince, declaring that Ed was trying to cover up his identity. Soon afterward another man accosted him as Fred and stated that if he was not Fred Blank he was exactly like a fellow of that name with whom he had recently worked in a distant city.

Ed was by this time rather disturbed about the matter and told his parents about it. Reluctantly, the parents were forced to admit that Ed was an adopted son and that he was one of a pair of twins; the other of them had been adopted by a couple who lived in their home town but with whom they were not acquainted. They also revealed the fact that when the twins were small boys they had attended school together for a short time and that the other children often noticed their close resemblance. It occurs to us that this early association of the twins may have led to the above-mentioned mutual feeling about a brother who had died. Needless to say, Ed lost no time in getting in touch with Fred.

The latter was out of work at the time and came to visit Ed. It was during this time that we succeeded in inducing them to come to Chicago to see the Fair and, incidentally, to be examined. Their visit with us was made even more interesting to them and to us by reason of a confusion of dates which resulted in their coming to us at the same time as a pair of young women twins, Ethel and Esther, whose story comes next in this series. The two pairs of twins became great friends and were much impressed by similarity in the circumstances that led to their discovery that they were twins. The visits to the Fair were made together, each young man taking one of the young women. When they walked about people were startled to see one couple walking ahead and a duplicate couple following behind. Everywhere they went they attracted attention and enjoyed the sensation they created. On one occasion they attended a side show featuring a pair of Siamese twins and, according to their statement, stole the show, attracting more attention than the exhibits.

They resembled one another closely in IQ and less closely in personality. Perhaps the degree to which heredity determines development diminishes from size to IQ to personality. Or perhaps the correlations were highest on concrete physical growth because here is where the best, most exact and most reliable measuring instruments are available. Devices for measuring intelligence are less precise and reliable than devices used to check physical dimensions. The reliability of measures for personality is low even at the present time and was certainly a good deal lower at the time of the Newman et al. study in the 1930's. Actually, the reliability of most tests was so low in the 1930's that it was surprising to find any resemblance at all between twins. Since the measures of intelligence were most central to the matters that concerned psychologists at the time these tests have been the most widely discussed. Woodworth offered both IQ and environmental data for the 19 sets of twins studied by Newman and his associates, and for three other sets as well.

The correlation obtained between identical twins reared in separate environments was +.767. This was a more substantial relation than was obtained between fraternal twins raised in the same environment. Although Newman, Freeman, and Holzinger considered their data to support an environmentalist view, heredity seemed to have played an important part in determining the level of intelligence. A more recent study of variations in intelligence among a comparable sample of identical twins who were raised separately has turned up similar results. In this case it seems clear that some variability can be attributed to environmental circumstances, even though the heredity factor is quite strong. One other intensive study of a single pair of identical twins supplies considerable information about the interests and personalities of the twins, as well as the more customary measurements of intelligence and physical size.

The twins were girls, who had been separated before they were two week old. At the age of 12, personality ratings showed them to be quite similar to one another, despite a variability in certain areas of adjustment, which was produced by familial and environmental influences. The girls differed markedly in Strong Interest Test scores. At 18 they seemed even more similar to each other then at 12 and their interest profiles showed a distinct increase in comparability. Moreover, Rofschach tests at 18 indicated a high degree of likeness; the patterns of response were more alike than might have been anticipated even from previous studies of identical twins who had been reared together.

The greater likeness at 18 suggested that as one grew older and, hence, freer from parental dominance, innate predispositions became more apparent. This study, the only known one to have measured separately raised identical twins with adequate devices for assessing personality, suggested that the extent to which individuals displayed certain personality traits was in large part the consequence of genetic inheritance. Studies of identical twins who have been separated also have bearing for one particular aspect of the subject of heredity and environment. This is the aspect of how enrichment affects intelligence-test scores and, presumably, innate ability. Wellman maintained that kindergarten experience increased the ability of the child. More recently, Bowlby, Goldfarb, and Spitz asserted that a child's level of intellectual performance was largely determined by the closeness and richness of the mothering it received.

However, Pinneau and others, among them Dennis and Najarian, have taken a contrary position. The latest phase of enrichment to be explored is that of very early enrichment. This is the area of enrichment that is most relevant to the study of identical twins. Thus far, most of the experimental work has been conducted with laboratory rats. Hebb reported that rats from an ordinary strain of laboratory species who were reared as home pets performed in significantly superior manner on a learning task to rats from the same strain who were reared in a normal laboratory environment. Other well-controlled experiments have extended these findings. In a representative study of this sort conducted by Forgus, infant rats were exposed to visual forms from the time they first opened their eyes at the age of 16 days until they reached 41 days of age.

A second group of rats was exposed to these same forms during the interval from 41 to 66 days of age. In both cases control groups of littermates were reared without the visual experience. Tests of both enriched and both control groups showed that the two enriched groups learned more rapidly than the control groups, and that the group that had been enriched early learned more rapidly than the late enrichment group. Several similar studies concurred in this finding. These indicate that deprivation retards later learning, whereas early enrichment increases the rate of learning. Studies in the early enrichment of lower organisms contain implications for problems of human development.

This has been suggested by Hunt, McCandless, Smith and Stone, and Thompson. Perhaps, for example, the enrichment or deprivation of problem-solving experience to which a human is exposed before the age of two or three may be related to later ability. If early enrichment or deprivation bears on the intellectual ability of humans, then identical twins who are exposed to a common early environment and share the stimulation it offers should resemble each other more closely in IQ tests than identical twins who have not shared a common environment for any length of time. The 19 pairs of separated identical twins studied by Newman et al., plus one pair each studied by Burks, Gardner and Newman, Muller, and Saudek constitute 23 pairs. Of these 23 pairs of identical twins, 11 were separated before the age of six months and 12 were separated after their first year. The mean age of separation was two months for the younger group and 24 months for the other. The respective medians were one months and 18 months. If early environmental stimulation influences later ability, those twins who shared a common environment for a longer period of time should show a greater resemblance in intelligence than those separated at an earlier age.

Evidence from Selective Breeding

Selective breeding is the breeding of organisms for the presence or absence of some particular trait. If the breeding can be achieved, the trait must necessarily have some hereditary base. The speed at which selective breeding progresses indicates, in part, the importance of heredity in determining how much of the trait is present in any organism. Galton's study persuaded him that humans should engage in selective breeding. The able person should seek an equally able mate in order to improve the human race. This process of selective breeding Galton called eugenics. Although eugenics societies still exist, human beings have not taken Galton's ideas very seriously. They continue to fall in love without giving the slightest consideration to what the eugenicist might think of their choice. Yet even if people turned about and suddenly adhered to Galton's formula, problems would remain.

What should be the goal of the breeders-vigour, beauty, intelligence? Often these are not found in the same individual, as the well-known story about George Bernard Shaw, the playwright, and Ellen Terry, the beautiful actress, illustrates. Miss Terry suggested to Shaw that they could produce a true wonder kind with her beauty and his brains. Shaw rejected the proposal, replying things might turn out the other way around; the child might inherit his beauty and her brains. The difficulty in any sort of selective breeding is thus the matter of choosing the objective of the process. The few situations in which humans have bred selectively are indeed odd, since only eccentric people could and would indulge in such experiments. Frederick the Great is said to have married off a large number of his tallest guards to a group of strapping peasant girls and provided them with villages in which to live so as to ensure future rulers of Prussia a ready source of tall soldiers for honour-guard usage. Hitler attempted to breed Aryan Supermen.

The most interesting example of selective breeding among humans stemmed from the ideas of an American religious sect. John Noyes believed that the violent, antisocial emotions, such as jealousy and anger, resulted primarily from the existence of the nuclear family the family composed of father, mother, and children formed into a tightly knit unit. Doing away with this family, Noyes held, also does away with possessiveness and, hence, with greed, jealousy, and anger. In its place he advocated a utopian scheme as part of a religion he called Perfectionism. At Oneida, New York, Noyes and his followers maintained themselves for years in a communistic community.

They practised what outsiders called free love but what they themselves considered multiple marriage. Although sexual behaviour was, in a sense, free, Noyes and other leaders of the Oneida community decided who could have children, how many they could have, and who would be the partner of a particular individual in conceiving a child. Noyes desired only the brightest, most capable adults to reproduce. Long before Galton he practised eugenics, though he called it stirpiculture. The community flourished long enough for two generations, in some cases, to be bred selectively. Then federal prosecution of Mormon polygamy in the 1880's spilled over into Oneida, forcing the end of the experiment, the only one in which humans were bred for general physical and intellectual excellence. Although there have been assertions that children of the community have demonstrated high levels of ability, only an empirical study of the group's descendants can truly assess the success of the venture. Among lower organisms it is easier to observe the results of selective breeding.

Physical size and structure, ability, and emotionality are the variations between organisms that can be genetically determined. By selecting and breeding dogs for smallness, as well as for other characteristics, one obtains the Chihuahua, whereas for largeness, one obtains the Great Dane. Moreover, dogs of different breeds vary in temperament and in ability almost as widely as they do in size. Since the ancestry of pedigreed dogs is known for generations the researcher has purer strains at his disposal than he can obtain among humans. Scott has reported studies conducted by Fuller and himself which disclose the effect on temperament of hereditary differences produced by selective breeding.

In several of these studies, they compared cocker spaniels with basenjis. Basenjis proved considerably shier and more fearful than cockers, even when they were reared by cocker mothers. As a result of breeding cockers to basenjis, the hybrid progeny were as shy as full-blooded basenjis, suggesting that shyness was a dominant genetic trait in dogs. Breeds of dogs, which differ in parental stock and in the traits for which they are bred, also differ widely in other respects. By shifting from dogs to rats, we move from the domain generally inhabited by the animal fancier to the domain of the animal scientist. Many rats have been bred by investigators to study the influence of genetic inheritance on a variety of animal characteristics. The most famous rat-breeding experiment was conducted by Tryon. Krech and Crutchfield have succinctly summarized Tryon's work.

Tryon started with parental generation of 142 male and female rats. Each animal was run for 19 trials through a 17-unit maze. The brightest animals made a total of approximately 14 errors in learning the maze, the dullest, about 174. The bright females were then mates with the bright males, the dull females with the dull males-the other animals being discarded. Then the offspring of these matings were tested on the same maze. On the basis of their performance, the brightest rats within each of the bright litters were mated, and the dullest within each of the dullest litters were mated. This testing and selective breeding procedure was followed for 18 generations. The results are summarized in the distribution curves of showing the errors made by the parental group, the third generation, the seventh generation and the ninth generation.

With successive generations the two strains of rats pull apart, until by the generations the dullest of the bright rats are about as bright or brighter than the brightest of the dulls. The Tryon experiment is itself of considerable significance and has led to further work in the biochemical aspects of brightness and dullness. Conceivably, this might be a key to the treatment of certain kinds of mental defect. If, in eight generations, one can produce differences so great that strains of organisms do not overlap in a trait such as brightness or emotionality, then genetic factors are indeed powerful in establishing individual differences.

The many studies in selective breeding, although dealing for the most part with lower organisms, strongly support the notion that human beings do not enter the world as a tabularasa-a blank tablet. Instead they are born with certain abilities and propensities which are further accentuated by the environment. In fact, it might be said that any characteristic that has a structural base, such as activity level, tendency toward schizophrenia, emotionality, or intelligence, in inheritable.

7

Learning and Motivation

The learning process is fundamental in all theories purporting to explain the psychological development and changing behaviour patterns of the growing child. There is ample evidence that maturational processes set the limits for behaviour change, and determine to a large extent the rate of learning. There is also a large body of data demonstrating that the child's behaviour is continuously modified during the growth period in a manner that permits him to adapt himself to his natural and social environments. Since a large part of the child's adaptive behaviour is directly dependent on the particular social-cultural milieu in which he develops, this interaction between the child and his environing conditions is extremely important to an understanding of the dynamics of behavioural change. The results of this interaction between the child and his environment have been variously designated as conditioning, learning, problem solving, and acculturation, depending upon the relative molar or molecular perspective of the expositor.

What is Learning?

Probably the most general definition of learning is that given by Guthrie, "to respond differently to a situation because of past response to the situation..." The definition offered by McGeoch and Irion is similar although somewhat less general because of the inclusion of the concept of "practice", "Learning as we measure it, is a change in performance which occurs under the conditions of practice." Hull's definition is probably the most acceptable to the average American psychologist because it stems more directly from the Pavlovian Thorndikian tradition, "Just as the inherited equipment of reaction tendencies consists of receptor-effector connections, so the process of learning consists in the strengthening of certain of these connections as contrasted with others, or in the setting up of quite new connections." The latter definition leads very directly to hypotheses and postulates about the nature of these intervening "connections" - the construction of conceptual systems based on inferences from empirical relationships has been approached very differently by various psychologist. (Hilgard)

Learning can also be considered as the resultant of an individual's attempt to solve a particular problem. For example, consider the hungry infant. The motivating condition depends on the complex of physiological conditions of the organism that result from food deprivation after the passage of time following previous food intake. The neonate will demonstrate the sucking response to a variety of stimuli, such as a pinch on the toe or a tap on the chest. Through practice the infant learns that some of these stimulating conditions are not associated with or do not lead to a satisfaction of the motivating condition of hunger. With sufficient practice the infant learns to suck only when a nipple is placed between his lips, since this response has so often been followed by the presence of milk in the oral cavity and a subsequent reduction in the need for nourishment. In this case the infant has temporarily solved the problem of what response leads most directly to a satisfaction of the motivating condition of hunger. As the infant increases in age he aces many new problems related to the search for nourishment, e.g., motor skills of self-feeding, verbal requests for desired foods, and so forth. The growing child is continuously faced with new problems that must be solved in ways that satisfy his basic needs and by behaviours that do not come into serious conflict with the need satisfactions of the various individuals in his social environment.

There are a few things the baby does not have to learn. These responses are present at birth. The baby does not have to learn to breathe, to make his heart beat, to digest his food, to sneeze, to grasp a rod, or to make random movements. Given the proper stimulus, certain movements result. The touch of a rod in the hand is the stimulus which evokes the response of grasping. The touch of the nipple on the lips is the stimulus that calls forth the sucking response. The feeling of pain if the knee is pinched is a stimulus that is followed by defensive movements of the other leg.

A variety of stimuli-such as pressures, fatigue products, digestive movements and secretions, resultants of preceding reactions, and growth of the nerve cells-probably gives rise to the random movements of the arms and legs and muscles of the face and throat. These movements are or at one time in the history of the race were necessary to life. There was no time to stop and learn them. They furnished as it were, the minimum essentials of living. Learning actions less immediately necessary is a slow and complex process.

The importance of Motivation in the Learning Process

In any consideration of learning it is important to remember that the child is a striving organism, an organism whose seeking behaviour continues until a particular need (such as hunger, social recognition, etc.), is satisfied - or until fatigue or some other condition dissipates the need - tension system. Most psychologists assume that all behaviour is motivated, although it is usually difficult to identify the particular social needs and rewards which motivate and direct the behaviour of older children. Teachers, parents, and other individuals who have frequent social interactions with children usually find that a child's behaviour is more understandable after they reflect on the question, "What is this child trying to do, what does he want, what lies behind this behaviour?" An understanding of children's wants and interests is of extreme importance in attempts to guide their learning activites.

Learning to Bring his Hand to his Mouth

The ability to bring the hand to the mouth is learned in a similar way. Random movements towards the face are frequently made. By chance the baby happens to put his hand into his mouth. The sensation is pleasing. He fumbles around and does it again; more satisfaction results. The act is repeated until he can put his hand into his mouth every time he wants to. Objects which he grasps go the same way. This reaction is very common at six months. After that time the hands should find other interesting things to do, and the hand-mouth pathway should fade out.

If the baby is left alone too much of the time with nothing to look at or to play with, he will often amuse himself by sucking his thumb. Bright coloured balls and birds hanging a few feet away for him to look at will occupy his attention. Various home-made and ready-made toys should be available for him to handle. Rattles, celluloid and rubber rings and animals, unbreakable dolls, blocks, untearable picture books, nests of hollow blocks, spools, buttons and beads on strings that do not break, small lids and covers, aluminium spoons and cups, post cards, sheets of clean crisp paper-these are some of the toys that Mrs. Fenton suggests for the first year.

Learning to Pick up Objects

The baby, as has just been said, does not have to learn to make random movements of the hands. These movements are the capital he has to invest in new combinations. His hands beat about over the bed covering in the third or fourth month and happen to encounter a little rubber toy, a rattle, an aluminium spoon, or other small objects which are strewn over the bed. Having a number of objects near the baby will insure his coming in contact with some of them. The child will never learn to grasp objects unless the stimulus-an object of convenient size-is provided. At first he fumbles with it. At last he succeeds in grasping it.

The feeling of the little object in his hand is pleasing. In other words, grasping results in satisfaction. The baby repeats activities which please him. He should be allowed to try, again without interruption and without much help from adults. Occasionally he may be shown a way of grasping more convenient than the one he learns by chance. After a time, the sight of a little object will stimulate him to reach out and grasp it. Eventually he may desire an object out of sight. In such a case he will look for it and, finding it, pick it up.

These, then, are the steps in learning to pick up an object: random movements which bring the fumbling fingers in contact with an object; an accidental success in grasping it, which results in satisfaction; repetition of the act of grasping; seeing an object, reaching for it, and picking it up; wanting an object not in sight, looking for it, finding and securing it. What can the mother do to help the baby learn to pick up objects? When he is in the fumbling stage, she can provide many objects small enough to be grasped easily and large enough not to be swallowed. When the baby has learned to grasp objects and needs practice in looking for and recognizing things, she should provide only a few objects at a time. She should leave him alone to solve the little difficulties he meets in picking up objects, and thus help him to develop initiative, reasoning, and independence in these simple situations. Overcoming difficulties give even a young child a satisfying feeling of mastery.

Learning to Look

The development of long-distance and meaningful vision is best encouraged by a similar method. Allow the child to look as long as he likes without interruption. Give him many kinds of objects which he can look at and handle. Move him about occasionally from room to room and outdoors on the street or in the garden, because a change of surroundings increases his interest in learning to look and see.

Learning to Walk

This important activity follows a similar trial-and- success pattern of learning. In general, the steps are as follows: random arm and leg movements, pushing and kicking movements, sitting with support, kicking with alternate movements of the legs, learning to wriggle about on the bed and turn over at will, pulling himself to an erect position, creeping, standing by holding on to the side of the pen or table, standing alone, walking with help, walking alone. Some of these abilities seem to develop suddenly, but the process of learning to walk has many ups and downs. The course of learning does not always run smooth.

One twelve-months-old baby, for example, was making steady progress in learning to walk without help. One day he slipped on a small rug and feel on the slippery hard work floor, hitting his head. This one painful experience markedly delayed his progress in learning to walk. The fall resulted in an unwillingness to continue his attempt to walk. As long as walking resulted in satisfaction, progress was made. When it resulted in pain and annoyance, progress was interrupted. What can the mother or nurse do to help the baby learn to sit, stand, and walk? At least two things are essential-food and freedom. Adequate food is needed to build muscle and bone. Freedom is needed for developing and learning to control the muscles.

A clean sheet spread on the floor is a safe place for the baby, unhampered by clothing, to turn and kick and squirm freely. A little pen by which the child can pull himself up to standing position in helpful about the sixth or seventh month. Again the laissez-faire policy is best-do not interfere with his own efforts or force him to walk before he is ready. To prevent serious injury from falls, the baby should never be left alone except in a crib with raised sides, in a baby pen, or some other place from which he cannot possibly fall. Four-months-old Jean fell from the bed one day. Her mother thought the baby was safe on the bed because she 'had not yet learned to creep or crawl. But while her mother was out of the room, Jean had managed to wriggle herself to the edge of the bed and tumble over. When the baby is learning to creep, a good way of substituting a desirable response for the undesirable one of tumbling off the bed is to teach him how to slide down the side of the bed until his feet touch the floor and to drop to creeping position. Sliding down stairs in the same careful way step by step should also be taught before accidents have a chance to occur.

Learning not to be Afraid

The baby learns to fear by the same process by which he learns to act. It, as Watson claims, there are only two inherited causes of fear, how does it happen that children are afraid of so many different things-animals, strangers, snakes, ghosts? They learn to be afraid of these other things. How? A neighbour comes in to see the baby. She takes him in her arms less securely than the mother does. The baby is afraid that he will fall. He cries. Is he afraid of the neighbour? No, he is afraid of falling. But the neighbour and the fear of falling occurred together.

The fear response is thus easily attached to the neighbour. Another example: The family dog barks every time it is introduced to the baby. The baby cries and tries to creep away. He does not like that loud noise of barking. If the dog had been still, the baby would doubtless have stretched out his hands in a friendly way. After the dog and its noisy bark have occurred together a few times, the baby is afraid of the dog even when it is quiet. The animal and the noise have been associated so many times that the fear-at first called forth by the barking-now becomes attached to the dog-perhaps not only to that one dog, but also to all dogs, to all animals, even to all furry objects.

One element of a situation-the furry quality of animals in this case-calls forth the same response that was made to the whole original situation of the loudly barking dog. Thus fears are built. The more fears the baby has, the more readily will he acquire other fears. They accumulate at an increasing rate. The greater the number of fears, the greater the possibility of shifting the fear reaction over to objects previously unconnected with fear. Watson failed to find any of the six or seven babies, four months to one year old, who had never been outside of the hospital afraid of animals and other things which arouse fear in many one year-old who reached for and wanted to play with a very lively, friendly black cat, a pigeon cooing and flapping its wings, a rabbit, and a white rat.

This baby showed no fear when taken into a dark room by a stranger. All the animals in the zoo failed to arouse any fear response. The same lack of fear was found in all the babies tested. What can the parent or nurse do to prevent unnecessary fears? One obvious suggestion is to avoid as far as possible those two natural causes of fear-loud noises and loss of support. Papers may be folded quietly, water turned on gently, pots and pans handled with care, and other very loud noises controlled as far as possible when the baby is around, until he gradually becomes accustomed to the ordinary household noises. The best technique of handling the baby can be learned. A trained nurse should show the inexperienced mother exactly how to bathe and dress the baby.

A mother who does not know how to do this is very likely to give the baby a feeling of insecurity-of imminent danger of being dropped. Moreover, the mother is not under any obligation to pass the baby around to unskilful strangers to hold. A second suggestion for preventing fears is to introduce objects and people to the baby under favourable conditions. The pet dog should not be brought to the baby when it is barking violently. The neighbour should be introduced while the baby is safe and happy in his mother' arms. A third suggestion is to associate things that commonly arouse fear with laughter and playfulness.

A baby's attitude toward many things is frequently determined by the clue he gets from his companion. One baby on the beach who was about to cry as a wave rushed up around his feet laughed and gurgled and splashed in the foam when he saw his sister do this. Moods may be communicated. Joyousness, calmness, and confidence are contagious, and babies are very susceptible to them. A fourth rule is to avoid the use of fear in discipline. Ignorant or wicked nursed often build fears of policemen, burglars, or animals in order to secure obedience. The temptation to use fear for this purpose is great because it is such an easy way to control the behaviour of little children. Shutting them in a dark closet after having created a fear of the dark, telling them the bears will get them, shouting at them, spanking them, telling them the policeman will carry away bad children-these means of discipline are still to frequently practised.

Two types of children are likely to result from the use of fear as a means of controlling their behaviour. One is the defiant child, who gains control of his fear and refuses to be intimidated. The other is a nervous, timed child, who is afraid of innumerable things. Chronic anxiety in adults may be due to excessive fears of things and people acquired in young childhood. Locke, in his Essay Concerning Human Understanding, first printed in 1690, gives some very modern suggestion on this point: Those who have children, or the charge of their education, would think it worth their while diligently to watch, and carefully to prevent the undue connection of ideas in the minds of young people.

This is the time most susceptible of lasting impressions... The ideas of goblins and sprites have really no more to do with darkness than light: yet let but a foolish maid inculcate these often on the mind of a child, and raise them there together, possibly he shall never be able to separate them again so long as he lives, but darkness shall ever afterwards bring with it those frightful ideas. If a baby is already afraid, he should not be forced to do something in the face of an intense fear. A baby afraid of the water should not be plunged into it regardless of his cries. This is a favourite masculine way of meeting the situation, but is not the wise way. Re-education by gradually associating the thing the child is afraid of with something pleasant is the approved method.

A child afraid of the sea or a bath tub full of water is quite willing to play with little toys in a small pan of water.

The amount of water and the amount of splashing may be increased day by day until finally the child is willing to have the water come up all around him. A child who has been frightened by an animal should be shown, after the first fear has subsided, some small gentle animals, such as chickens, little kittens and puppies, while he is held by his mother.

If she talks soothingly, laughs, names the various kinds of animals, and encourages the baby's attempts to reach for and play with the animals, interest and curiosity will gradually drive out fear. If the baby has been frightened by a stranger, it is best to wait until the baby is clam and happy before trying to establish friendly relations. The mother's mood in meeting the stranger will furnish a clue for the child. Reasoning and explaining are of little value in overcoming the fears of babies. Even older children and adults, who understand how foolish it is for them to be afraid of a certain thing, experience the fear reaction in spite of themselves. The best procedure is to discover the cause of a given fear and to see that this cause does not occur, or if removal is impossible, gradually to attach other associations and responses to the stimulus which originally tended to produce fear.

Frequently pleasant associations may be formed from the beginning with objects that most commonly call forth fear. Babies should have playful experience with gentle pet dogs before big, rough barking dogs are met. The child can learn to like the nice dark, before his imagination confronts with terrifying inhabitants. During the first year the baby should become accustomed to going to bed alone in the dark. The attitude of the parent toward real dangers is communicable to a year-old baby, and may affect more or less permanently the child's response in similar situations. The mother should guard against showing fear herself. An indirect way of combating fear is to improve the baby's physical condition. Poor health increases the tendency to fear.

A characteristic of many diseases is increased fear and anxiety. When fatigued, adults are more easily frightened and start more violently at a slamming door than when they are rested. The habit of meeting new situations with interest and curiosity rather than with suspicion and dread may have its foundations laid in this very early period.

Learning to Speak

This significant achievement follows the same general pattern of learning. Random sounds are made at first without any special intention on the baby's part. Next, sounds are called forth in response to something in the environment or to an internal feeling which seems to require vocal expression. If crying when hungry brings relief, the baby will learn to use this method in summoning food. A pattern of associations is built-feeling of discomfort-crying-mother coming-relief of discomfort. The baby learns to make the appropriate cry to complete the pattern. There comes a time when the baby chances to make a new sound which he enjoys, just as he chanced to grasp an object and to enjoys, just as he chanced to make a new sound which he enjoys, just as he chanced to grasp an object and to enjoy the ensuing sensation.

He tries to repeat the enjoyable sound and, if successful, babbles that sound interminably. Every baby at first has a vocabulary of his own. If parents learn it, they deprive the baby of a strong motive for learning adults' words, since he can get what he wants by using his own vocabulary. Motive is important in learning even in the first year. If the baby can secure everything he wants by making gestures, or if his wants are detected and supplied before he makes any attempt to fulfill them, he has no incentive to use other means of getting satisfaction. If the more primitive form of language-gestures-will secure the things he desires, there is no urge to acquire the more difficult form of communication-speech. Something that is greatly desired is worth making an effort to name, if naming will secure it. Interesting sights and sounds also provide stimuli to speech.

Outdoor trips furnish new experiences that encourage recounting. Looking out on a busy street stimulates conversation about its sights and sounds. Animals furnish interesting, easily imitated sounds. Picture books help the baby to enlarge and interpret his experience, and so aid language development, especially if the objects are named as the child looks at each picture. Picture books of familiar objects such as the common domestic animals are better for the little child than pictures of unfamiliar wild animals. The adults' manner of speaking to the baby is also a factor in his speech development.

The child's auditory patterns must be made very distinct. Speaking clearly and slowly and directly to a child whose attention is fixed on the speaker helps him to hear and comprehend the meaning and to reproduce the sounds of the words more accurately. Correct pronunciation is extremely important in the early years. The child carries through life not only the language of the group in which he is reared, but also, to a certain extent, the language of the individual who cares for him most constantly through the first years of life. If this person is his mother, he is likely to have the accent of his mother. If it is someone else, then her dialectic sounds will colour it. Adults should not use baby talk in speaking to children because this helps to fix infantile pronunciation which must be corrected later on. A good rule is, teach the child only those things which are permanently useful to him-not those which he will have to unlearn later. The babble stage is necessary for a time, but baby sounds should be dropped after they have made their contribution to the development of real words. From the babble period, language may develop in a number of directions, depending on the way people respond to the child's first attempts at speech.

Mrs. Fenton says that "the child who is talked to a great deal, who sees many interesting sights, and has a kind and patient companion to explain the sights he sees and name them for him will make the best progress in acquiring a rich and varied vocabulary. The meaning of words should be known before the child attempts to say them. Miss Shinn's niece knew the meanings of eighty-four words when she was able to say only five. What a dog looks like, feels like, sounds like, and does, should be known before the child learns to say the word dog. Accordingly, the best words to learn first are the words which are most like the child own sounds, those in which he is most interested, and those describing his everyday experiences and his familiar environment-milk, bread, table, chair, coat, hat, shoe, water, drink, and the like.

While the baby is being dressed, the mother can name rhythmically the various articles of clothing as they are put on. Mrs. Lucy Sprague Mitchell has shown the poetic possibilities of such rhythmic enumeration. Further training in speech in the preschool and school periods in largely an extension along these same lines.

Learning not to get Angry

How many anger frequently be prevented, and how should it be treated when it occurs? In the first place, unnecessary hampering of the baby's movements in bathing and dressing may be avoided by knowing the best technique of handling him and by providing clothing which is easily put on-garments open all the way down the back and fastened with a few easily adjusted tapes or buttons. Awkward and uncomfortable handling is a source of irritation. Since many babies thoroughly enjoy the bath, a bath battle is usually due to lack of skill in giving the bath. Even putting on winter clothing may be done with smiles and frolic.

The mother should give care and thought to teaching the baby to accept cheerfully bathing, dressing, and other necessary details of everyday living. If the baby is interested in helping to put his arms into the sleeves, and his legs into the leggings, and in otherwise taking an active part in dressing himself, anger will be avoided because his movements and desires are no longer being thwarted, but rather are being aided by the mother. Every time the baby succeeds in helping himself, nods and smiles should be bestowed to encourage repetition of the desirable activity. In the second place, unnecessary interference with the baby's activities should be avoided. If carrying the baby away from some interesting activity is necessary, his attention may first be attracted to some little object which he may carry with him without interfering with his mother's plans. In the third place, continued failure to get things he wants should be avoided.

If the baby cannot reach something which he desires, the object should be moved a little nearer so that it may be obtained with reasonable effort, or a stick should be provided with which he can secure the object if he has sufficient sagacity to see the relationship between the stick and the object. Helping the baby in these indirect ways prevents the response of anger from occurring, and gives the infant a sense of achievement in place of a sense of failure and thwarting. Of course, there are some things he cannot do and some objects he should not touch, but in a home built for babies, such objects are not numerous, and the baby soon learns not to bother with them. Helping the baby to avoid frequent failure is not incompatible with the suggestion previously made to interfere as little as possible with the child's activities, in order not to remove stimuli to effort and reasoning.

The assistance given should be just enough to bring the task within the physical and mental capacity of the child. Sometimes anger may be checked by merely diverting the baby's attention to something else. It is not possible however, to prevent all outbursts of anger, except at too great cost. The baby must learn that he cannot always have what he wants, and the best time to begin learning this is early in the first year. Temper tantrums may occur and should be dealt with in a firm manner. One baby stiffened, kicked, and screamed when his mother brought the sleeping bag and began preparation for bed. What should she do? Should she spank him? Should she let him play a little longer? Should she let him cry it out?

She decided to follow the latter course, and went away and left him alone until he stopped screaming. The performance was not repeated. If she had let him play a little longer, the fit of anger might have become a regular part of the bedtime program. If she had spanked him, the anger response might have become still more intense. Being left alone is annoying to a sociable baby. Crying did no good. It didn't work. The baby did not get the thing he wanted. The result was that the fit of temper in this situation was not repeated. As is true of fear, physical irritations-sore gums, chapped skin, mosquito bites, and indigestion-predispose to anger. Regularity in feeding, dressing, going for an outing, and all the other events of the day is the best background for growing, placid, jolly babies. Happiness should be the predominant note of babyhood.

Summary of Suggestions for the Education of the Child during the Rust Year

1. *Provide an environment which furnishes the stimuli needed for the child's development in this period. If suitable materials are provided, the baby may be trusted to make good use of them.*

(i) Place near the baby two or three interesting objects when he is learning to look for, reach for, and recognize special objects.

(ii) Take the baby from room to room and outdoors on the street so that he will have new sights to look at. Toward the end of the first year interesting familiar sights, sounds, and objects which stimulate the impulse to look, listen, handle, and talk are needed.

(iii) Plan all the mechanical details of bathing and dressing so that unnecessary fear and irritation will be avoided.

(iv) Remove from the house as many things as possible that may harm the baby or necessitate many don'ts. Glass bowls and heavy ornaments placed on a table cloth may be pulled down on the baby. Vases and dishes which the baby may break should be placed entirely out of reach. Scissors and knives should be kept where only adults can use them, until the baby is old enough to learn to use them safely.

(v) Place within reach of the baby, when he begins to want to handle things, a number of objects of a convenient size.

(vi) Provide coloured balls and birds and other objects for the baby to look at when he is lying awake.

(vii) Provide a little pen or something by which the baby can pull himself to standing position when he feels so inclined.

(viii) Talk to the baby a great deal with clear, slow, accurate articulation.

(ix) Provide a pleasant, sanitary nursery with washable walls and floors, low shelves, a box, or cupboards in which to keep toys; a sunny window; a low rocking chair; a low firm table; a bassinet of the simplest type; harmonious colours; one or two beautiful pictures changed from time to time; a few artistically illustrated books, such as those illustrated by Caldecott, L. Leslie Brooke, and M. Boutet De Monvel; a wicker wardrobe; and home-made or ready-made toys such as have been previously mentioned. If the baby cannot have a room of his own, a corner of the shared room may be furnished for him.

2. *Leave the baby alone- i.e., do not interfere unnecessarily with his activities.*

(i) Do not interfere with his looking at things long and steadily.

(ii) Do not do everything for him, solve all his little difficulties, nor give him everything he wants. Let him do things for himself and try to find a way out of his own difficulties.

(iii) Do not hamper the baby's movements with unnecessary and unsuitable clothing.

(iv) Do not constantly try to amuse him. The baby is not a plaything. He is easily fatigued by unusual experiences either pleasurable or painful.

(v) Do not urge him to walk or stand before he is ready. Leave him free to kick and wriggle and creep, so that he will be ready in time to pun himself up to standing position. Mechanical devices for teaching babies to walk have not proved practical.

(vi) Do not anticipate his desires. This removes his motive for trying to make his wants known through speech.

3. *Avoid as far as possible stimuli which evoke undesirable responses.*

(i) Handle the baby skilfully so as to avoid arousing fear of falling or anger at having his movements interfered with.

(ii) Avoid slightly burned or spoiled food which might cause a permanent aversion to that particular food.

(iii) Never allow anyone to tease the baby.

4. Treat the baby consistently-respond in the same way to a situation each time until he knows what to expect. For example, maintain uniformity in the bedtime program. Do not hurry him to bed one night and permit people to frolic with him at bedtime another night. Do not sometimes leave him alone when he cries for attention and at other times take him up and cuddle him. Parents who wobble in their treatment make habit formation difficult for the baby.

5. Do not be so careful and troubled about many details that the baby cannot be enjoyed as well as roved.

6. Plan a suitable daily schedule and adhere to it, thus maintaining regularity in feeding, sleeping, bowel movements, and exercise.

7. Make desirable behaviour satisfying to the baby. Certain routine habits can most easily be formed by the same method that a trainer uses in teaching an elephant to play ball or a bear to beg-namely, by getting the act performed each day and immediately rewarding success. Solving his little difficulties is decidedly satisfying to the baby. In general always try to make the things which the baby ought to learn pleasant, and the things he ought not to learn, unpleasant. Anatole France sums up this most important education principle when he says: "I would make lovable to her everything I would wish her to love.

How to Study the Baby?

Parents, teachers, and other persons closely associated with children are constantly studying them to some extent, noticing especially inatteption, disobedience, evident symptoms of communicable disease, favourite toys and games, and manifestations of fear, rage, and love. How does this incidental study differ from scientific child study?

Kinds of Observation

There are two kinds of observation-uncontrolled and

controlled. In uncontrolled observation, the observer watches the baby in his customary environment, and notes from day to day the movements he makes with his hands and fingers, legs and feet, and other parts of his body; the sounds he utters; he evidences he gives of memory, imagination, and reasoning; and his responses to other people. Gesell describes ingenious methods of observing and recording observations of children in their familiar environment.

The investigators are concealed from the children whom they can easily see and hear. Tiedemann's observations are an early, and Brainard's, a recent example of this method of studying the baby. A modem parent's Baby Book is no longer a stork-and-forget-me-not-decorated little book interspersed with pretty poetry and spaces in which to paste a bit of the baby' hair, or a pattern of his first shoe. A modem Baby Book is nothing more than a note book of a utilitarian type filled with jottings such as: April 3. Baby sat with very little support, grasped a bottle with her feet, enjoyed kicking feet in the air, and often used an alternate movement, said check-boo, moo, in response to talking. The value of a method of observation depends more upon the interpretive attitude which accompanies it than upon the method itself. There is great danger, Gesell points out, that the infant's emotions and actions will be interpreted in terms of the adult's own psychology.

Characteristics of Scientific Child Study

In the first place, scientific child study requires more definite observation. An ordinary observer might merely notice that a child is crying. A scientific observer makes detailed, definite, observations. Darwin, for example, noted that infants, when suffering even slight pain, moderate hunger or discomfort, utter violent and prolonged screams. Whilst thus screaming their eyes are firmly closed, so that the skin round them is wrinkled, and the forehead contracted into a frown. The mouth is widely open with the lips retracted in a peculiar manner, which causes it to assume a squarish form;

the gums or teeth being more or less exposed. In the second place, scientific child study requires skilled observers.

A skilled observer knows what to look for. Some observers do not see certain characteristics of children because they do not direct attention to these specific things. The skilled observer knows the kinds of behaviour which may be expected from children at a certain stage of development and notes the extent to which a given child deviates from the average in any direction. Moreover, the skilled observer has through practice become more accurate in his observation than the incidental observer. He looks intently, disregards the unimportant details, and makes immediate and accurate records of his observations. In the third place, scientific child study requires systematic and repeated observation. Ordinary observation is usually spasmodic and irregular. Miss Shinn made observations of her little nice day by day, not merely when some particular behaviour attracted her attention.

The parent or teacher who is using a scientific method observes a child during all period of work of play, not only when he has done something to annoy her. Herbart expressed this idea very well: Nothing is learned from one experience, and just as little from scattered observations; but one must repeat the experiment twenty times with twenty variations before a result is obtained, which even then opposing theories can explain each in its own way. In the fourth place, scientific child study requires immediate and accurate recording. Often ordinary observation is not written down immediately, but is held in mind, becoming increasingly vague and worthless as time elapses.

Various means of recording observations are used: writing, stenography, phonographic records, moving pictures, and special apparatus such as that used to record respiration, eye movements in reading, and motor ability. Keeping records helps the parent to view an annoying problem more objectively and less emotionally. It enables her to find out why Mary is stubborn by noting the occasions on which she says no and I won't the part that the mother plays in these situations, and the treatment that works. As the record of the responses of the mother and the child grows from day to day, the mother will get an illuminating picture of inconsistencies in her treatment, common recurring factors and unexpected changes and improvement.

Value of Studying Individual Children

If a large number of parents or fond relatives kept accurate records of this kind, a knowledge of the common characteristics and abilities of children and of the steps in their development might be built up-knowledge which research workers alone would be unable to secure. For although research workers have stenographers, moving-picture machines, phonographic plates, and other apparatus for recording exactly what the baby does and says, they do not see large numbers of babies under absolutely natural home conditions. In addition to obtaining data on the development of children, these records help the mother to maintain the calm, objective attitude toward the child's behaviour which experts say should supplant the tense, highly emotional attitude frequently found.

Such records would hold a mirror, as it were, up to the mother and disclose the inconsistencies in her treatment of the baby, as well as behaviour trends which are developing in the child. She would see more clearly the behaviour she would encourage, the objects she ought to provide in the environment, and the effect on the child of her own and other people's responses to him. While the baby is small, a fairly complete diary record of his daily activities may be obtained. The best way to learn about an individual child is to study him directly, not to read about children in general. In the method of controlled observation, the observer treats the baby in certain definite ways-or in other words, presents certain stimuli to him-and watches carefully the responses he makes. Gesell's work is an excellent example of this method.

The stimuli presented to the child are described so clearly and definitely that they may be presented in a uniform way to any child, the results carefully noted, and the responses of a given child compared with those of other children of the same age. A trained person can gain a more adequate knowledge of the child's ability by notion the child's response to these tests than by using the method of uncontrolled observation only. The method of controlled observation is valuable in discovering what the baby can do in certain situations and in comparing his responses with those of other babies. Parent's study groups are most valuable for increasing interest in child study, bringing to parents the findings of recent research, helping them to apply facts and principles to concrete situations and giving them opportunity to exchange experiences and to work out tentative solutions for specific problems.

These groups are also an important means of securing cooperation in improving the neighbourhood by providing playgrounds, health service, and regulation of commercial amusements, and in agreeing upon certain common policies such as time for and kind of parties given families in the community. Less technical outlines are suggested each month in children, The Magazine for Parents. Better still is a trained leader who can make an outline to fit the needs of the group and the development of their interests.

Two methods of studying the baby are especially useful. One is the biographical or uncontrolled method, in which the spontaneous reactions of the child are accurately and immediately written down. This type of study describes the responses which are made under natural environmental conditions. The other is the experimental or controlled method. In this method definite stimuli-such as a rod touching the baby' hand, a loud noise, a bright light-are presented to the baby and his responses are noted. When these stimuli are described so accurately that anyone can present the same stimulus in exactly the same way, the responses the majority of infants usually make may be determined, and the responses of the child being studied may be compared with these.

8

Intellectual Growth

Since intelligence is related to so many aspects of behaviour and psychological growth, it is a topic of great interest to parents, teachers, and other adults who wish to promote children's welfare. The following questions, raised very frequently by parents, teachers, and students in child psychology, reflect this interest: "What is intelligence, anyway?" "What does an IQ of 130 mean?" "Are very bright children usually abnormal in some way?" "Can the IQ be raised by any kind of drugs?" "Can an infant's intelligence be measured?" "Can you tell whether a six-year-old child has enough 'brain' to go to college when he grows up?" "Are children with very large heads brighter than other boys and girls?"

What is Intelligence?

Intelligence is first of all a descriptive concept. It represents a dimension which can very from some very low to some very high value. The layman often uses this concept to describe the appropriateness and reasonableness of his associates' general behaviour. In this setting, intelligence becomes synonymous with "brightness", "house sense", "brainy", and the like.

The psychologist employs the term intelligence as an intervening variable or as a theoretical construct. It is an intervening variable (inferred and measured by indirect operations) with certain descriptive and predictive properties. Intelligence, in this sense, is not a unitary and unchanging concept, since it can be altered in definition and design to suit the needs of the scientist. However, even for the psychologist, intelligence has some social connotation. It is a generalized reflection of many examples of intelligent behaviour. Intelligent behaviour implies, of course, the making of value judgments, e.g., "That is correct", "That is incorrect", "That was a 'smart' thing to do", "That was a 'stupid' thing to do". Since intelligent behaviour (and intelligence, by definition) derives its meaning from a social context, it has certain cross-cultural limitations. For example, a child in our culture might be praised and evaluated as "bright" for making a quick decision in a problem situation. In certain oriental cultures such behaviour might be censured and evaluated as "stupid". In the construction of intelligence tests, the psychologist usually attempts to reflect with fidelity the value judgments of some specific culture, usually his own.

A very brief summary of the chief point of the last lecture and their practical lessons for the educator may perhaps be not altogether superfluous. Thought is an activity dealing primarily with ideas, and aims at bringing these into an order and connection corresponding with the order and connection of things, as experienced not by this man or that but by men general. Language is a sort of philosopher's stone which precipitates the fleeting and soluble imagery of thought and fixes it in solid form comparatively safe from further transmutation in the flux of consciousness. It is this, where we think for ourselves; but, when we receive the works of others without corresponding thought of our own, such forms are hollow and yet opaque: they make a dreadful rattle and keep out a deal of light.

Hence the desirability of rather stinting the supply of this useful but dangerous article. To have fewer words than ideas is a less evil than the converse, and the habit of using words without knowing what they mean is one which the teacher should do his utmost to check. And especially is he bound to avoid himself employing terms which the pupils cannot for the present understand, or be made to understand. But words do more than fix our concepts; they make them manageable, for our control of works is more complete than our control of ideas, so that symbolic thinking, like the fairy power of riding on gossamer, enables us to reach points of view and gain a knowledge of things which would be else impossible. Here, again, however, it is rather the danger than the gain that the teacher must attend to. His own familiarity with his subject enables him to feel quite at home gliding, as we say, with the speed of thought above the terra firm of concrete facts: he forgets that he ever lived upon the ground.

And his poor pupils, if their interest is not stifled by disgust, come groping after him like bean stalks in a cellar straining towards the light. Knowledge so attained must at best be thin and meagre, like all forced growth. Mischief of this sort is often the work of clever and conceited men and women, who are small enough to rejoice in their own mental superiority and to forget the steps by which they climbed. Since, then, we must have many impressions before we can have lived ideas and many ideas before we can have complete and powerful concepts, it is evident that the more haste the worse speed.

Resort to the time-saving process of manipulating general terms and rules, without constant recourse to the realities symbolized, means mental collapse at a later stage. Festinalente should be our rule; we should advance slowly for the pupil's profit but seem ever advancing in order to retain his interest. I lay the more stress on this because of my own juvenile experience. I am not sure even if it would not be worth while to make school books, as often as possible, consist of small separate volumes, to have the same dirty arithmetic for a couple of years is apt to produce the dispiriting impression of being no forwarder.

But, whatever be the risk of thinking by means of works, it is a risk we have to run. Abstraction at the same time that it is a mark of man's finiteness is also the source of his strength, and without words to fix our abstractions we should, as we have seen, rise but little above the perceptions of sense. The cardinal point, however, is to know what it is we have abstracted and to know this clearly and distinctly, that is to say, so that we shall not only confuse it with anything else but be able to state what it contains. This is after all the gist of the rules laid down by Descartes in his epoch-making Treatise on Method. Definitions as well as instances must be forthcoming if obscurity and confusion are to be avoided. To give instances of law, for example, instead of stating whether uniformity or coercion is implied will never clear up the obscurity that invests the term. Similarly, to say England and France, Greece and Rome are civilized countries will not do much to determine whether by civilization we refer to social organization or to the progress of the arts of life, to individual culture, or what. But to insist continually on a knowledge of the meaning of works, i.e. on clear and distinct conceptions, necessitates gradual and regular advance. And, as I have already mentioned Descartes method, I will quote his rules, which are to this effect:

- To divide each difficulty we examine into as many parts as possible, or as may be required for resolving it.
- To make in every case enumeration so complete, and reviews so wide, that we may be sure of omitting nothing.
- Never to accept anything as true, which we do not clearly know to be so; that is to say, carefully to avoid haste or prejudice, and to comprise nothing more in our judgments than what presents itself so clearly and distinctly to the mind that we cannot have any room to doubt it.
- To conduct our thoughts in an orderly manner, commencing with the most simple and easily known objects, in order to ascend by degrees to the knowledge of the most complex.

It may seem strange that so much stress is laid on

systematic thinking. And yet the reason is evident enough. Unless we think systematically, we cannot think clearly and distinctly; and, unless we think clearly and distinctly, we do not really think at all. It must be remembered, too, that I am not discussing the imparting of knowledge, but the training of the mind. The question what particular study will afford the best training in connected thinking and the best corrective for loose thinking is not a question for us just now. But, by whatever means obtained, such training must be afforded if education is not to fail of one of its chief ends. And, certainly, we are now in possession of sufficient bodies of reasoned knowledge to furnish such training, if only the most be made of it and of those to whom it is taught. And yet is it not pitiable to see the exhibitions even clever men are continually making of themselves-men who have been everywhere and read everything, but whose ideas, like the odds and ends of half a dozen picture puzzles in a child's toy-box, jostle each other in their brains and come to the top in their turn but never, fit?

I do not forget how much prejudice and self-interest have to do with the inconsistency of our opinions, but even prejudice and self-interest cannot pervert the multiplication table. Strong light is dry light. At all events, I cannot help suspecting that our schools and universities must largely share the blame with those ancient preservers of the truth. And, if they are to blame, it is because they make learning the first thing and thinking the second, place the tradition of knowledge before the training of the mind. But logical training involves something more than precision in the formation and classification of our ideas. To use the analogy most in vogue now-a-days we have not only a statics but a dynamics of thought, not only a logical structure but logical function. Having elaborated our system of ideas up to certain stage, we must use it. The products of past thought which we have embodied in words must aid in turn in the elaboration of new thought. If we thus look at thinking in progress, rather than at thought settled and complete, we shall find that we have more to do with judgments and reasonings than with concepts. The mental attitude to be acquired here is what I have already spoken of as the feeling for proof, i.e. both the need of it and the ability to appreciate it.

The educator must do all in his power to develop this feeling, and this is to say that he must largely guide thinking, instead of supplying ready-made thought. How, then, is he to go to work? Now, there are two chief methods of exposition,

(i) the method of discovery, or the heuristic method, and

(ii) the dogmatic method, or method of instruction.

Of the latter probably the most perfect example on the whole would be found in a good text book on mathematical physics. Euclid's Elements, though the most convincing book in the world, is not the most systematic; it continually sacrifices the classification of its subject-matter to the exigencies of the original proof. Of the heuristic method it is not easy to mention any well-known example. And natural it is not, because first routes are rarely the shortest, and so are abandoned and forgotten when they have made a better way possible. It will save some time, if, in order to make quite clear in what this method consists, I quote what Professor Jevons says in elucidation of it: The method of discovery begins with facts apparent to the senses, and has the difficult task of detecting those universal laws or general principles which can only be comprehended by intellect. It has been aptly said that the method of discovery thus proceeds from things better known to us, or our senses, to those which are more simple or better known in nature. The method of instruction proceeds in the opposite direction, beginning with the things notion naturae, and proceeding to show or explain the things nobis notiora.

The difference is almost like that between hiding and seeking. He who has hidden a thing knows where to find it; but this is not the position of a discoverer, who has no clue except such as he may meet in his own diligent and sagacious search. Now, it has been much disputed which of these two methods the educator should use. Pestalizzi with his usual unbalanced enthusiasm, proclaimed the method of discovery as the only true and natural method. Describing his method Pestalizzi says: The child that is educated after my method, will be set down upon the road, which the first discoverer took and must have taken, and in its hand will be placed the clue which the human race itself has followed in extending and unfolding his science. There is truth in this; and it deserves attention especially in view of the exclusive employment of the opposite method, universal, perhaps, in Pestalozzi's time, and still far too common.

But, if it be wrong to treat the pupil's mind as a mere repository of useful knowledge arranged in the clearest and concise form, it does not, therefore, follow that it is right to deprive him of all the advantages of past systematization. The true educational method, if there be a single method, if there be a single method, is probably neither the one nor the other. Nature, to whom Rousseau and Pestalozzi were so fond of appealing, would have taught them better, had they lived in these days. There is much truth, I suppose most of us believe, in the hypothesis of Darwin that the present perfection of the more complex organisms, such as that of the barndoor fowl, is due to a long series of tries of which we have a partial record in certain of the lower organisms, is due, in other words, to the method of discovery. Nevertheless, if you open egg in process of hatching, you will find Nature taking very much shorter cuts to a chicken than she took at first. Yet still there are indications of the old road, indications which make the study of embryology one of such enchanting interest.

Nature roughs out the whole first, and then gradually elaborates every part, following the leading lines but not all the windings of the long and tedious process by which the primeval chicken was evolved. And this in general must be our plan; for there is, we may be sure, a profound analogy between the order in which the human race has evolved its knowledge and the order in which any given descendant of the race can best appropriate it. Among the many qualifications of a first-rate teacher I should include this, a knowledge not only of his subject as it stands today also of the steps by which it has been brought to that position. One of the reason why the teaching even of science so often lacks the freshness and charm which men like Faraday and Hugh Miller could give it, is, I am disposed to think, that the teacher from the very first has known the science only in its latest phase. And the feverish hurry with which we all now hasten to acquaint ourselves with the newest thing leads to a neglect of the history of knowledge, a neglect which is both un-physiological in itself and mischievous in its effects.

In this respect, we English contrast very unfavourably with the Germans, who appear to have escaped the contempt, or at least indifference, for the history of knowledge which has made its mark on us. It is a favourite commonplace with those who boast of the enormous strides knowledge has made in these latter days to say that even a schoolboy now would be able to puzzly Aristotle. Perhaps he would. Certainly Aristotle would very soon mightily puzzle him. To suppose that a boy, who is told in a moment the answer to a question which engaged the world for ages, in then and there as wise as he would have been if he had first felt the pressure of the question and been intellectually hungry for the answer, is as absurd as to suppose that a stake driven into the ground will stand as firmly as a tree that has grown and rooted on the spot. As a child cannot begin to talk like a philosopher, neither can he begin to see and think like one.

His knowledge must have its childhood as well as that of the race. To the uninitiated, the acids and alkalies, air and water are very much what they were in the days of Priestly and Lavoisier; and the structure of the hills and valleys appear much as they appeared to Werner and Hutton rather than as they appear to the coming geologist, whose name has not yet got wind. But to the young savant, with his head full of original memoirs and his interest centred in the debateable outposts of his science, all this is otherwise. Such an one invites his pupils to come up higher, but does not see that his ladder has no rungs, no steps near the ground. Men like Davy and Faraday, on the other hand, who were largely self-taught, knew from their own experience how to connect the new with the old, knew how to preserve the continuity between everyday observation and scientific theory. The chief educational value of science lies in its method; its dogmatic presentation renders it almost useless.

The educator's problem in this case, then, should be so to supply the material of knowledge and so to direct his pupils in their mental manipulation of it as to awaken and foster the habits of mind by which new truths were discovered and new hypotheses tested. To do this, it is of the first importance to keep distinct the principles of the science and the evidence on which these rest. When a science is wrought into what the old logicians called a doctrine, the principles come first, and what is really the evidence is deduced from them, so that the original relation of the two is inverted; and a generalization, which is really grounded on a number of particulars, appears to prove them instead of being proved by them. This is what is usually meant by the synthetic or deductive method. Now, this more systematic arrangement certainly affords a much more complete command and oversight of the subject-matter. Such ideal arrangement is in fact the end at which we are to aim; the more a science allows us to use general propositions, the more perfect it is. But, on the other hand, the specially scientific training is lost on this method; nothing is learnt of the way in which general laws are established, but only of how they are applied. Hence, a combination of the two methods seems to suggest itself.

First, what the logicians call the analytic method, i.e. the method of discovery, so far as discovery is methodic, apart, therefore, from its fruitless and for beginners uninstructive deviations. According to this plan, then, we shall start from facts familiarly known, but not necessarily those from which the original investigator set out, although in the hands of an enthusiastic teacher these when skillfully handled can, if otherwise suitable, be made much *mote* interesting. From such facts, so far as possible, the pupils should be able either themselves to detect, or at once to recognize, the general law. And I may add, by the way, that even when, as often happened, the original investigation did not proceed inductively but deductively, i.e. started from a hypothesis which was established by its consequences, it is none the less true that the inductive method is the best educationally at the outset. But, when, in this manner, one or two of the leading principles of the science have been reached and appear to the young student to have some flesh and blood and life about them, when he is in no danger of taking them on authority; or remaining oblivious of the ground on which they rest, then the smoother and more potent synthetic method may be adopted.

Even now, however, as little as possible in its dogmatic dress, but wherever possible as what the logicians call the genetic method, a longer but educationally a more valuable procedure-in plainer words, the applications of the general principle are to be reached by working a series of problems. The advance to new and more complicated principles will call for a fresh resort to the analytic method; and so on continually. The proportions in which the two methods will be employed will necessarily vary with the science and to some extent too with the stage at which afford full opportunities for both methods. And foremost amongst these I should place experimental physics.

Chemistry, on the other hand, is certainly of little value as a mental training for the young; because, notwithstanding the entertainment it affords and the interest it awakens, the thinking required is either very easy and mechanical, little more than remembering analysis tables, or it is very difficult-quite beyond the power of a schoolboy and moreover requiring extensive knowledge of facts, and being into the bargain largely hypothetical. As Archdeacon Wilson, formerly Headmaster of Clifton College, well said: The notions of force, cause, composition of causes, are too abstruse in this subject for boys to get any hold of them.

Hence it is, as matter of fact, accepted as a mass of authoritative dogmas. The difference between certainty and probability or conjecture, between truth and opinion, is one which the educator should not fail to make felt. It is not of course desirable that subjects which are still mainly in the hypothetical stage should be taught in schools and to beginners. But what is merely probable or supposable, or matter of opinion, so far exceeds in quantity what is certain, that we cannot go far in any direction without coming upon it. Nor, if matters of probability and opinion could be wholly excluded from the scholar's attention, is it desirable that they should be. To keep him in an atmosphere of real or apparent certainty, when in after life three-quarters of his intellectual occupation will be to deal with uncertainties, is as foolish as it would be to keep him out of the water till he has learnt to swim. It is one of the most serious objections and, so far as I can see, almost a fatal objection to mathematical training, that it deals so exclusively with matters of demonstration in which there is no room for doubt, and, therefore, no exercise in the balancing of probabilities, a study, which, as Huxley said, knows nothing of observation, nothing of induction, nothing of experiment, nothing of causation.

Of course, the whole point of this remark bears against the exclusive study of mathematics; as furnishing a training in connected thinking, in formal exactnessematics are invaluable. To know that you do not know is also knowledge; and, perhaps, there is no knowledge a man can possess that will do more to save him from error than a clear perception of high ignorance, of the line at which certainty ceases and doubt begins. To know this well is the first step towards suspension of judgment and deliberation. He who has but vague ideas of proof, who knows nothing clearly and distinctly, or he who has taken his knowledge on trust, cannot distinguish the certain from the uncertain, the obscure and the doubtful from the self-evident and demonstrative, opinion and prejudice from truth and knowledge. We see here again, then, that no efforts should be spared to make the young mind intellectually exacting; and, where certainty is not forthcoming, proportioning its conditional assent to the evidence.

But this is much more than an intellectual matter. To know what truth is, to have a feeling for proof, is necessary but not sufficient, Descartes used to maintain that the will as well as the understanding is concerned in judging and that it is to the will's share in the process that error is due. Perhaps there is not much more in this than in the common adage the wish is father to the thought; but, at any rate, Descartes exposition of it is worth our notice. Our understanding he says in limited: there are many things of which we can form no clear idea, many of which our ideas are obscure and indistinct. In such cases, the form of a judgment is necessarily presented to us as, for example, in the moot questions whether the world had a beginning in time or whether matter in infinitely divisible. Here I have, let is be supposed, no clear idea; yet, none the less, in thinking about it, the two contradictory judgments, the world had, or had not, a beginning, matter is, or is not, infinitely divisible, present themselves to my understanding. Now, there are but two ways to avoid error: first to know absolutely and perfectly what is true, and secondly, in the case of ignorance, to know clearly that I do not know and to refrain from deciding.

The latter is my only alternative here, and so long as I refrain from affirming either of the possible propositions, I am only ignorant but not in error. And this no doubt would be my position if intellect were alone concerned; but then the will comes in. And the will, unlike the intellect, has no limits: it embraces everything, the unknown equally with the known: where the intellect is indifferent, the will has a choice and affirms or denies accordingly. Descartes' motive in all this was theological. He was concerned to show that error is due to man's volition and could not be charged upon God. Man's ignorance as distinct from man's error did not give Descartes much trouble; because he could easily show, at least to his own satisfaction, that the imperfection of a part taken alone and ignorance is only imperfection is quite compatible with the perfection of the universe as a whole. Though largely a piece of special pleading, Descartes doctrine is psychologically sound. As I remarked at the beginning of this lecture, there are some truths we cannot pervert, however, anxious we may be; but, so far as our power to determine the movements of our ideational mechanism reaches, so far we have the power to deceive and cheat ourselves, and this is the case in the whole region of probability.

If our interests incline us to one side, then, unless our love of truth is superior to them, and the less we have acquired a logical cast of mind, the more certainly shall we concentrate our attention on the pros and thereby exclude the cons, or on the cons and exclude the pros, as the case may be. Not merely so, but it is one of the effects of this emotional preference to heighten the intensity of such ideas as are allowed to occupy consciousness. How great this intensity may be we can see in the illusions sometimes consequent on strong desire. The upshot is clear. The opposing reasons have been scattered and banished, the concurring reasons have become consolidated into a mental concept, perhaps have received a favourable name, and thickly there concretes around them a mass of error and prejudice, having the semblance of truth, because shielded from all that can expose or refute it. Nevertheless, that very word prejudice which I have just used and its troop of synonyms, prepossession, preconception, bias, one-sidedness, obliquity of judgment, and the like wake one up to the fact that without the help of psychological exposition the world is well enough aware of the chief source of error. And yet, is it well enough aware? Are parents and school teachers well enough aware?

That a man is more liable to error the less he is inured to reflection and the handling of evidence, the less he has learnt to require and to submit to proof; that, above all, he is more liable to error the less a love of truth is paramount in him and the more he is swayed by his own interests and feelings all this is as trite and commonplace as it would be to say that bread is the staff of life. The unfortunate difference, however, is that we live up to the one truth so much better than to the other. If action is the measure of conviction, then I doubt if educators are adequately convinced on this point. But I am not going to be guilty of the impertinence of exhorting you to be more urgent in this than your predecessors; and that, not because I do not feel strongly myself, but because I should be unwilling to believe that you do not feel as much. It is a question not of the will but of the way, that concerns us; and, as to that, I can only summarize what I have already said. In the first place, I would urge that, from the outset, the pupil should learn as little as possible on authority and shape his ideas as far as possible for himself, his activity being directed but not superseded.

It is on this ground chiefly that I urge an early training in observation and simple mathematics, and doubt the propriety of crowding out such lessons in order to make the most of the greater retentiveness of early years to impress paradigms and vocabularies, in all of which the scholar has to depend on his teacher, and has less scope for intellectual exercise. However, no doubt, there is time for both, if the literary teacher is not too greedy. At any rate, it is true, as Descartes-whose greatest service to mankind has been to teach them to doubt well clearly saw, that the habit of receiving knowledge and opinions on authority during childhood and youth becomes in manhood so confirmed that an average man thus treated has almost lost the power to think independently. In the second place, when the scholar comes to deal with general and abstract terms he should make clear and distinct to himself in what sense he uses them.

For without cleat conceptions it is impossible to have clear judgment: the mechanism of thought being bad, the work performed must be defective. In the third place, his judgment should be exacting, and, where certainty is not forthcoming, should proportion its conditional assent to the evidence, answering to evidence as a ship does to her helm, and to nothing but the evidence. Long and careful training will be required to secure an ideal so soon stated in words. To attain this end, as well as on account of the preceding considerations, it is every way desirable, if not necessary, that the teacher should be acquainted with logic. True, men think correctly without logic, but they think more correctly with it. As Mill well says, where there is a right way and a wrong way, there must be a difference between them and it must be possible to find out what the difference is; and, when found out and expressed in words, it is rule for the operation. If anyone is inclined to disparage rules, I say to him, try to learn anything for which there are rules, without knowing the rules, and see how you succeed. And, as part of a liberal education, I even think that logic should not be confined to the teacher.

The exorbitant pretensions of the earlier logicians and the foolish disputations they encouraged have brought logic into undeserved contempt. No doubt, it requires to be taught with discretion and not by a logical pedant; but, well taught, it affords training by exercises and problems, as Professor Jevons has shown, quite as valuable as the training afforded by mathematics, and a very desirable supplement to the latter. But, over and above logical training, a profound love for truth must be quickened and kept vigorous in the student's mind. This is the crown and glory of an intellectual education, and to produce it is the sublimes office the teacher has to discharge. And here, as in so many other things, his example will be more effective than his precepts.

9

PERSONALITY INTEGRATION AND ADJUSTMENT DURING CHILDHOOD

Personality is the theoretical construct employed to focus attention on the individual as in integrated, striving organism. As a theoretical construct, personality is related to the many dimensions of a human being's behaviour at every developmental period as well as in his adult life. It involves: (1) the overall organization and the relative potencies of his psychological needs; (2) the manner in which he customarily tries to satisfy these needs, the various psychological - adjustment functions; and (3) the ways in which his individual "style of living" affects other people. A more complete definition of personality by Murray and Kluckhohn is an elaboration of these functional components: Personality is the continuity of functional forces and forms manifested through sequences of organized regnant processes in the brain from birth to death. The functions of personality are: to allow for the periodic regeneration of energies by sleep; to exercise its processes; to express its feelings and valuations; to reduce successive need-tensions; to design serial programs for the attainment of distant goals; to reduce conflicts between needs by following schedules which result in a harmonious way of life; to rid itself of unreducible tensions by restricting the number and lowering the levels of goals to be attained; and finally, to reduce conflicts between personal dispositions and social sanctions, between the vagaries of antisocial impulses and the dictates of the superego by successive compromise formations, the trend of which is towards a wholehearted emotional identification with both the conserving and creative forces of society. Understanding a personality requires following its development through time, study of the processes of differentiation and integration, knowledge of the personality's endowments.

Perhaps no concept in psychology is as important or as elusive as personality. Like intelligence, personality might be thought of as a hypothetical construct. Psychologists observe an individual's behaviour and on the basis of their observations draw inferences about his personality. However, too often personality is more than a descriptive concept; it becomes explanatory. Susie stays apart from the other third graders because she has an introverted personality. Thus, the child's behaviour has been explained by assuming that it reflects her "basic nature" and by attaching a label to it. Further, she can be linked with other children who are introverts. She has been typed, pigeonholed. Her behaviour has been elucidated.

This, of course, is one of the perils of employing the concept of personality. Inferences are drawn from selected observations of behaviour in which attention is focused on only one aspect or characteristic. The notion of personality is really thought to include all aspects of the individual. To understand this child more fully necessitates rating her on many different bases. It is not enough to consider just her tendency to remain apart from others in a group situation. This neither explains her behaviour nor describes her personality. Now will a summation of her characteristics constitute a portrait of the individual.

The interaction among these characteristics, their organization, and the unique manner in which each modifies and alters the others is what truly matters. For the purposes of this chapter, personality may be defined as the distinct and unique organization of traits in an individual as reflected in how he reacts to himself and others and in how they react to him, and also in how he meets frustrations and conflicts-that is, in how he adjusts to his environment. The chapter is divided into three general areas: first, a reprise of the antecedents of personality; second, an analysis of the self concept and of self-consistency; and third, a treatment of those phases of personality that appear to be of particular significance in development. Many attempts have been made to describe stages in personality development.

It is not certain whether there are specific, inevitable, well-defined stages, but one assumption concerning their existence is worth attention. This assumes that an individual can move on to the next, more mature stage only after having successfully completed the demands of the previous stage or having satisfactorily met its requirements. For understanding the personality development of children, this is invaluable. It also has far reaching implications for understanding adult behaviour and adjustment. Erikson described the following either stages in personality development, each with its own distinctive goal normally to be attained in that period.

Early childhood - *a sense of autonomy*
School age - *industry and competence*
Play age - *a sense of initiative*
Adolescence - *personal identity*
Mature age - *integrity and acceptance*
Adulthood – *generativity*
Infancy - *a basic sense of trust*
Young adult - *intimacy*

The advanced stages of psychological maturity cannot be approached unless the goals of the preceding period have been met successfully. For example, a sense of trust is necessary before a child feels sufficiently secure to strive for autonomy. This is a trust in both the reliability of people and the satisfaction of basic physiological and psychological needs.

Security gives freedom. The child who is led to mistrust others and his universe may be wedded forever to a need to seek the security he lacks. In the normal progression to personality adjustment as a mature adult, an individual may be more vulnerable to certain influences during some periods of his life than during others.

For example, some say, as noted earlier, that the effects of maternal deprivation are more severe in the second half of the child's first year. Perhaps in general a child cannot move on to a new and higher phase of personality development until he has achieved a certain amount of personality integration at his current level. Perhaps also the appearance of a more mature phase may be blocked or retarded by the interference of some event with the child's present degree of adjustment. The same principles apply as the child grows. Not just the first year or two of his life but the entire period from infancy through adolescence lays the groundwork for adult personality.

The Self Concept

The term self concept has, sometimes conflicting, definitions. For the purpose of this discussion, let it be considered one's attitude toward one's physical self and own behaviour. Recent perusal of the self concept have hit upon two bases for it: one's social roles and the attempts to synthesize them; and second, the body image, "the body as a psychological experience...the individual's feelings and attitudes toward his own body. In the pages that follow we shall dwell on these two aspects of the self and then turn to the relation of the self concept to behaviour.

Role Theory

"All the world's a stage, and all the men and women merely players." The words were Shakespeare's. The idea did not originate with him. Centuries later the scientific study of roles and the use of role theory as an explanatory device had its beginnings in the work of such sociologists as Durkheim and Tonnies. These were first elucidated clearly by Cooley to be further developed in the social psychology of George H. Mead. Mead did not publish his ideas himself. After his death, his lecture notes were edited by his students so that his ideas have become available in written form. Cooley originated the notion of the social or "looking glass" self. To him, man's ideas about himself were reflections of how others saw him. Mead divided personality structure into the I and the me.

I was the part of the self that was partly-perhaps largely-genetic in origin, the continuing part of personality present in every special situation. The me was basically social, a reflection of society's demands. Each individual was made up of many me's, of as many as he had distinct social roles. The expectations and demands of all social groups of significance to the individual influenced his behaviour at all times, but their relative influences shifted with the behavioural situation and the roles it required. The me that is in the forefront at any time depends on the composition of the group toward which behaviour is referred. For example, a boy in a Little League game has his team-mates as his main reference group. They provide him with the most accurate information as to whether he is playing this particular role of baseball player adequately.

As he changes roles to son, brother, or pupil, the Little Leaguers lose their power as a reference group while other groups like the family, teachers, and classmates gain in this respect. Role assignment has much to do with personality. This has been clearly shown at many points throughout this book; individuals have a strong disposition to perform the roles assigned to them, even when the roles are damaging to self-esteem, as in the case of the stutterer, or to adjustment. A wide range of social and biological factors, as well as chance, enters into the roles assigned to an individual. Once assigned, however, the individual tends to respond in terms of the roles. This makes for regular, consistent behaviour, as long as the roles are clearly defined and do not clash too sharply. Across those situations the I aspect of personality persists. And a good thing, too!

One can see that the individual whose behaviour is determined only by the demands of the social group would be the ultimate of the other-directed person, with no core of personal integrity. To use Freudian terms, this type of person would have an externalized superego; a conscience dependent only on the values of the group to which one belongs at the time. The roles assigned to an individual determine a fair portion of his behaviour; when roles are central and significant and yet conflict directly with one another, there is behavioural disturbance. Romeo and Juliet is a classic example of role conflict in which romantic love and family honour collide. But it is of little significance today since family honour means less now than it did to individuals in Shakespeare's day-and perhaps the same is true of romantic love. Crime and punishment is more pertinent because Roskolnikov's conflict between conventional upper-middle class values and those of the poverty-stricken, amoral student world is a more immediate one in the contemporary world.

The classic primary-group tragedy involving a clash of central roles still exists, and along with it in contemporary industrial society goes the problem of nonexistent roles and a loss of personal identity. The breakdown occurring as a result of ambiguous role definitions has been well described by Dunham and forms the basis of most contemporary literature. Kafka's heroes, whether on trial for some unnamed crime or for changing overnight into a gigantic cockroach, are the ancestors of Beckett's and Sartre's existential men-individuals without a governing 'Set of roles and values'. Whereas having clear and conflicting roles is one basis for tragedy, the tragic nature and emptiness of a life in which one has no roles to play is doubtless greater.

The Self Concept and Adjustment

To many interested in psychotherapy, the self concept plays a vital role in adjustment. They say that the fundamental problem of the neurotic is that he is self-rejecting. The objective of their therapy is to cause him to come to terms with himself and adjust his behaviour and perception of himself to the point at which he is able to accept himself. Raimy demonstrated that successful cases in psychotherapy enabled patient to acquire a more favourable view of themselves, whereas unsuccessful cases did not. The overwhelming evidence from Wylie's review of the literature on the self suggested that self-acceptance was related to adjustment. A high regard of the self generally meant a high level of adjustment, except in a few cases where high self-esteem worked as adversely as self-rejection.

In general, moreover, those individuals who were self--accepting were seen to be accepting of others. What this means, of course, is that the individual who can accept himself can withstand aggression and disparagement from others; his personal psychological security grants him an objective view of the behaviour of others and an understanding of the bases for their behaviour. Such an individual can also sustain adversity better than a self-rejecting person. He can return aggression directly toward others, if necessary. He therefore need not develop neurotic defences or take out his hostility on innocent victims. Quite obviously it would be to the benefit of the culture to raise children who are self-accepting.

From McCurdy's work on extremely creative individuals as well as from the researches of those directly concerned with the self concept, it would appear that individuals who are regarded highly by their parents, who are aware of this regard, and who enjoy a great deal of parental contact are most accepting of themselves. They are best able to face the possible rejection stemming from their own creative efforts, which are considered deviant from the majority standpoint, and are presumably more accepting of others.

The Body Image

Awareness of the physical self and its separation from the non-self comes about, in part, from body movements, internal changes such as hunger, and such things as laryngeal activity in which the infant feels movement simultaneously with hearing sound. It also comes from observing the effects of one's behaviour on the external world. Generally the body image is assumed to be closely tied to physical reality; distortions in it relate to psychological disturbance. In the following case a distorted body image seemed to be the source of some other side inexplicable behaviour. Occasionally distortion of body image can be discerned in an individual and explain behaviour that appears highly unreasonable and illogical.

Hence, body image exists-though not tied as closely to the physical self as it widely assumed. Attempts to assess body image in a scientific manner and to predict behaviour from it have not been successful. Typically, individuals are requested to draw a human figure; it is assumed that they will project into the drawing their own ideas about their physical selves. These drawings are then interpreted. If, for example, the individual draws his figure with hands concealed behind the back, he is believed to disclose a feeling of impotence, of inability to deal with problems. Perhaps the individual feels impotent only in the fine art of drawing hands! Very few individuals represent their own bodies when instructed to draw a person, suggested Swenson. Even when they do, the interpretations of their drawings seem largely based on conjecture.

Thus, though the body image quite likely exists as a significant part of the self concept and plays an important part in determining behaviour, proper techniques for measuring the image do not yet seem to have been developed. One further point on body image. If body image determined behaviour, and especially the self concept, which promotes consistency in behaviour, then the demeanour of individuals would become *more* variable as the physical self changed more rapidly. This is what happens in adolescence; rapid shifts in children's behaviour often baffle parents. And, of course, data cited earlier on the relation of physical maturity to social adjustment are themselves suggestive of the impact of the physical self and one's attitudes toward it on adjustment.

Consistency and the Self Concept

Personality presupposes consistency. Without consistent patterns of response, behaviour would be chaotic and unpredictable. Since personality refers to persisting continuing, predictable, social aspects of the self, there can be no personality without consistency. There are many reasons to expect consistency. Man remains the same biological entity throughout life, and many determinants of personality, as we know, are biological in character. To the degree that man's biological composition does not change during lifetime, consistency may be expected. No matter what else may change in the course of development, humans carry around the same physical self, and with it, their own responses and the responses of others to it. Consistency would also be expected from what is known of the incorporation of social roles into the concept of the self as well as from what is known about identification. Role assignment is sufficient cause to play a social role.

The performance of a role leads to increased expectancy on the part of others that the performer will not relinquish it. These firmer and more explicit expectancies impel one to act even more consistently in harmony with them. Since roles even in childhood have some constancy and with age become more so as well as invariable, and sharply defined, some consistency is foreseen at all ages, more in later than in earlier years. A recent psychological theory, Festinger's theory of cognitive dissonance, is based on the notion that humans fundamentally need to maintain consonance or consistency among various aspects of the self, and between the self and the outside world. These are some examples of dissonance: an individual believe that his children deserve the best possible education. He regards federal aid to education as creeping socialism.

The school district which operates on a skimpy tax base cannot finance an adequate school system. There is a dissonance between two sets of social attitudes; if the individual has enough ability he will recognize the dissonance in himself and attempt to resolve it. The dissonance may occur between two aspects of the self, as in the foregoing illustration, or it may arise between behaviour and belief. This is exemplified in the parent who believes that his children should make their own decisions, yet refuses to allow them to do so, because the errors initial grave consequences. There is evidence that the need for consonance, consistency, or the synthesis of conflicting values increases with age, and among children is also associated with IQ.

This need for self-consistency plays a major part in achieving consistent behaviour. Yet if people were I completely consistent, life would be extremely dull, and change, as in psychotherapy, difficult if not impossible to achieve. To what degree, then, 'do humans reflect' consistency?

Trait Consistency

At one time psychologists studied types, such as introvert versus extrovert. But as research findings failed to support predictions based on type psychology, many personality theorists abandoned types and turned to traits. Admitting that type psychology had not worked out, these theorists assumed that personality was composed of a set of consistent, continuing traits. This assumption was soon subjected to experimental test, and this test, the Hartshorne and May study of honesty, had a profound effect on psychology. The objective of Hartshorne and May was simple: to find out if there were a general and consistent trait of honesty. If there were, individuals should be consistently honest from one situation to the next. Those who lied should also cheat and steal whereas those who were honest in one instance should also be honest in the other two.

Testing a large number of school children in a wide selection of real-life situations involving cheating, stealing, or lying, they interpreted their findings as indicating only a very minor zone of common response to all three areas of honesty. Nor could they predict behaviour in one situation from knowledge of the individual's behaviour in other situations similarly involving honesty. Their results indicated there was no general traits of honesty. This meant presumably that any assumption of trait consistency was unwarranted and argued against a notion of human consistency altogether. It correct and applicable to broader situations, the Hartshorne and May conclusions would lead to the belief that the study of personality should be abandoned. Actually, this general hypothesis, based on their data, gave the Hartshorne and May study great significance, for it led to a series of investigations and critiques of trait consistency. From a brief but general interview, MacKinnon predicted whether college students would be honest on tests modelled after those used by Hartshorne and May.

His predictions were more accurate than chance might expect; this corroborated the idea of a general trait of honesty whose existence was rather easily discernible. Furthermore, he had much greater success in predicting honesty than dishonesty. His dishonest subjects feel into two groups: one that appeared basically honest but yielded to temptation and a second that was generally dishonest. For most of these individuals, honesty or dishonesty seemed to be the result of a general and consistent trait; for some, their behaviour seemed largely determined by the stimulus of the moment. In general, MacKinnon's findings and conclusions presumably contradicted those of Hartshorne and May, perhaps because he used a brighter and older group of subjects, and individual consistency apparently increases with age and IQ. Yet even the Hartshorne and May data, though interpreted as showing inconsistency, really represented a substantial degree of consistency.

Burton analysed the same data and concluded that they disclosed the existence of a moderately general and consistent trait. Other studies also indicate that honesty is sufficiently consistent as a trait for one to predict children's responses on measures of different aspects of conscience development and to anticipate behaviour from paper-and-pencil tests. But investigations of consistency in traits have not been limited to honesty. Murphy found consistency in sympathetic responses to others among three-year-old though not among two-year old. Kagan and Moss reported on the stability of passive and dependent behaviour in childhood and adulthood. Though part of a longitudinal study to which we shall return presently, their findings supported the notion that much trait consistency existed among different behavioural situations at any time in an individual's life history.

They obtained reliable measures of subtle aspects of personality even at preschool age and reliability implies consistency. How much consistency will be found depends on the effectiveness of the measuring device, the characteristics of the individuals measured, and probably on the complexity of the social forces bearing on the trait in question.

Consistency Over Time

To what extent does the individual remain consistent and how much does he change in time? One of the first studies of this question was conducted by Buhler and her students. They divided infants into four types: those easily stimulated by both pleasant and unpleasant stimuli; those easily stimulated by pleasant but not by unpleasant stimuli; those easily stimulated vice versa; and those not easily stimulated by either. The result of the study suggested that most children remained in the same category, at least up through middle childhood. Cited often among studies of consistency and change is Neilon's. After a 15-year interval, she followed up the individuals who had been studied by Shirley from birth to the age of two. Shirley's personality sketches of the 13 male and 6 female infants she studied were published with pseudonyms attached to each so that neither Neilon nor her associates knew the true names of the children represented by the sketches. Neilon collected rather full and autobiographical sketches of 15 of the original 19 children at the age of 17 -ten boys and five girls.

She then requested a panel of judges composed of faculty

members and graduate students to match the six infant sketches with the five adolescent sketches of girls and the 13 infant sketches with the ten adolescent sketches of body. Ten judges matched the girls, five the boys. Shirley's original data were then consulted to find out the real names of the children associated with each infant sketch so that the accuracy of the matching could be seen. The judges succeeded in matching the girls to an extent that could be obtained by chance less than once in a million times; with the boys, a somewhat more difficult task, they were correct to an extent that could occur by chance only once in 4000 tries. Although considerable individual difference existed among individual children, one girl being matched correctly by all ten judges and another by none, it was evident that there was much consistency in personality over a period of time; accurate matching occurred so much more often than would be expected by chance. Several subsequent studies have corroborated the idea that an individual's personality is usually consistent over time.

These include children, in which he found that 82 per cent of a group of 106 youngsters disclosed a consistent pattern in this area from nursery school into adolescence. Escalona and Heider predicted behaviour at the age of five from observation of infant in the first year of life. At five, they found their predictions correct much oftner than by chance but saw that prediction was more accurate in some areas, such as motor skill and sex-role interests, than in others, such as shyness and striving for achievement. Tuddenham, following up individuals studied as adolescents 19 years earlier, observed a significant stability in more than one-third of the traits studied, despite the low reliability of ratings in adolescence and adulthood. The stablest trait for man was aggressive motivation, with a correlation of +.91 between ratings; for women, it was a desire for social prestige, with a correlation of +.81. The latest and most extensive study of consistency over time was undertaken by Kagan and Moss who analysed the Fels longitudinal data.

In general, they found that consistency was greater up

to the age of ten than thereafter. It seemed likely, as noted in reference to Burks's study of a single pair of identical twins, that a person could be more himself at later ages when parental pressures played less of a role in shaping behaviour. Perhaps the lessening relationship between earlier and later personality, on the one hand, and between adolescent and adult behaviour, on the other, stemmed in part from the greater independence from parental influences in later years. Even with this qualification, correlations between childhood and adulthood were generally substantial. Where the correlations were minimal, the shifts in societal pressures seemed most accountable. For example, dependent behaviour in females was permissible throughout life, whereas extreme pressures were imposed on males from adolescence onward to become independent.

Personality Antecedents

In a sense, the entire book to this point could be considered as composed of antecedents of personality: maturation, learning, cultural factors, the home and family setting, including parental and sibling influences, the peer society, and finally, aspects of community. It may be argued, however, that the influences that occur earliest in the child's life tend to have the broadest impact on the individual's personality because they are the first incorporated into it and thus they play a part in determining the effect of subsequent experiences. Because personality is conceived of as the product of interaction between hereditary and environmental factors, let us examine both areas of influence. Since from birth onward, heredity and environment interact, it is impossible even at the age of two to say how much of a child's personality is attributable to one or the other. A child may inherit in irritable temperament from his father, but it is his mother who reacts to it, with resulting consequences for the child's personality.

Environmental Factors

What a child brings to a situation helps to shape the responses of others to him in the situation. This, in turn, determines how he will approach future situations. Let us deal here, then, with the social influences that bear on personality development. These include social expectations for child behaviour as well as some cultural differences in expectations for behaviour and personality. First, to several non-psychological factors that have some potential psychological bearing.

Acceptance

Too frequently physical handicap engenders resentment and frustration in the child. Deviation from normality, especially if it restricts and curtails the child's active participation with his peers, can affect personality development. So can parental non-acceptance of the child and his handicap which is particularly damaging to the child's sense of self-worth. The underlying psychological mechanism of this non-acceptance is complicated. Parents blame themselves for abnormality in their offspring. This was the case, for example, with mothers of children with cleft palate. Actually, any condition in the child which adds to child-care responsibilities often irks the parent. This irksomeness is bound to affect the parent's attitude toward the child. The point is that parental acceptance or rejection, as we have seen earlier in this book, influences the child's attitude toward himself which is a significant factor in personality development. Similarly, peer acceptance is an important element in self-acceptance, though it is not always clear which causes which. Perhaps the child's lower self-acceptance may generate hostility and resentment which reduce his acceptance by his peers.

Sociometric studies have shown that children with speech defects are chosen less often than children without them when play and friendship are the bases for selection, and that children with defective hearing are not as acceptable among peers as those whose hearing is normal. Case studies spotlight strong differences in the degree to which physical handicaps become psychological burdens among children. What causes these differences? The major factor is doubtless the parent's attitude toward the child the extent to which they accept him prior to and then with a handicap. Though bodily injury and physical handicap may exacerbate and complicate a prior hostile, non-accepting parent-child relationship, it is doubtful whether real acceptance of the child for his own sake would be substantially altered by such an occurrence.

One five-year-old, severely affected with cerebral palsy, was light-hearted, gay, and full of mischief. With much effort and exertion he would manage to propel himself up the ladder of a slide and then slide down, screaming with delight, to land at the bottom, arms and legs twisted appealingly. Every day at five-thirty his father came to fetch him at the Day Care Nursery Centre, engulf the child in his arms, and wipe away the boy's uncontrolled saliva as the youngster jabered on about the day's events. He would never watch his son hit a home run or score a touchdown, but, because of his acceptance of the body, he would be able to see him grow and develop into a fine, worthwhile young man.

Organic Factors

Anything that affects the individual's willingness or ability to respond to his environment is certain to influence his view of himself and his interaction with others. For example, vitamin deficiencies may be reflected in such psychological symptoms as depression and irritability. More important perhaps is the lowered vitality of a child suffering from general nutritional deficiency. Illness, injury, and physical handicap undoubtedly impede the child's personality development. Yet research which has sought to find the precise impact of these factors on personality development is largely inconclusive. To begin with, information concerning the child's personality development prior to illness of injury is seldom available. This limits the extent to which certain aspects of a child's personality may be attributed to them.

The use of a control group, of course, would be advantageous, but it is difficult to obtain an adequate one suitably matched with the experimental group. Furthermore, present instruments for assessing personality are largely inadequate in this area of research. The children on whom personality measures were standardized are not comparable with, say, children with physical handicaps. Comparisons are therefore inappropriate. Similar responses by a healthy and a handicapped child on a personality inventory may have quite different meaning for the two. Prolonged illness reduce the child's contact with the environment and his interaction, which results in decreased stimulation. Coupled with increased bodily concern, this induces the child to withdraw his interest from the world about him and focus it upon himself. Egocentricity, selfishness, and undue concern with oneself follow.

Because illness handicaps feelings of helplessness and dependency are born. These, together with parental resentment, rejection, over-concern, or overprotection, may have long-range effects on the child. Beverly found, for example, that an overwhelming majority of hospitalized children whom she interviewed answered the question, why do children get sick? With the assertion, because they are bad. Indeed such an attitude can pervade the child's concept of himself and his sense of self-worth. In discussions of the effect of physical injury or handicap on personality the notion of body image has often been invoked. An infant gradually becomes aware of his physical self through a variety of physical sensations. At first the distinction between me and not me is not a sharp one. Then experience furnishes countless clues that assist in the process of self-differentiation. Later, psychological attitudes toward the physical self develop out of the child's social interaction with others so that ultimately the most significant aspect of one's body image are those psychological attitudes that involve evaluation and consequent acceptance or rejection. Because of the circular nature of an individual's attitude toward himself and the attitude of others toward him, there is not necessarily a close correspondence between the objective aspects of one's physical composition and the psychological attitudes associated with it.

In any case, one's image of one's physical self becomes

increasingly consistent throughout childhood. For this reason any alteration in one's body requires some adjustments in body image. Perhaps one of the most difficult and yet most imperative adjustments is acceptance of the changed physical condition. This requires acknowledgement of dependency on others when physically handicapped and recognition of the fact that participation and achievement in some areas of life are impossible. Realization of this avoids needless frustration.

Socio-cultural Factors

The differences between cultures are so strong and pervasive that modal personality types are often noted by anthropologists. They use the adjective modal to signify common or fashionable as in a model. This modal type may be essentially paranoid and suspicious as among the Doubuans studied by Fortune, or open and guileless as were some of the Doubuans neighbours studied by Malinowski. It has been suggested that there is a model American personality and that it is changing largely as a result of technological, educational, and economic development within the culture. Within the range of behaviours deemed acceptable by the culture, the specific behavioural pattern of an individual, based on his unique biological composition and social experience, takes from. Behaviour and personality vary among individuals within the culture.

Some of this variance results from social class, occupation, racial background, and place of residence. These broad sociological variables, as previously noted, have considerable bearing in the certain of individual differences in personality and behaviour. Also contributing to the shaping of an individual' web of responses are various aspects in the family setting. The biological forces on one side and the social forces on the other fix the limits within which parents and others in intimate association with the child may mould character and personality. Parental personality, attitudes, and behaviour all influence the developing child. The development of dependence or independence, of activity level, and of ability to resist stress result, in part, from the child's interaction with his parents. A host of social influences exists. How these shape the concept of the self and in so doing dispose the individual toward becoming consistent in personality and behaviour will be discussed in some detail.

Innate Pre-dispositional Factors

Flexible and resilient, the infant selects those aspect of the environment to which he responds. Innate characteristics determine both this selectivity and the infant's initial responses to the environment.

Body Structure and Physical Abilities

The child's basic physique is primarily a product of heredity. Despite a history of effort to link type of body to personality and temperament, present evidence indicates only a slight relationship between physical and psychological make-up. Sheldon, the leading protagonist of the body-type theory of personality, devised a scheme for ascertaining the portion of each of three body types in an individual's physique: endomorphic-a roundish build weak in bony and muscular development; mesomorphic-large bones and muscles with an athletic physique; and ectomorphic-long, slender extremities, lacking in muscular development.

In addition, three basic types of temperament were described, each associated with one of the body types: with the endomorphic, viscerotonic-sociable, relaxed, love of comfort, slow reaction; with the mesomorphic, somatotonic-need for activity and action, assertive, courageous, energetic; and with the ectomorphic, cerebrotonic-restrained, inhibited, tense, preferring solitude. The Glueck found at least twice as many measomorphic physiques among delinquent boys as among non-delinquents. Another investigation observed some differences in IQ test performances of seven-year-old boys grouped into the three categories of body types. In addition, more signs of emotional disturbance in the boys were reported by mothers of the ectomorphic group. These findings cannot be discounted, but their explanation may be more important here. Some physiques more than others permit an individual to perform certain motor and physical behaviours successfully.

Competence in the motor area is an important attribute in childhood, especially among boys. The competence of the mesomorph wins favourable reaction from the group. This leads him to solicit further approval in the particular area of activity; thus, an assertiveness induced by social considerations may emanate from the self-confidence he develops. Similarly, a child who is unsuccessful in the motor area will seek rewarding experience elsewhere. Success in the classroom may compensate for failure on the playground. A second and related factor is social expectation. The stereotypes of the jolly, plump individual, the thin bookworm, and the aggressive mesomorph may not be scientifically derived, but they establish certain expectations of behaviour for children of these body types.

A father is less likely to spur his ectomorphic son to athletic prowess. Diagram demonstrated that excitability and outgoingness were related only minimally to parent attitudes, whereas other traits, such as empathy, and clusters of traits, such as meeting cultural demands, were closely related to them. Possibly excitability and outgoingness result more from genetic factors-perhaps body type-than from strictly social forces. Attractive appearance has been seen to have some relation to popularity among children. Although popularity may be a result rather than a cause of an individual's personality, the extent to which a child is accepted. This, in turn, affects his subsequent personality development.

Endocrine and Nervous System

Malfunctioning of the endocrine glands produces deviant behaviour in only a limited number of individuals. Nevertheless, there is a link between behaviour and glandular secretion. An under active thyroid, for example, causes a low rate of metabolism, resulting in sluggish behaviour and lack of endurance. Contrarily, too high a rate of thyroid secretion engenders restlessness and nervousness. Hormonal secretion from the gonads, though it can be changed by environmental factors, stems primarily from innate sources. The sex hormones influence a number of behaviours and characteristics. Secondary sex manifestations, such as lower voice pitch, facial hair growth, and growth in musculature appearing in boys at puberty, exert broad influence on personality and adjustment. Further, the rate of sexual maturation, which is largely determined by hereditary forces, bears an important relation to certain personality tendencies at adolescence. Findings from the California Adolescent Growth Study indicate that the girl who matures early and the boy who matures late both encounter problems of adjustment.

Marked behavioural differences were noted by Jones and Bayley between boys who matured early and those who matured late. Late maturers persisted in childlike patterns of activity, eager and animated. Their peers considered them restless, talkative, attention-seeking while viewing early maturers as popular, having older friends, a sense of humour about themselves, and good appearance. Quite clearly the rate of maturity relates to several aspects of adolescent personality because of the premium on maturity at this age level. Thus, one has an excellent example of the interplay between innate factors maturity level-and environmental factors-social responses based on values and social expectations-which then affects personality adjustment. Among infants the differences in the reactive tendencies of their nervous systems influence both their responses to their environments and the manner in which the significant individuals in their environments respond to them. Newborns differ widely in level of activity, irritability, and general emotional excitability-all of which reflect differences in nervous systems.

Whether or not these particular characteristics have long-term consistency in the individual, their influence on the child's psychological surroundings and in turn on his personality at one point in his development suggests they have some importance. For example, Steward concluded from her observations of crying behaviour in infants that too much crying tended to generate insecurity in the mother which, in turn, is transmitted back to the offspring. There is no doubt that emotionality, the physiological portions of emotional experience, has a base gas in the autonomic nervous system. This is borne out by a study by Gottesman in which identical twins resembled one another more than fraternal twins, especially with respect to sociability versus withdrawal. It does not mean, however, that differences among adults in emotional behaviour are due exclusively to constitutional factors.

Environmental factors play a tremendous part. Nevertheless, infants and children differ in the functioning of their autonomic nervous system, thus occasioning differences in emotionality and in the responses of adults. Finally, and trait or characteristic based on the structure and operation of the nervous system is hereditary in origin. Admittedly, research has hardly scratched the surface in detecting relations between behaviour and organic structure. But there seems to be enough evidence to conclude, for example, that intelligence has a physiological source in the central nervous system whereas such a trait as selfishness almost certainly has not.

Intelligence

To consider intelligence as an innate predispositional factor is not to imply that intellectual functioning is entirely inherited. Indeed, it is an excellent example of the continual interaction of hereditary and environmental factors. Yet it is probable that by determining an individual's central nervous structure, he imposes limits within which environmental influences work. It is not easy to determine the precise role of intelligence in the development of personality. Despite the conclusion from a survey of 200 studies that no uniform relation exists between intelligence and emotional and personality traits, evidence is at hand showing a tie between intelligence and adjustment. Anderson, in studying prediction of adjustment over a seven-year span, found IQ to be a significant prognosticator of adjustment and concluded: "Our results can be interpreted either as showing how difficult it is to separate our an intelligence factor from the complex of personality characteristics with which we are dealing when we talk about adjustment, or as indicating how important intelligence is in the adjustive process.

Through factor analysis of various personality ratings and measures of analysis, Cattell has shown intelligence to correlate highly with self-control, reliability, industriousness, emotional independence, conscientiousness, and perseverance-all of which are traits of character. Intelligence was less closely associated, however, with basic emotional integration and adjustment. Several explanations account for the relation of intelligence to adjustment in American society.

First, brighter children have brighter parents who handle the emotional problems of childhood more wisely, thus establishing a sounder psychological foundation in childhood.

Second, brighter children perceive social expectation more accurately and conform accordingly. Their behaviour is rewarded, which leads to good adjustment to the demands made of them.

Third, brighter children are more resourceful in meeting social expectations and demands; therefore, they are more likely to be successful.

Fourth, a moderate relation exists between intelligence and ingenuity, curiosity, and creativity, traits that abet popularity and adjustment in peer society.

Fifth, a closer relation between intelligence and adjustment may be postulated for middle-class than for lower-class children because of middle-class emphasis on academic achievement and educational progress.

Just as intelligence exerts a board and complex influence on personality development, aspects of personality affect intellectual functioning. In a longitudinal study of mental growth and personality development, children who gained or lost in IQ during elementary-school years were seen to differ significantly in the following personality traits: independence, aggressiveness, self-initiative, problem solving, anticipation, and competitiveness. And in Terman and Oden's 20-year follow-up of a group of highly gifted children, comparisons were made between successful and unsuccessful male adults, the measure for success being the extent to which an individual has made use of his superior intellectual ability. The successful received higher ratings on perseverance, self-confidence, integration toward goals, and absence of inferiority feelings, leading to the conclusion that the two groups differed markedly in achievement drive and all-around social adjustment. To be sure, the interaction between intellect and personality is complex, and a great variance in personality adjustment exists at all levels of intelligence.

Certain problems of emotional adjustment are more frequent at the lower intellectual levels, yet highly endowed individuals are not entirely immune from personality difficulties. Thus, it is apparent that even if there is no clear-cut tie between aspects of intellect and personality, intelligence does influence an individual's interactions with other people; it also affects one's adjustment to the demands of the environment.

Principal Components of Personality in Children

Personality seems to gain complexity and consistency as the years pass. It grows more complex because the number and range of its antecedents increase, producing more intricate interactions. It in creases in consistency because as physical growth terminates the body image becomes stable and roles played become clearer, more consonant with one another, and more tightly incorporated into the self concept. Considerable research has been amassed on particular components of personality which seem to be rather central in the personality fabric of childhood, yet relatively independent of one another. These are dependence-independence, aggression, anxiety, conscience development, dominance-submission, and social acceptability. We propose to explore each in some detail, with emphasis on their antecedents.

Conscience Development

Conscience is sometimes defined with tongue in cheek as that which keeps us from doing what we shouldn't do even when no one is looking. Indeed, this definition lights upon a major element in the idea of conscience: inner controls based on an individual's acceptance of values concerning right and wrong behaviour. Yet there are other kinds of control of behaviour. Control may be external in origin, resting in the prohibitions and demands of others. Between the Hartshorne and May study and the late 1950's, little concern was shown over conscience development in children.

Matters of values and conscience were apparently not thought to be appropriate topics for scientific research. Sears noted that the identification of the child-rearing antecedents of inner controls and sanctions signified one of the most important problems facing students of personality development today. Miller and Swanson saw moral standards in terms of inner conflict. Three reasons were advanced for this approach: moral needs, that is, internalized standards, are frequently the cause of conflict within the individual; the manner in which these conflicts are resolved depends on the particular moral values held by the individuals; and each individual employs characteristic ways of resolving conflicts, and these are thought of as his "character structure." Among adults, some are faced more frequently than others with conflicts over moral issues.

Such conflicts are likelier, however, to involve a position taken on some moral issue than overt behaviour, as in childhood. For example, is racial discrimination in public housing acceptable? Is nuclear war justified? Can unfair business competition be condoned? Most likely the mature adult resolves such issues in a rather consistent manner, and when he does employ defences such as rationalization to avoid facing the conflict, they are a stable part of his personality.

No wonder an understanding of conscience is essential to an understanding of human behaviour.

Antecedents

There are three principal elements that affect that development of conscience. First, a culture's values or standards form an important part of the legacy transmitted to a child by his parents. One culture may discourage aggressiveness, another emphasize self-effacement, a third espouse personal recognition. The second factor is the child's better able to perceive what is expected of him; he can understand the reasons for certain restrictions and standards; he is able to generalize a principle and apply it to a variety of situations. More than the younger child, the older one can comprehend some of the abstract concepts behind social issues-unselfishness, equality, justice, truth. Third is the child's relations with his parents. Several research techniques have been used to study parental influences on development of conscience. In the Pattern Study, mothers were asked to indicate signs of conscience in their childhood. Two criteria were used; the child's tendency to act the parental role, that is, his attempt to teach parental standards to siblings and friends; and the child's behaviour following a wrongdoing, that is, his attempts to confess, apologize, or make amends. Evidence of the development of a conscience was rated on the following scale:

- Little evidence of conscience.
- Considerable conscience.
- No evidence. Child hides, denies, does not seem unhappy when naughty.
- Strong conscience. Child feels miserable when naughty; always confesses; never denies; strong need for forgiveness.
- Moderate conscience development. May not confess directly but looks sheepish; seldom denies.

The concept employed most frequently to explain the

child's internalization of adult standard is identification. Factors producing a strong identification with the parent tend to encourage development of conscience. Kindergarten boys who were highly masculine, presumably because of identification with their fathers, were also high in conscience development. Research has dealt with two factors, in particular, regarding this antecedent of conscience development: the type of parental discipline and the warmth of the parent-child relationship. As to disciplinary activity in the home, the Pattern Study indicated that psychological or love-oriented techniques exemplified in praise, isolation, and withdrawal of love aided the development of conscience more than the materialistic or physical methods embodied in tangible rewards, deprivation, and physical punishment. MacKinnon's investigation of college students found that those who transgressed prohibitions in an experimental setting were likelier to be children of fathers whose disciplinary tactics had been physical rather than psychological. Yet a study a four-year-old or resistance to cheating did not support these findings.

In this investigation, scolding and physical punishment were more closely related to resistance to temptation than were psychological punishments or use of reasoning. Direct, physical techniques seemed most effective in the young child, although psychological techniques encouraging identification with the parent look over as the child grew older and gained in cognitive development. Similar to the distinction between physical and psychological disciplinary methods in the differentiation between techniques of induction and of sensitization. Reasoning with the child, ignoring or rejecting him, and explanation are all inductive techniques. They elicit in the child reactions to his own transgressions, which may become independent of the original source of punishment. For instance, reasoning with a young child and explaining the consequences of an act should encourage him to examine his actions and to accept responsibility for them.

These may simply make the child extremely susceptible

to fear of external punishment following transgression and attach importance to the demands and expectations of others. Through use of a story-completion technique among sixth graders, a relations was found between the child's type of moral response and the mother's disciplinary technique. Children whose mothers used inductive techniques were more prone to include notions of reparation and acceptance in their stories, whereas others whose mothers relied on a technique of sensitization oftener introduced external consequences of transgression in theirs. In the Pattern Study, love-oriented techniques characterized most middle-class mothers and physical types of discipline, most lower-class mothers. In the Aronfreed study induction was the predominant choice of middle-class mothers and sensitization the major choice of lower-class mothers.

The physical types of discipline espoused in lower-class home, however, neither encourage identification nor produce inner controls. Turning to warmth, most efforts to find conscience development to specific child-rearing practices, such as the age and severity of toilet training, have not borne fruit. Perhaps, as noted in the chapter on parental influences on children, the general psychological atmosphere of the home may be more important. In this connection, facts in the home which produce strong identification with parents are also conducive to early development of conscience. In the Pattern Study, the threat the withdraw love, a psychological device, had little effect if the mother was relatively cold and rejecting. Conversely, it proved most effective when the child's relationship with his mother was warm and accepting.

Thus, the non-accepted child has little to lose by displaying disapproved behaviour. To cite the record, only 18 per cent of the rejected children covered in the Pattern Study were judged as having high conscience, compared with 31 per cent of the accepted group. And in support of the MacKinnon finding about the import of the kind of discipline practised by the father, stronger consciences were observed in boys with accepting fathers than boys with fathers who tended to reject them. No such difference was detected, however, in girls. Two major family qualities are tied to a strong superego in children, that is, to the "presence of an effectively behaviour-guiding conscience-consistency and a combination of mutual trust and approval. Logically, a consistent pattern a parental control and expectations provides a clear-cut setting for the development of positive conduct. In addition, an atmosphere of mutual trust inspires the child to absorb his parents' values and standards, which the child accepts for his own. Development of conscience, then, needs to be understood in order to understanding the development of personality.

For the manner in which the individual resolves a moral conflict is a stable aspect of his personality. As significant as are the cultural lessons transmitted by parents, the child's own intellectual growth, and also his identification with parents which leads to adoption of their values and to acquisition of inner controls, nothing counts as much as an atmosphere of warmth in the relationship between parents and child. Mutual trust, acceptance, and consistency combined with warmth are likely to assure strong conscience when childhood gives way to adolescence.

Dependence-Independence

Dependency is the condition of the human infant. The infant is instrumentally dependent on his mother. Because she is associated with the satisfaction of his basic biological needs, the infant also develops a rewarding emotional dependence on her. How then does independent behaviour develop? It comes about through maturation and learning. The young child grows increasingly capable of functioning independently. Moreover, independent behaviour is in itself rewarding to the child because of the satisfaction gained from exploring and manipulating the environment and from interacting with peers. Normally, therefore, there is an increase in independent behaviour with age.

In nursery school, children exhibit less behaviour

reflecting infantile reliance on adults and a shift toward a more active, assertive dependence on peers. However, emotional or psychological independence does not inevitably accompany physical or instrumental independence. Further, some children manifest greater independence of behaviour than others.

Symptoms and Causes

What are the earmarks of dependent behaviour? Of independent behaviour? To Beller the following behaviours were signs of dependency: seeking help, seeking physical contact, seeking proximity, seeking attention, and seeking recognition. These were the behaviours denoting independence: taking initiative, trying to overcome obstacles in the environment, trying to carry activities to completion, getting satisfaction from work, and trying to do routine tasks by oneself. By and large, dependent behaviour is characterized by reliance on someone else for assistance and assurance. A child is said to be dependent when he manifests behaviour that, at his age level, should be superseded by independent behaviour.

The six-year-old who does not dress himself alone, the four-year-old who does not feed himself, the five-year-old who does not play with his peers unattended by his mother all exhibit dependency; Why does dependent behaviour persist? No single explanation accounts for either dependence in children in general or its occurrence in any one child. All explanations, interestingly enough, have focused on various aspects of the parent-child relationship. An early study concluded that dependent behaviour resulted from maternal over-concern; the mother was not only permissive about dependency behaviour but also encouraged it.

This view was reached by identifying independent and dependent behaviour in children and then applying Fels ratings to the psychological atmosphere of their homes. The homes of the dependent youngsters rated higher on child-centred and babying counts. Widely held at the present time is the view that dependency increases and is intensified when the parent does not adequately meet the dependency needs of the child. Frustrated through lack of parental warmth, nurture, and affection, the child cannot proceed to greater emotional independence. This notion has its supporting evidence even though the results of various studies are not in full agreement. In an extensive study of the antecedents of dependency and aggression the amount of dependent behaviour in nursery-school children correlated positively with the severity of their weaning in infancy.

However, no such relation was found with respect to toilet training. And even the weaning finding was not supported by data obtained in the Pattern Study. Conceivably the extent of the frustration of a child's early dependency needs is not adequately assessed through the mother's feeding the toilet-training practices.

A Cultural Phenomenon

The concern of American psychologists over dependence versus independence reflects the importance attached by society to the development of independent behaviour. The individual who is able to operate as an independent agent is regarded as a maturer adult. However, anthropologists have shown that American emphasis on early independent training is not shared by all other cultures. Take this illustration, for example, of the attitude and behaviour of parents in a New Guinea tribe. Similarly, a study of child-rearing practices in Puerto Rico found little parental encouragement of independent behaviour in the young child. Children are not given regular tasks to perform and little is expected of them. This stems partly from the culture's view of the child. Children are regarded as sin capacidad-without capacity.

Dependency and Other Behaviours

Is independent or dependent behaviour related to other aspects of behaviour? Among preschool children a negative connection has been shown between dependence on adults and popularity among peers. Actually, those children depending most on adults participate least with peers. Thus, dependence on adults presumably hinders a child's interaction with his peers whereas independence seems to be a valued trait event the preschool level. In adolescence, independence and popularity go together; however, the inverse relation between dependence on adults and popularity is by no means a simple one.

Dependent boys were seen in the McCord study to display heightened anxiety and internal stress, which perhaps interfered with peer relations. Independence relates to achievement and motivation for achieving. High-achieving nursery-school children depended less on adults for help and emotional support than did children lower in achievement, according to a study conducted by Crandall, Preston, and Rabson. One might infer that independence as a sign of security enables the child to function autonomously and apply effort toward personal accomplishment and attainment of goals. Furthermore, children who rated high in emotional independence from parents showed increases in IQ during preschool years.

Some Conclusions about Dependency Antecedents

To begin with, there is probably a curvilinear relationship within the normal range of dependency behaviour between how parents meet of frustrate a child's early dependency needs and the persistence of such needs in the child. If the parent strongly rewards dependent behaviour and takes a permissive attitude toward it, preventing or discouraging independence, dependency persists. Similarly, frustration of the infant's needs for dependency might intensify the yearning for dependency. The Pattern Study, for example, found dependency increased in children whose mothers punished them for such behaviour. The same thing applied to children of homes where rejection was evident and withdrawal of love was used as a disciplinary technique. Parental conflict and rejection of the child were prominent in the family backgrounds of extremely dependent boys. Low parental esteem for one another and for the child pervaded their homes.

From this point of view dependent behaviour was a manifestation of feelings of insecurity in the parent-child relationship. Gewirtz noted a high frequency of attention seeking in children when the adult was relatively unavailable. Thus, dependence on adults appeared to increase when the children perceived them as psychologically distant. Finally, the curvilinear relation between dependency and the extent of frustration by the parent may actually hold for only the broad normal range. If parents or parent-substitutes show a nearly complete absence of nurture, or if parental rejection exists to a pathological degree, the child may develop an intense independence. This is dramatically illustrated by six German-Jewish orphaned refugee children who spent the first two or three years of their lives in a concentration camp. The children had been reared together with a minimum of adult nurture.

When transferred to a rehabilitation centre, they were excessively distrustful and wary of adults. Their hostility toward adults was replaced by positive feelings only after a long period of time. Among a group of aggressive adolescent boys, Bandura and Walters found their fathers to have been rejecting and to have punished early dependent behaviour after the affection of their mothers had established a motive for dependency. Thus, anxiety over dependency developed. The aggressive behaviour, Bandura and Walters reasoned, was born in the early frustration of their dependency needs. Treatment of this anti-social behaviour was hampered by the boys' suspicion and fearfulness of establishing a dependency relationship in therapy. Although the socialization process is characterized ordinarily by increasing independence in the child, certain parental attitudes impede this development. Stendler maintained that there were critical periods during the early years when over-dependency might result.

The first of these occurred toward the end of the first year of life when the child becomes aware of his dependence on his mother. Recognizing her importance, the child tested her to see if he could really depend on her. Separation at this time might produce a child low in ego strength and toleration of frustration. The second critical period appeared between the ages of two and three. At this time the pressure of the culture for independent behaviour increases on the child. Disturbances in his relation of dependency with his mother during this period might touch off attempts to cope with the resulting anxiety by developing an extremely strong conscience. To support this notion of a critical period, Stendler showed that a larger number of discontinuities in personality adjustment turned up in dependent children than in others. Moreover, her data corroborated those of Bandura and Walters in notion the importance of paternal influence in the learning of dependency. Two further considerations merely brief attention.

First, because independence grows out of dependence, the two must not be considered distinct from each other. Several studies have observed that despite a negative correlation between the amount of independent and dependent behaviour shown by nursery-school youngsters, the two are not entirely inversely related. That is, even though some children display generally less dependent behaviour than others, some of both kinds of behaviour can be seen in all children.

Second, long-term consistency in dependent behaviour is of great concern to child psychologists interested in predicting behaviour. In their study of the display of passive and dependent behaviour in 54 adults, Kagan and Moss collected information on how much dependency these individuals showed as children between the ages of three and ten. Comparisons of the two sets of data indicated that passive and dependent behaviours "remained stable over the years among women but not necessarily among men." Kagan and Moss inferred that passive and dependent behaviour was punishable in males while perhaps actually being encouraged in females. More males proportionately than females shifted from high dependency in childhood to independence in adulthood, implying a sex difference in the extent to which pressures for independence are applied in America. Even in adolescence, girls enjoy less independence than boys.

Dominant-Submissive Behaviour

A hierarchy of behaviour ranging all the way from dominance to submissiveness has been seen many times in the social interaction of a wide assortment of organisms including rats, dogs, monkeys, and humans. Implied in this range is the jockeying for position, the manoeuvring for power that is virtually an integral part of all social interaction, regardless of species. Here, too, comes into relief the structure of group whose members can be ranked with respect to dominance and submission.

Both the struggle and the structure are vividly illustrated by the pecking order of the domestic fowl. Factor analyses of personality tests and ratings almost invariably find a factor designated ascendance, or dominance, or assertiveness both at child and adult levels. In the paragraphs to follow we shall summarize some of the early studies that contributed methodologically to the investigation of ascendant behaviour in children and then turn to the antecedents of dominance and submissiveness.

Dominant-Submissive Antecedents

Dominant behaviour is observable in children at least as young as three years of age. It is also observable in lower organisms. Conceivably, therefore, constitutional factors predisposing an individual to dominance play a role in such behaviour. Nevertheless, this does not eliminate the role of environmental antecedents. Part of the problem of identifying the antecedents of ascendant behaviour results from a confusion in nomenclature. Jack clearly did not differentiate between acceptable and unacceptable kinds of behaviour in the type she selected to define ascendance. This distinction largely appeared later. Children embraced both dominating and cooperative behaviour in the term assertiveness. Anderson, it will be recalled, distinguished dominating from integrating behaviour.

In a similar vein, Parten described two types of leaders, the bully, who used brute force and bossing, and the diplomat, who used artful and indirect suggestion. Finally, Mummery spoke of socially acceptable and socially unacceptable behaviour. Various distinctions between socially positive and socially negative types of domination aid in resolving some of the disagreement over parental antecedents of dominating behaviour. From some of the Fels studies, Baldwin concluded that democracy in the home, especially an actively democratic home, tended to produce an active, aggressive child, likely to be a leader. Children from restrictive, controlled homes tend to be unaggressive and fearful. Baldwin reasoned that freedom in the home encouraged active exploration of the environment and a high degree of social participation. In agreement with the Fels data, Miles noted that parents of adolescent leaders were less restrictive in handling their children.

The child enjoyed the freedom to make his own decisions and judgements and to experiment with new opportunities. Yet these findings contradicted those of an investigation by Meyer who, in rating homes of 29 preschool children on the 30 Fels Parent Behaviour Scales, found significant negative correlation between their dominating responses under experimental conditions and such home atmosphere as democracy of policy, readiness of explanation, understanding of child's problems, and rapport with child. The homes of the dominant children were characterized by disciplinary friction and general discord. Similarly, Radke reported that children from autocratic homes tended to dominate their companions more readily than children from democratic homes.

They were also less considerate of their peers. To Mummery the chief effect of democracy in the home was perhaps to influence the child's self concept in terms of self-acceptance and self-confidence. Because democratic parents respect the individuality of the child, it is likely that he will show respect for his peers in social situations. If such a child displays assertive behaviour it will generally be socially acceptable, integrating, and cooperative in nature.

Early Studies

Noteworthy is the Jack study which sought experimentally to modify behaviour. Jack observed four-year-old in pairs in a room supplied with a sandbox and three types of toys. The following eight types of behaviour figured in defining ascendance.

- Forceful attempts to secure play materials
- Defence and snatching back of materials taken from one's possession
- Companion compliance with direction
- Providing pattern of behaviour which companion imitates
- Verbal attempts to secure play material
- Success in securing material from companion's possession
- Verbal attempts to direct behaviour of companion
- Forbidding, criticizing, reproving companion

Concluding that the most significant difference between ascendant and non-ascendant children was degree of self-confidence, Jack applied special training materials in her effort to modify the behaviour of the five least ascendant youngsters. Later, when she paired them again in the experimental room, the ascendance scores of these particular youngsters showed significant gain. Therefore, she questioned whether the results of the training spread to the environment beyond the training room.

Though lacking data on long-term effects of training, psychologists find it significant that by increasing a child's self-confidence through developing certain skills and proficiencies in him they can alter his behaviour in a social situation. Similar modification of behaviour was reported by Children. She provided special tutelage to ten preschool children who were most dominating in their relations with other children. Conflicts involving dolls were analyzed, with the social and emotional consequences of certain kinds of behaviour emphasized. Tests conducted after the training disclosed that these children had increased their cooperative behavioural.

Leadership Behaviour

Although not synonymous with dominating behaviour, leadership has much in common with it. Leadership implies the successful use of techniques to guide and direct the behaviour of others toward an agreed goal. Dominating behaviour, on the other hand, mayor may not succeed and mayor may not involve a shared goal. Whether children who are dominating in the preschool period assume leadership in elementary-school years is not certain from the scant evidence at hand. Equally sparse is the evidence relating to the transferability of leadership from one group to another although more of this does exist. Yet leadership is a topic of interest to social psychologists who deal with adult behaviour. In general there are two approaches to the subject. The structuralists regard leadership as a trait or a set of traits. The functionalists view it as a function of the situation.

The two positions may be synthesized if leadership is seen on the basis of role theory and role expectancy. It is likely that children who later become leaders possess in childhood the earmarks of leadership. The inclusion of leadership capacities in the child's concept of the self results from the successful use of these characteristics in opportunities to lead. Effective leadership in one situation inspires the child to assert it in others. Through repeated successes the notion of leadership becomes an integral part of the self concept. Furthermore, as others expect the individual to continue to lead this contributes to further exhibition of leadership demeanour. Reputation occasions the repeated display of specific behaviours in children even if the repute is under-observed. Having reviewed the available data on the qualities inherent in leaders, Stogdill listed these characteristics in which leaders surpassed the average members of their groups: intelligence, scholarship, dependability in exercising responsibilities, activity and social participation, socio-economic status, initiative, persistence, knowing how to get things done, self-confidence, alertness to and insight to situations: cooperativeness, popularity, adaptability, verbal facility, athletic ability, originality, desire to excel, judgement, humour, chronological age, heights, weight, appearance, energy, dominance, integrity, and mood control.

Those factors associated with leadership, Stogdill concluded, could probably be classified under the following headings.

- Achievement
- Responsibility
- Capacity
- Participation
- Situation
- Status

As much as the traits seem to support the structuralist approach to leadership, Stogdill pointed out that the qualities and skills enabling an individual to function as a leader depended on the demands of the group and the situation. In preschool years, mere activity level is enough to determine leadership; in late elementary-school years and throughout adolescence, athletic ability and physical prowess are the important requisites for leadership among boys; in college empathy is the key to leadership. Since the functionalists are also correct, leaders are made as well as born.

Aggressive Behaviour

Our culture seems uncertain as to how aggressive behaviour should be regarded. During childhood aggression is discouraged; attitudes toward it are highly restrictive. Yet aggressiveness carries a premium in adult society. The ambitious, hard-driving, aggressive male represents the epitome of success in the competitive, free-enterprise system. His quiet, contemplative, introverted opposite is outdistanced in the race to the top. Aggressiveness appears to be approved in covert; sophisticated forms, but frowned upon in the overt, primitive, physical sorts that characterize children's behaviour, except in such formalized events as athletic contests and war. Aggression may be defined as any act or behaviour that is intended to harm or injure. Thus defined, it is inimical to friendly, social intercourse.

The rights and wishes of others are ignored or abridged. In this sense, aggressive behaviour is maladaptive. There is also evidence that the behaviour of highly aggressive children is inflexible and stereotyped. The implication is that children evincing a great amount of aggression have failed to develop inner controls and have not learned more appropriate, adaptable, and acceptable types of behaviour. The social interaction of young children is marked by aggressive and conflict-ridden behaviour. Anger, hostility, quarrelling, and combativeness are observable frequently in children' relations with each other.

It is impossible to determine how early these aggressive feelings appear in the child. However, the infant lashes out very early at the source of events that frustrate, restrict, or irritate him. The child uses any means at his command to eliminate unpleasant and undesirable stimuli. In the young child this usually means crying, screaming, and direct physical attack. As children grow older overt aggression decreases. Inner controls are learned. More effective and more socially acceptable ways of solving conflicts are developed, and rules governing the rights of property become incorporated. However, at every age there are side disparities among individuals in the amount of aggressive behaviour, and in some children a marked persistence of aggression pervades a great number of behaviours. Among the notions advanced to explain aggression in children, three stress various aspects of the parent-child relationship.

In the first, frustration-aggression, any situation, condition, relationship, or experience that produces frustration in an individual is seen to generate aggression. The second notion emphasizes the parent as a model for the child; identifying with the parent, the child models his own behaviour after the parent's. Third, parental permissiveness of aggression is said to increase the child's tendency to behave aggressively. Clearly all three notions are centred in the environment since these stress the child's learning experiences, particularly as they occur in the family setting.

There is also an argument for a biological basis for aggression. Diamond, who examined studies among animals, found strain and sex differences in aggressiveness and concluded that genetic factors were influential in determining aggressive behaviour, even though learning experiences were important. Reviewing some of the same research, Berkowitz saw no evidence of an instinctive drive to hostility or aggression in animals. He accounted for the relative rare occurrence of spontaneous aggression by frustration or through prior learning that rewarded aggressive behaviour. Although environmental factors contribute heavily to the appearance of aggressive behaviour, it would be a mistake to overlook inherent differences in individuals which might indirectly increase their tendency to react aggressively to environmental events.

Certain innate characteristics, then, may determine the kinds of learning experiences to which the child is exposed and these, in turn, influence behaviour and personality. Among nursery-school children, Walker obtained significant correlations between mesomorphic type and clusters of behavioural traits labelled energetic-active and aggressive-assertive. He concluded that variations in physical energy, in bodily effectiveness for assertive or dominating behaviour, and in bodily sensitivity appear as important mediating links between physique structure and general behaviour. Whereas no cause-and-effect statements can be drawn from studies showing a relationship between physical factors and personality, it is not possible to ignore entirely the role such factors play in moulding responses to the environment.

The Parent as a Model

The parent serves as a model for the child. The child adopts his values and imitates his behaviour, irrespective of whether such behaviour is rewarded or expected. In general, adults set examples for children. Logically, then, it would seem that the more aggressive the adult's behaviour, the more aggressive would be the child's. This view is buttressed by several studies. Preschool children imitated or reproduced the behaviour of the conductor of the experiment who was their model. An aggressive model elicited a greater amount of aggressive behaviour than a non-aggressive model. Interestingly enough, boys showed more aggression than girls after exposure to an aggressive male model.

In the development of aggressive behaviour the father played a particularly pivotal role, just as he was more important source of frustration than the mother. Indeed, a correlation of +.33 was obtained by Eron et al. between ratings of paternal aggression and child aggressiveness at home. And Winder and Rau in a study of the parental attitudes of deviant pre-adolescent boys found parents of the aggressive boys to score higher in aggressiveness than parents of non-aggressive counterparts. One study pertinent to the notion that parents serve as models for a child's aggression observed that children most closely identified with their parents displayed the most aggression in the doll-play sessions.

This was particularly true for boys whose fathers did the punishing. Since boys from homes in which the father was absent showed less aggression in doll play than boys from intact homes, boys might be thought less likely to act aggressively in the absence of an aggressive male model. In similar manner, more aggression is evident in lower-class children than in those from the middle class because the lower-class male who serves as the model is seen as typically aggressive, at least in the overt physical mannerisms that might prove most significant.

Frustration-Aggression

Most people experience frustration in the course of a day's events. Goals are blocked. Rewards are not received. Desires remain unfulfilled. Developed by the Yale group the frustration-aggression hypothesis holds that aggressive behaviour is the typical response to frustration. Support for the hypothesis appears in experimental studies as well as in observation. To mention on briefly, 63 preschool children were exposed to eight consecutive repetitions of a mildly frustrating situation. Observed and recorded for manifestation of aggressiveness, the children displayed an increase in aggressive conduct from the first four to the last four trails. Quite likely this finding is particularly significant in supporting the Yale group's hypothesis because the frustration was mild and the children were not greatly involved in the situation.

Certainly plausible, then, are findings that point out the severe consequences of parental frustrations of the child's emotional needs. The findings of several parent-child research studies concur in noting a bond between aggressive behaviour in children and punishment for aggression. The Pattern Study explained this relationship along the following lines: the child receives some reward in resorting to aggression through the satisfaction realized from hurting others or expressing danger. But when this aggressive behaviour incurs punishment, great frustration is felt, which incites the child to further aggression. Moreover, the Pattern Study noted a tendency for severe punishment of aggression toward parents to be one aspect of general strictness in child-rearing. One study relating parental behaviours to aggressiveness in school children found aggressive boys likely to have fathers who severely punished aggressive deportment in the home.

That there was no significant correlation between aggression at school and maternal punishment of aggressive behaviour at home suggested that father, more than mothers, were an important source of frustration in the home, especially for boys. So much for restrictive and autocratic techniques producing frustration. As we have seen, the young child is totally dependent on his parents. When one or both parents fail him, frustration results. Hostile, aggressive behaviour appears. In their book on adolescent aggression, Bandura and Walters attributed the development of aggressive behaviour to disruption of the child's dependency relation with his parents.

Their thesis is corroborated by the findings of another study of family correlates of aggression in non-delinquent boys. Here, 95 per cent of the aggressive boys come from homes in which at least one parent was emotionally rejecting. Thus, there seems to be ample evidence for the frustration-aggression hypothesis. It is likely that parents who reject the child's needs for dependence and affection also establish a relatively restrictive home atmosphere which itself is frustration to the child. Both these behaviours seriously affect the child and his development.

Permissiveness of Aggression

This notion rests on the fact that aggression is more likely to occur when it is permitted. An increase in doll-play aggression in a permissive situation has been observed from session to session. This has been taken to signify that in a permissive atmosphere, the child's fear of punishment *for* aggressive behaviour diminishes and his inhibitions concerning the show of aggression lessen. The accepting, non-reproachful attitude of the adult is perceived by the child as granting him permission to exhibit aggression. However, another interpretation is plausible.

The amount of session-to-session aggression manifested by pairs of seven-to-ten-year-old boys in a permissive, free-play situation was observed under two conditions: the presence of a permissive adult and the absence of any adult. Under the former condition, the typical session to the next. Under the latter condition, however, there was a drop in aggressive behaviour from the first session to the second. Thus, when an adult is present the child presumably tends to transfer certain ego functions, such as control of disapproved or punishable behaviour, to him.

In the absence of the adult the child must exercise his own self-control. The Fels studies indicated that one effect of democracy in the home was to raise the child's activity level. Since there is a connection between sheer level of activity and aggressiveness, this helps to explain the greater aggression noted in children from democratic or permissive home. Democratic parents incline toward tolerating all child behaviours, including quarrelling, activeness, and aggression. In the Pattern Study a slight relationship was seen between aggressive conduct in the child and the mother's permissiveness of aggression. Sears argued that maternal permissiveness signalled the child that aggressive behaviour was acceptable; it was not punishable and was expected by the mother to occur. Yet Lynn, in testing the Pattern Study's finding, could not discover such as link between aggression in children and maternal permissiveness of aggressive behaviour.

However, Lynn did observe a relationship between scores of a mother's extroversion and both her tendency to be permissive and her child's aggression in school. Lynn suggested the existence of a genetic factor since other studies also found a connection between extroversion and aggression. Weatherly, through ratings of aggression found in TAT stories told by college girls, detected no difference in the amounts of aggressive behaviour among girls whose mothers had been low in permitting aggression and those whose mothers had been relatively permissive of aggression in child rearing. However, the former group exhibited a sharp increase in fantasy aggression as a result of frustrating, aggression-arousing conditions in childhood, Although maternal permissiveness of aggression may not be highly related to aggression in children, it does increase the likelihood that the child will respond aggressively to various environmental stimuli. The case for the notion that aggressiveness in children is abetted by a permissive atmosphere in the home is not clear-cut.

The idea does not explain the original onset of aggression. Possibly, however, parental reluctance to punish various sorts of child behaviour tacitly encourages such behaviours when their exercise is rewarding to the child. Regarding aggression, a child's frustrations are relieved by striking someone interfering with or interrupting his activity. If allowed by parents, the tendency for aggressive behaviour to recur in similar situations is reinforced.

Social Acceptance

Social psychologists who contend that Americans place too much emphasis on sociability, adjustment to the group, and other-directedness support their complaint by pointing to the amount of research on social acceptance in the field of child psychology. Yet there are a number of reasons to believe that a child's degree of acceptance by his peers is of more than fleeting or superficial significance. Children not well accepted by their peers tend to express less positive feelings toward them, and it is reasonable to consider positive feelings toward others as one sign of mental health.

In the classroom, poor pupil-to-pupil relationship is one indication of an unfavourable climate for learning and for positive group interaction. The second reason for attaching importance to peer relationships is that the adjustment to peers is a good barometer for adjustment in adult life. Roff has been able to predict the adjustment of individuals to military service from comment made about them years before concerning their childhood relations with their peers. Early detection of difficulties in adult adjustment is possible, Roff held, from knowledge of the attitudes and opinions of an individual's associates regarding him. Undoubtedly, a vast number of persons who are not highly accepted by their peers in childhood make an adequate adjustment to adult life.

There is a difference, though, between lack of acceptance and active rejection. The Roff data seem to indicate that it was active rejection to which he referred. Finally, it is important to find the personality correlates of social acceptance because knowledge of them may make it possible to help children develop better relations with their peers. We have seen the negative correlations between social acceptance and aggressiveness, anxiety, and dependence. How can these aspects of personality be altered, modified, or altogether prevented?

Modifying Social Acceptance

If social rejection reflects basic maladjustment of personality, raising the level of an individual's social acceptance is not easily accomplished. Because of the role of antecedent parent-child relationships, in social acceptance, changes may involve the entire family. But this may be true only of extreme social rejection. For children in the intermediate zone, it may be profitable to concentrate on the self concept. Increasing their self-confidence, self-assurance, and self-esteem is most desirable. Children who manifest unacceptable behaviours usually know that they elicit unfavourable reactions from others but are unable to mend their ways. Feelings of inadequacy interfere with behaviour and lead to deeper feelings of inadequacy.

Somehow the treadmill must be stopped. And it is likely that modifications in self-feelings and in behaviour are best achieved in the early elementary years. The prime responsibility for assisting the child to more positive and acceptable social relations is the parents. In the case of the boy, since athletic skill plays so great a role in his acceptability, the father can increase the child's self-confidence by practising various games with him. This also serves to increase the boy's feeling of parental acceptance. In fact, the child's problems in acceptance by his peers may have their genesis in parental non-acceptance. The teacher also has a role. An alert, sensitive teacher can do much to create a classroom atmosphere of mutual assistance, mutual understanding, tolerance, and acceptance of others.

Constancy of Social Acceptance

Several factors indicate the likelihood of relative constancy in social acceptance from one group to another and one time to the next. First, Bonney found that a child's social position in grades two, three, and five was as constant as his intellectual and academic achievements throughout the elementaly-school years. Years later, upon interviewing 25 first-grade children throughout the school year, Medinnus obtained correlations of about +.85 between scores of social acceptance from one interview to the next. Thus, there is certainly short-term constancy in social acceptance. Second, a number of studies concur on the personality characteristics associated with acceptance and non-acceptance.

Further, researches into children's friendships report an increasing constancy in friendship choices throughout childhood and adolescence. Prior to school, constancy probably results from the restricted range of choice imposed by limitations in mobility. Later, it may become accounted for by the increasing consistency of personality. In adolescence, friends are chosen on a deeper basis-on aspects of personality that are fairly stable. That social acceptance is fairly constant while growing up points to its influence on the child's personality and adjustment. As awareness of social position increases with age, a long-term pattern of acceptance and non-acceptance exerts direct and indirect influence on behaviour, until knowledge of one's social status becomes an important part of one's self concept.

10

SOCIOLOGICAL INFLUENCES ON CHILD'S BEHAVIOUR

The child's most difficult adjustments involve the behaviour of other people. Physical things to which he must make perceptual and motor adjustments are relatively static. A behaviour pattern that permitted him to climb a fence yesterday has a high probability of accomplishing this same goal today. This stability of adjustment conditions is the exception rather than the rule in most of the child's interactions with other children and adults. Since human behaviour is fluid and dynamic, the child is faced with an ever varying stimulus configuration when he makes social adjustments to another person. This adjustment difficulty is compounded by the child's having to adjust his behaviour patterns to many different people, each of whom displays numerous inconsistencies in response to a social situation.

In view of the complexity of social adjustments, it is little wonder that the majority of children's problems and maladjustments lie in the social area. Growing up in a highly social environment in which so many conflicting demands are made on one's behaviour involves an increasing series of baffling frustrations. The child's potentialities for psychological adjustment and growth are often sorely taxed in this process of learning to live in a social world. Parents and teachers sometimes censure children for failing to make social adjustments without an adequate appreciation of their earnest efforts to resolve these conflicts in a socially acceptable manner.

The school transmits the values of the society to each succeeding generation of children, thus perpetuating the basic facets of a culture. Its significance in the child's life becomes clear from the realization that it is the setting for much of his relationship with his peers. Because of the social interaction occurring within it, the school, through its personnel, attempts to guide and facilitate the personality development of its pupils. This list is far from complete; the school has many other functions. No longer the centre of community life as it was in rural America, the school continues to play an important role in the lives of young people from five to eighteen. The concern of the present chapter is essentially the various aspects of school experience that influence the child's development of personality.

Nursery school, the beginning of formal schooling and what it means to the child, the teacher's role in the classroom, especially her part in establishing a psychological atmosphere, the factors involved in achievement, social-class membership, and competition all these will be considered in turn. Educational methodologies and materials are better left to texts on educational practice. Besides, the teacher's fund of knowledge, her enthusiasm, and the kind of psychological and emotional relationship existing between her and her pupils are the really crucial matters in the classroom most significantly affecting the child.

Formal Schooling

The beginning of school marks the end of an area for the child, chronologically and psychologically. Before the age of five the child interacts more with parents and siblings than anyone else. They are the greatest influence on him. To be sure, he has playmates in the neighbourhood but his parents are the only adults he knows intimately. They set much of the pattern of his daily life. It is their approval that is most important to him. With the beginning of school the child's world expands and becomes more complex. He spends more of his time away from home in the company of people other than his immediate family. The opinions, approval, and demands of these people now become of increasing importance. Yet he may now need his parents more than ever before-at least they wish this. Entrance into the conventional first grade marks a sharp break in the actual structure of the child's experience.

For the first time in the case of many children, they are expected to conform to a group pattern imposed by an adult who is in charge of too many children to be constantly aware of each child as an individual. Flash cards are flashed at the group all at once. Stories are told and everybody must listen whether he will or not. Drawing paper and crayons are meted out whether you happen to feel like drawing at that moment or not. One child who found this shift quite beyond endurance remarked after his first day in school, It's awful; all you do is mind all day long. And another day he added, it really is awful. All you do it sit and sit and sit.

School Entrance and the Child

It is only natural to expect some changes in the child as a result of exposure to the formal school situation. Conformity to the demands of a new adult, intimate contact with a number of other children, separation from the mother for a substantial part of the day-all these must impinge on the child's behaviour and his concept of the self. Information pertinent to this point was obtained by Stendler and Young in interviews with more than 200 mothers before their child began school, after he had been in school for approximately two months, and finally, after eight months of first-grade life. An overwhelming majority reported that their child was looking forward to the beginning of school with some eagerness.

The children's anticipations dealt with learning to read, write, and do numbers. Although middle-class parents are more likely than lower-class parents to teach the child various intellectual skills, the six-year-old generally knows the alphabet, some nursery rhymes and songs, and counting, and can usually write his name. Perhaps more important than these is the fact that the parents portray the school to the child as a socializing agent. Certain kinds of behaviours are required by the teacher and she has the authority to enforce them. Most of the mothers said the child's behaviour changed with school entrance, mainly in a positive way. The children took more responsibility, they helped more at home, and they showed greater self-control and more independent demeanour at the table, in dressing, and in going on errands. Two kinds of difficulties encountered by the child, both arising from social relations, were mentioned by the mothers.

In more than half the interviews, they spoke of aggressiveness on the part of other children or of exclusion from a group. Thus, school attendance clearly involves much social learning. The child learns new behaviours, new ways of adjusting to other children, new roles to play. No doubt some children are more successful initially at social interaction and some are more capable than others in meeting new social demands and in making the necessary social adjustments. For these reasons teachers must remain alert to children who run into difficulties in peer relations. Guidance and encouragement can be effective in aiding a child to build up self-confidence and confidence in others. If the wrong pattern is established early in the school career it may be difficult to modify. Toward the end of the first year, a preponderant number of the mothers reported continued improvement among their children in such traits as maturity, self-control, helpfulness, responsibility, self-confidence, and getting along with playmates.

Perhaps in consequence, more than half of them felt the first-grade year had been an easier one on them in their relationships with their children. Most of the children themselves continued to like school and the teacher, a liking that grew for many throughout the school year. The beginning of school, then, is a significant moment for a child. Persons other than his immediate family begin to play an important role in the socialization process. His success in this new venture and his adjustment to its demands depend intimately on the skills and attitudes he brings to the new situation. However, the child's relationship with his parents continues to exert its influence on his behaviour and so it shall continue to be.

School Readiness

Some children adapt to the new conditions imposed by the start of formal education, whereas others encounter difficulties. How can these differences be explained? Are they predictable prior to school entrance so that some ameliorative measures might be applied? What sort of pre-school experience facilitates successful adjustment in the first grade? Although, of course, there are no final answers to these questions, data are available which permit some fairly certain conclusions. One investigation that made use of anthropometric assessments of physique Simon, 1959 found that students who were failing in first grade were less mature physically than a group of successful students. Thus physical maturity would seem to pertain to school readiness. To check school readiness and adjustment to the first grade, Medinnus subjected a small group of five-year-old to a series of tests in the year prior to their starting school.

He also interviewed their mothers, made ratings of the psychological atmosphere of their homes, and had both parents complete a standard parent attitude questionnaire. Upon the children's completion of the first grade, he correlated their scores on several criteria of achievement with their scores on academic skill-type tests. In addition, he related teacher ratings of general adjustment in the first grade to the scores obtained through assessment of the home psychological atmosphere. What he found was a moderate correlation of about +.50 between the children's IQ scores on a Stanford-Binet test administered before school entrance and their achievement scores at the end of the first grade. Thus, although intelligence is important in academic success in the first grade, other factors such as motivation, interest, and application also seem to have relevance. Further, Medinnus noted that the amount of information possessed by a child prior to entering school predicted reading achievement by the end of the first grade. To discover how much children knew before their entrance into first grade, medinnus confronted them with a questionnaire which modified one used by Templin. These were some of its questions:

- Friday, Saturday, Sunday-what day comes after Sunday?
- What is a helicopter?
- What are the colours in the flag?
- How may pennies in a nickel?
- What are clouds made of?
- What is butter made from?
- What was the name of the boy who climbed the beans talk?
- Whom was Red Riding Hood going to see?
- In what game do you have a home run?
- What do we call a butterfly before it becomes a butterfly?
- What is the brake on a car for?

Among 40 five-year-old quizzed, Medinnus found a wide range of total scores. Because of a substantial correlation between the children's mental ages and their scores, it was impossible to attribute higher performance on the information test to a richer home environment. Of course, innately more intelligent children turn up oftener in the better socio-economic homes where parents provide a fuller, more stimulating environment than is supplied by lower-class parents. However, irrespective of socio-economic status, the amount of time a parent spends reading to a child and the variety of experiences to which the youngster is exposed-trips, museums, zoos-serve to expand the quantity of his information. Although IQ predicts academic success in the first grade better than any other measure, the importance of an intellectually stimulating home environment must not be underestimated.

First-grade children who scored high on a standard

measure of mental maturity, Milner learned, came from homes with more books available; these children were read to often by their parents and in general experienced a more positive emotional relationship with their parents than children who scored low. Time spent reading to a child accomplishes many things. It establishes a warm, friendly relationship between parent and child which increases the child's sense of security. The child's questions and comments inspired by the reading aids the parent's understanding of the child. And the influence of parent reading to child is certainly evident in the child's record of achievement. From what the mothers told him in their interview, Medinnus rated their homes on a number of the Fels Parent Rating Behaviour Scales.

The differences in the ratings of homes of well-adjusted and poorly adjusted first graders showed a higher rating on a Dependence-Encouraging factor for those of the well -adjusted children. This is borne out by study of academic achievement in the first grade. Mothers of the children who achieved above average In relation to intelligence favoured later independence for them than mothers of children whose achievement on the basis of intelligence was low. Both findings seem to contradict the common notion that parents should stress early independence in their children to prepare them for school life. To medinnus, great parental concern with the encouragement of independence perhaps reflected a basic rejection of the child.

Parental cliches that children must learn to stand on their own two feet, and fight their own battles may be attempts to justify an unwillingness to provide the child with emotional support, nurture, and acceptance. The teacher can teach the child to count but can never fully compensate for a lack of parental love and acceptance. Parents best prepare their children for school with affectional, accepting relationships.

Nursery-School Experience

In the 1930's child psychologists spent inordinate amounts of effort endeavouring to discover the relative contributions of heredity and environment to a child's intellectual development. One aspect of this issue-or indeed, controversy was the effect of nursery-school experience. According to one camp, nursery school produced a gain in IQ: according to another, this was not necessarily so. More likely, attendance at nursery school may increase IQ scores but most probably it does not exert any long-range influence on the functioning of the intellect. Actually any increase in IQ scores following from such exposure may result from a variety of non-intellective factors, such as increased familiarity with the materials and tasks contained in intelligence tests and greater adult-child rapport. The enriched nursery-school environment might have a salutary effect on children from deprived or impoverished backgrounds, but it is doubtful whether nursery-school experience will improve the IQs of children from homes offering an adequate amount of intellectual stimulation.

Yet even if one were to concede that nursery school stimulated intellectual development, it would be difficult to identify the specific factors in the nursery-school environment that accounted for this. By the 1940's interest had shifted to the effect of nursery-school experience on the child's social and emotional adjustment. Even before that time Walsh had found a number of personality traits to be more pronounced in a group of children who had six months of nursery-school training than in a similar group lacking such experience. The former group seemed more spontaneous in behaviour and showed more independence, initiative, self-reliance, and curiosity than the control group. Other early studies noted similar differences. Later, Bonney and Nicholson saw some indications that elementary-school children who had previous exposure to nursery school were more popular with their peers.

However, this was not found to be the case in several earlier studies reviewed by them; these showed negative findings regarding the relation between pre-school experience and pupil adjustment. Notwithstanding the inconclusive nature of the research available, some comments seem to be in order. They very nature of the nursery- school situation in which relatively large numbers of children interact under the supervision of one or two adults would tends to encourage the development of independent behaviour. In such a setting the child must learn to fend for himself. In addition, a certain amount of social learning inevitably occurs from participation in the group over a period of time. Some behaviours are discovered to be unacceptable to peers whereas other behaviours result in pleasant, favourable responses and are thus reinforced.

However, a follow-up study of a number of elementary-school children who had previously attended nursery school found consistency in behaviour from nursery school through the elementary years, thus implying that peer responses alone may not suffice to remedy behaviour difficulties. Since the source of such problems often lies in the parent-child relationship, which is a continuing one, influences outside the home cannot always counter those within it. Nursery schools vary widely in goals and procedures. So do the behavioural results they hope to achieve in children. Certainly the quality of the school and the characteristics of the teacher determine the effects of this experience on the child. The importance of the teacher is reflected in an experimental study which analyzed the impact on nursery- school children of two different types of teacher-child relations.

In one group the teacher was instructed to develop a warm relationship with each child and to stimulate the children's activities by providing information and assistance. In the other group contact between teacher and children remained at a minimum and the teacher participated in the children's activities only upon request. At the end of the school year the children in the first group in contrast to those in the second were seen to be more ascendant as well as more constructive in the face of possible failure. Moreover, they showed greater social participation and leadership. No noteworthy difference was detected between the two groups in nervous habits or IQ. Attendance at a nursery school for at least part of the day may have some bearing on the relationship between mother and child.

The time spent away from home may benefit both. The mother may enjoy temporary relief from her child-care responsibilities; the child enters a situation in which he learns to accommodate to the demands of an adult other than his parent. Very much like the effect of maternal employment on the child, the quality not the quantity of the mother-child interaction is the important thing. Quite possibly a reduction in quantity raises the level of the quality, or so it would seem from the typical report of mothers whose youngsters attend nursery school. The nursery school setting through its equipment and type of supervision is designed to reduce the amount of restrictions placed on a child and to encourage physical activity and self-expression. Few homes are arranged like it either with respect to schedule or physical facilities.

In consequence, fractions present in the home, such as sibling rivalries or mother-child antagonisms centring about certain areas of behaviour, can be minimized or voided in the nursery-school setting. However, this does not mean that compulsory school attendance should be lowered to the pre-school years. Early child rearing is a parental responsibility and should perhaps remain so. The value of the nursery-school experience is that it may enable the parent to gain some insight and understanding about the child-rearing process from a new perspective.

Some Special Problems of the Primary Period

A survey of undesirable behaviour in public school children showed the following types of behaviour to be most prevalent-disinterest in school work, cheating, unnecessary tardiness, lying, defiance of discipline, marked over-activity, unpopularity with children and temper outbursts. Some of these problems will be discussed in this chapter.

Stuttering

Causes

Stuttering often begins when a child is about four years

old. The sooner treatment is begun, the better. Why do approximately nine out of every 1000 children stutter? Frequently stuttering is acquired by imitation. One stuttering child in a class may start a mild epidemic of stuttering. Sometimes a child may be shocked or alarmed into stuttering. He catches his breath through fear or excitement. That catching of the breath is the characteristic feature of stuttering. Normally words and sentences are spoken on the outgoing breath. In stuttering speech is attempted during inspiration. A stutterer can often speak freely under certain circumstances. Under conditions of fear or anxiety, or in the presence of certain people the speech difficulty becomes marked. One mother took her eight-year-old boy to a speech specialist.

The boy talked to the doctor without hesitancy. In the classroom he stuttered very badly. Stuttering is own a symptom of some underlying emotional disturbance, such as fear or feelings of inferiority, inadequacy or insecurity. Factors in stuttering have recently been studied experimentally with great care. Wickes tells of a young girl who was so over burdened with a sense of inferiority that it caused an impediment in her speech.

Treatment

How should a stuttering child be treated? Very calmly and deliberately the child should be asked to repeat the sentence he is trying to say. The teacher or parent in a slow drawling voice, with no appearance of haste, anxiety or annoyance in her manner should tell the child to take plenty of time. The child should be encouraged to speak prolonging the vowels in the same slow drawling way that the teacher uses in speaking to him. When a child begins to stutter, the teacher should say, now try it again. Take plenty of time, and encourage the child to repeat the troublesome sentence until he does it easily. Making slow rhythmical movements with the hands while prolonging the vowels has been found helpful. Usually, stuttering children should be given more rather than less opportunity than average children to speak in natural home and school situations.

Otherwise they get little practice in taking part in social life. To put a little child into the care of an easy-going person such as a coloured mummy, has proved to be successful treatment. The child should be relieved if possible from influences at home and at school that cause tension and anxiety, and should be given the feeling of security which he lacks. It has been estimated that probably 50 per cent of stuttering could be prevented and that a large proportion of stutters are curable. Stammering, baby talk, or other forms of mutilated speech can be corrected by calling the child's attention to the differences between his pronunciation of a word and the current pronunciation.

He should be taught to listen attentively to speech and should not be confused by studying French or another language. Rewarding successful attempts promotes progress. One teacher gave a pupil a page of lose-leaf notebook to take home to his parents with a note stating that the child had pronounced certain words correctly that day. This gave the child a sense of achievement an additional practice in reading these words to his parents.

The Nervous Child

Individual Differences in Nervousness

Even cats show individual differences in their reactions to difficulty. Thornkike observed that some cats struggled with extraordinary vigour to escape from confinement while some do not struggle so vigorously or get so excited as the rest. On some occasions these more emotionally stable cats did not struggle at all. Great differences may be observed in the response of young child children to failure. In Marston's experimental situation of the duck hunt in which the child made a choice between two boxes, one empty and one containing a toy duck, some children responded promptly to each presentation of the pair of boxes showing no hesitancy or perplexity even after consecutive failures.

Other children sought to escape the discomfort of indecision and the disappointment of failure by turning to other activities. One girl after three successive failures said, 'I think it's time I much play now, and at the next failure, I think it's time to get to school now. Individual children's attitude toward failure may be observed in their everyday home and school activities. There are great individual differences in this respect not only between children but in the same child at different times. Brilliant people are frequently nervous in some situations.

Nervousness Defined

Some people are nervous when they have to speak before an audience. They feel inadequate to the situation. Some people are nervous about undertaking a new piece of work. They fear that they may not be able to succeed in it. Nervousness usually accompanies a feeling of inability to meet the situations life offers. One-third grade child of superior intelligence had not been taught to read in the first two grades. In the third grade he began to feel keenly his deficiency. The other children ridiculed him. He began to worry about it, lost interest in school and became nervous and restless.

The nervous child is one who is failing to respond satisfactorily to his school or home conditions. He is unhappy, unstable, maladjusted. By nervous stability is generally meant the power which an individual has of acting contrary to his impulses without loss of emotional control.

Characteristics of Nervous Children

How does a child show nervousness? He may lose his temper easily, show extreme timidity, or do the thing that is easiest regardless of whether it is best. The nervous child is unusually restless and fidgety and ill at ease. Since he has failed before, he approaches new problems with anxiety and a feeling of insufficiency. He is afraid he will not pass the test or win the approval of the group. He may become irritable, extremely sensitive to criticism, and laugh or cry over nothing. He may try to get satisfaction in other ways than by success in his work.

Day popular, lording it over smaller and weaker children and being very egotistical or very humble are ways in which a child may try to compensate for his lack of actual objective achievement. He cannot bear with equanimity any thwarting of desire, but responds to difficult situations as a very young child might, rather than as a child of his age should. Any or all of these symptoms may be observed in nervous children.

Treatment of Nervous Children

How should a nervous child be treated? The factors to consider are the child himself and the environment. In the first place, the child may have inherited a nervous system which makes him abnormally irritable to all kinds of stimuli. He takes things hard. His failures may really be insignificant, but they loom large to him. The teacher and parent should criticize such a child as little as possible. Approval of his successful responses should be bestowed heartily. The good points in less satisfactory behaviour should be mentioned and ways of improving should be stressed. Direct disapproval, however, is likely to check rather than stimulate further effort. In the second place, the child may being poor physical condition due to malnutrition, diseased tonsils or adenoids, eyestrain, too much dosing with cathartics, some error in feeding, anaemia, lack of sleep and rest, and over stimulation of any kind.

Such a child should be examined, and any physical defects or deviations from a desirable daily schedule should be examined, and any physical defects or deviations from a desirable daily schedule should be corrected. The causes of nervousness in the environment are more numerous.

1. A child may develop nervousness because of inability to adjust himself to a home situation in which he never knows what will be expected of him. The parents squabble over policies and methods of treating him. They do not consistently demand a few essential things. They are always making unreasonable requests. In some homes the child is exposed to a continuous bombardment of

commands from morning to night. He is talked at continuously. Another factor in causing a feeling of insecurity is the discrepancy which a bright child notices between the standards of the parents and those which they set up for the children. An environment of this kind aggravates a nervous condition.

2. Emotional conflicts on the part of parents frequently affect the child unfavourably. Parents who quarrel with each other, who are tense, gloomy, worried, anxious, and fearful may transfer some of their emotional disturbance to their child. Such a home atmosphere may make a child nervous.

3. A child may be nervous because too much is expected of him. The same situation would not disturb a better-balanced child. The work given him is too do it. One child in a family may not be so bright as his parents or his brothers and sisters. The same level of achievement cannot be set for him. It is no use trying to make him more ambitious if he lacks the ability to reach standards set for those of greater native capacity. In a case of this kind, the parent or teacher should provide work suited to the child's capacity so that he will be able to succeed reasonably often. They should not require too much work.

   In addition to the school work, some parents require the child to take music, French, and dancing lessons. Other parents require excessive work in the home or neighbourhood. Some home duties are desirable, but there can be too much of a good things.

4. A school program that is too confining, that provides little opportunity for physical activity and for working uninterruptedly on tasks that are interesting, increases restlessness and irritation.

5. The teacher as well as the parent frequently adds to a child's emotional instability. A dyspeptic, sarcastic, irritable or nagging teacher can lower health values and

bring about nervous disorders and emotional difficulties.

6. Poor training in the period may be the cause of nervousness in the primary grades. The child who has been protected from everything unpleasant, who has had all the rough places made smooth for him, and who is still mama's pet and dependent on her for everything, is very poorly equipped to adapt himself to the authority of the school and to meet the difficulties primary work presents. He feels a lack of power to adjust himself to school situations. Nervousness is the first sign of inability to cope successfully with the new problems of authority and the world of reality he meets in school.

Suggestions for Studying Nervous Children

A study of the physical condition of children will be described. Home conditions should be studied next. Are the parents selfish, moody, unfair, quick to fly into a rage, jealous, timid, gloomy? Parents of nervous children should check up on the habits which are interfering with their own success in adjusting themselves happily to home life. Children of parents with nervous disorders may inherit a tendency to nervousness which need not develop under proper management. Are unfavourable comparisons made between the child and his more gifted brothers and sisters? Does the child have frequent quarrels with his brothers and sisters?

What are the quarrels about? What does he cry about at home? The school program should be examined to see if it furnishes a healthful school environment for primary children. The child's mental abilities should be studied by means of intelligences tests and observation. The teacher should observe the child's behaviour in school-his habits of work, his reactions to other children, his lovable characteristics, his undesirable personality traits, his general attitude toward life, the things that satisfy him, the things that annoy him, his behaviour in difficult situations, causes for this behaviour, and his response to approval and to disapproval. She should try to look at things from his stand-point and *see* how certain of his acts may be justified.

A study of his heredity and developmental history is frequently illuminating. Mrs. Hollingworth suggests a few guiding principles in the management of unstable children:

- The parent should never fight the child's battles for him.
- Train for self-reliance from the earliest years.
- In the first place, the child must be trained to face the real world, with all its disagreeable facts and restrictions.
- The parent should avoid much coddling of the child. Slight illness should not be made an occasion of rushing all manner of satisfiers to the child, of making him the centre of attention, of removing all responsibilities from him.
- Do not show favouritism or partiality in the family. Let justice prevail.
- Do not communicate fear to the child through being yourself fearful.
- Give rational sex education. Answer the child's questions. Tell him or her the truth.
- See to it that the work of the child is appropriate to his capacities; that he or she is not being held at tasks which are too easy or too hard.

The Child who Lies

A recent study was made of 289 descriptions of situations in which six-year-old children intentionally misrepresented facts. These descriptions were written by adults who were in a position to observe some child. The type of situation in which these children most frequently lied was that in which the child had committed an irregular or non-conforming act and was called upon to account for the act. In 28 per cent of these cases, punishment was involved. The other kinds of situations often evoking lies were:

(i) the child wanted to obtain, keep or care for property,

(ii) he was competing with another,

(iii) he was being forced by another into performing some

act, and

(iv) his activity was being frustrated by another.

The Child who Cheats

Honesty is not an entity. It consists of many responses to many different situations. A child may be honest in an arithmetic examination and dishonest in playing games at a party.

Causes of Cheating

Why do children cheat? It is because they do not know any better? Probably not. Little relation has been found between moral knowledge and conduct, in experiments thus far performed. Is cheating due to lack of intelligence? Bright children as well as dull children sometimes cheat. Is cheating more common among children of the slums and poverty-stricken rural areas? All cheating may be a form of lack of inhibition. Children who cheat have been found to be more suggestible. Hartshorne and May summarize the results of their studies of factors in deceit as follows:

It is clear that there are significant differences between the extremely honest and the extremely dishonest in respect to intelligence, home background, and school deportment, and possibly in the matter of race or nationality and sex. It is not clear, however, that such facts, whether taken separately, added together, or considered in certain combinations, can account for deceit in individual cases, although, as illustrated, a close scrutiny of the details may lead to a better understanding of the subject and may suggest very definite ways of correcting the conditions that may possible be leading to the practice of deceit. Some classrooms promote cheating by placing an exaggerated emphasis on the importance of marks in tests.

This emphasis makes some children feel that any means may legitimately be used to prevent failure. In the primary grades the consequences of a child' first attempt to cheat may determine to a large extent his future attitude toward cheating. He may try cheating at first as an experiment. If he is caught in the act and dissatisfaction connected with it, he will tend not to repeat it. He might be spoken to somewhat in this manner: This is not your work. It is bobby' work. This score of 90 is a good score, but it is not your score. It is bobby' score. Your score today is 0. See how badly that looks on your record. The line goes way down to the bottom today. Which would have been better five correct examples which you did yourself giving a score of 50 or this paper you have handed in giving a score of 0?

In which case would you have learned more about arithmetic? Everyone likes children who do their own work. No one likes children who cheat. Come to my desk and let us see what is making the problems difficult for you. We will find out how you can make a score of 90 by solving the problems all by yourself. The primary teacher should be alert in detecting the first appearances of cheating, because letting it slip by and doing nothing about it is one way of promoting the practice.

Tests of Honesty

Significant tests have recently been devised to detect the children in a class who tend to cheat. In one test, directions were given to shut the eyes and make figures in a circle. This cannot be done successfully unless the child peeked, i.e., cheated, can be judged. In another test, cheating consists in adding points to the true score when correcting their own papers. The children are allowed more time than is required for scoring, and raising their scores can be done, apparently without risk of detection.

The Child who is Absent from School

What are the causes of absences from school in your situation? Some of the most common causes of absence are the following:

Absence Due to Other Causes

Absence is sometimes due to pupils being kept home by

the parents. In one kind of social environment children are kept out of school to work in factories, on farms, or in the home. On another social level, children are over-coddled and kept at home because the weather is too cold or too rainy. Occasionally, absence is due to forces over which neither child nor parent have control, such as a rail road tie-up, impassable roads and quarantine. Playing hockey doubtless still occurs, but less frequently in schools which appeal to children's interests and provide work suited to each pupil's ability, than in schools of the old autocratic type.

Absence Due to Sickness

In one large private school in New York City 12.5 per cent of the total number of school days in one year were lost on account of sickness. Slightly less than one-half of one per cent of these absences were due to mumps, measles, scarlet fever, and other acute communicable diseases. In some other schools three per cent of the absences were due to this cause. In the first school 2.4 per cent of the absences were due to colds; in the other schools, the per cent was twice as high. Twelve and one-half per cent of the absences in the first school were due to headaches, nervousness, indigestion, and similar miscellaneous ailments. January, especially during the days immediately following the Christmas vacation, was the worst month for absence due to illness.

What can be done about absence from this cause? The illness due to communicable disease can be greatly reduced by the vigilance of teacher, nurse, and physician in detecting early the first signs of communicable disease, a new cough, reddened eyes, running eyes and nose, flushed face, and isolating suspicious cases. It has been found profitable to require children and teachers having cold to stay at home. They lose a few days, but the total loss to the class is less. A second way in which disease is kept from spreading is by establishing habits of keeping things out of the mouth, washing the hands before eating, covering the nose and mouth with a handkerchief when sneezing or coughing, and avoiding too close contact with other children.

These are habits that the youngest and dullest primary child can be taught to form. New discoveries are constantly making it possible to protect children by immunization against certain specific disease such as diphtheria, scarlet fever, and typhoid. Other types of health disorders may be frequently traced to unhygienic habits of living such as eating unsuitable food, being irregular and hasty in eating, keeping late hours and disregarding other simple laws of health.

The Child with Special Difficulty in Reading

In every class some children, for one reason or another, have special difficulty with reading.

One Concrete Example

Miss Mary R. Lewis, teacher of third grade, hoarse man school, found that five of her pupils were below the passing score in the Thorndike-McCall Silent Reading test. The steps she took in diagnosing and correcting the difficulty were:

1. To find out anything in their previous school history which might have a bearing on their reading disability. The following facts proved to be significant:

- One boy cared only for nature stories.
- Two girls never volunteered to read because they felt they were poor readers.
- Two of the pupils who had been promoted directly from the first grade had read very little.
- Three had shown no interest in reading in the first two grades. *They* liked to have stories read to them but did not care to read for themselves.

2. To find out if the children were intelligent enough to attain average reading ability. The scores on their Intelligence Tests showed that they were.

3. To gain the children's cooperation and interest in improving their scores. The children talked over the situation with the teacher and made definite plans for study. Twenty minutes were used at first each day; later the same amount of time was used twice a week.

4. To find out the individual difficulties by a study of the silent reading tests of each child, by observing children as *they* read, and by hearing them read aloud material not previously prepared. The teacher examined the papers and talked them over with each child to ascertain if possible the child's mental processes.

5. To help the children see their own difficulties, to provide drills that would overcome these difficulties, and to check the results of each day's work.

6. To provide special incentives for wide silent reading. A chart with the names of all the children in the class and the books read by each one furnished a stimulus to the poor readers. The name of the book was written on the charts as soon as the child had read it and given a resume to the class or to the teacher. The number of books read during the year by these five poor readers ranged from sixteen to twenty-eight.

7. To give the children a clear picture of the results *they* were achieving. This was done by showing them on a chart their scores in the reading test as compared with those of the other children in the class.

8. To provide special incentives for effective oral reading. One incentive was furnished by the Story Hour Club membership in which depended on the ability of a child to read well enough to give pleasure to the other members of the club.

Other suggestions for dealing with special reading difficulties are given in next section, but for an adequate treatment of the subject the teacher or parent should consult a book that treats the subject at length.

Punishment of Primary Children

Is a parent or teacher justified in whipping a primary child? Primary children very often suggest, whipping as a suitable punishment for other naughty children. Older people in thinking back over their childhood sometimes say that whippings did them good. Others feel that harm was done by whipping. The first question to ask is, does whipping help to prevent future undesirable behaviour? In Boston in 1845 the average of daily whippings among four hundred children was sixty-five. Today children are rarely whipped in school and probably behave better than they did seventy-five years ago.

Of problem cases described by one hundred teachers, not one was solved by whippings. Visiting teachers frequently find a child's emotional difficulties aggravated by beatings at home. Parents have said the more I whip him, the worse he gets. Except possibly for a very simple offence and with very young children, whipping does not seem to work. The second question is, Why is whipping ineffective? Physical pain, to be sure, is annoying, and annoyance attached to an act tends to prevent its repetition. That sounds simple and reasonable. But the difficulty in a complicated situation is in knowing which part of the situation the dissatisfaction is being attached to. The punishment may not be connected with the wrong act, but with the teacher, the parent, the entire school situation. Whipping may make a child think, I'll not do that particular thing again. Very well.

It might also make him think, I got ought this time. Next time I'll be more cunning, or if I had run away from home, I wouldn't have been punished. Whipping is so often ineffective for character building because attitudes of fear, anger, and dislike for the persons and institutions concerned grow out of it. These attitudes are sure to develop if the child feels the punishment was unjust because he was innocent, he could not help it, he did not mean to do it, others were more to blame, or the thing he did seemed right to him. The third question is what can be substituted for whipping? If possible, the offence should not be allowed to occur in the first place. Children who have something definite, interesting, and important to do are not likely to get into mischief.

In the second place, understanding the rules and why

they are necessary aids a child obeying them. The rules of course must be sensible and reasonable. Children who as a group make their own rules governing conduct in the classroom understand such rules better and obey them more willingly that ready-made rules. In the third place, scolding, not nagging, may be tried. If a child has done something that is harmful to himself or others or that is contrary to social customs, he may be shown clearly how his act affects himself and others. In the fourth place, he may be allowed to suffer the natural consequences of the act and may be shown a better kind of behaviour to use in the future. Physical punishment is the lowest level of appeal and should be used as a last resort. Punishments which build up fears should be avoided.

In one of E.V. Lucas's Forgotten Tales of Long Ago a child is punished by being forced into an empty cellar, and left with no other companion than a glimmering rush light. The iron bars kept him from getting out on one side, and the door was padlocked on the other. This is one of the types of punishments of long ago which modern parents no longer use.

The Problem of the over-age Pupils in a Class

Many teachers in small schools have said, My greatest problem is that of the big over-grown boy or girl in my second grade class. Some of the characteristics of these children are: slowness in thinking, lack of comprehension of abstract academic subjects but skill in mechanical work. They frequently have considerable stability and common sense. Children with an I.Q. of less than 75 who cannot do the work of the grade and are left in the same room year after year should be put into a special class where they have work suited to their capacity. The following types of classes were used in an experiment in the public schools of New York City to provide for different kinds of ability:

Superior Classes, for children of considerably more than average intelligence. They have the regular curriculum, and usually complete the eight-year course in seven years.

- Average Classes, for children who deviate but little from

the normal.

- Opportunity Classes, for children definitely backward but not mental defectives. This group is most in need of a special curriculum...The registers are smaller than in the average classes.
- Slightly-above-Average Classes, for children able to do the same work, but a little more intensively than the average, and occasionally to make an extra term.
- Neurotic Classes, for children who are not mental defectives, but behaviour problems, who are temperamentally peculiar, or in need of a period of study and adjustment.
- Terman Classes, for very superior and gifted children. A specially enriched curriculum is provided; the skipping of grades by bright children is avoided. The eight-year course is covered, without skipping, in six years.
- Un-graded Classes, for children much below the average in mentality. Here the curriculum has been completely made over by those in charge of the Un-graded Department.
- Foreign Classes, for children of families newly arrived in this country.
- Slightly-below-the-Average Classes, for slower children who are not definitely backward. These children can complete eight years in nine.
- Classes for Physically Handicapped, including classes for children who are underweight and need special physical attention, and cardiac classes, for children who have heart trouble. Health is made the centre of the curriculum. Home visits and mothers classes are used to get the necessary attention to construct health habits.

But if there is no special class, what can the teacher do? All the children described above frequently present behaviour problems. Continued failure is likely to result in sullenness, disobedience, resentment against the teacher and school and other undesirable character traits. They cannot gain any feeling of importance through success in the class work; so they try to attract attention by bad behaviour. The best thing to do with such children is to help them to succeed in work suitable to them. Every one needs the stimulus of success. If the dull child has the chance to do something well, he will seek approval for that just as he seeks notoriety by his bad conduct. In working out a group project, the brighter children in one class planned and executed the more difficult abstract parts of the work and the duller children carried out the mechanical details.

In giving an entertainment to another class, the more gifted children composed the invitations, wrote the play and looked up references. The pupils with low intelligence made the scenery, sewed the costumes and made the little boxes which were to be used for favours. Good work of any kind was given hearty approval. The dull children were delighted with their share in the class activities, and were learning how to work with others. If the teacher is required to keep the mentally deficient children in her room, she should plan a special course of study for them including a large amount of useful manual work. She should emphasize habits of cleanliness and health. The teacher should not hold these children responsible for the standard academic work of the grade. Four things to keep in mind in dealing with these difficult children are:

- To explain what they are to do very slowly, clearly, concretely, and patiently, and use methods of teaching most suitable to them. Dull children frequently appear to understand directions but are unable to carry them out without further directions.
- To judge the child's achievement in relation to his ability, not in relation to the achievement of other children.
- To provide enough suitable work to keep them busy all the time.
- To praise heartily the good work they do and let them

see concretely the progress, however small, which they are making.

The attitude on the part of parents and other people toward the less gifted children should be one of eagerness to honour and commend anyone who is working up to his ability whether that ability be large or small to say well done just as heartily to the individual who has made good use of his one talent as to him who ten talents to begin with. There is injustice to the child if parents and teachers do not know his mental capacity, and scold him for doing less than average work, when that is the best he is capable of. There is a great need to educate the entire community in the proper attitude toward mentally deficient and dull children.

The Child who is Tardy

Suggested Remedies

Some readies are:

- Make school more interesting than the other things that cause delay. One teacher of retarded children noticed that they were always on time on the morning when they went to assembly with the other children, while they were frequently tardy on morning which began with their regular class periods. A story, a game, a class program, or a favourite subject scheduled for the first period in the morning would furnish a stimulus to come early.
- Even first grade children can participate in a well planned morning schedule which allows enough time for everything. The teacher may help by having them dramatize what to do in the morning before school. A cardboard clock may be used to point out the hours, and all the little details of bathing, dressing, eating, collecting books and wraps, starting for school, walking or riding to school and entering the classroom at the appointed time may be worked out and made vivid by dramatization.
- Develop time sense by asking the child to see how much

you can read in five minutes. See how many arithmetic problems you can do in ten minutes, etc.

- One requisite for getting up early in the morning is to go to bed early the night before. This is the first step in starting the new day right.
- Develop time sense by asking the child to see how much you can read in five minutes. See how many arithmetic problems you can do in ten minutes, etc.
- If the parents keep late hours at night, get up late in the morning, or fail to help the child plan his early morning efficiently, the child is greatly handicapped in his efforts to be to school on time. The younger the child, the more difficult it is for him to leave for school without the cooperation of the parents. If the teacher helps plan the morning schedule with the parent as well as the child, and they all work together on it, the best results will be secured.
- If the child has chores to do at home which make him late, some arrangement must be made with the parent.

A bright Italian boy was constantly late because he had to keep store while his father went to market. The boy offered to leave school rather than spoil the attendance record of the class. Arrangements were made so that the boy was permitted to come an hour late without being marked tardy.

The dissatisfaction which may be attached to the undesirable response of coming to school late are:

(i) disapproval of teacher;

(ii) disapproval of the class. In some cases to ignore the child is more annoying to a child who likes to attract attention;

(iii) disappointment at missing an interesting activity.

The satisfactions which may be attached to coming on time are:

(i) Approval of teacher and class;

(ii) pleasure in taking part in an interesting activity;

(iii) sense of mastery in having achieved a perfect record of prompt attendance.

The Causes

The most frequent causes of tardiness in primary children are:

- Other interests greater than interest in school.
- Poorly planned morning schedule.
- Lack of cooperation of parents in helping the little child to get to school on time.
- Dislike of school.
- Undeveloped sense of time.
- Late hours the night before.
- Work to do at home.
- Satisfaction in the attention attracted by late entrance.
- Forgetting something and having to go back for it.

The child who does not eat the right kind of food

In spite of advances in the newer knowledge of nutrition the number of children who are not eating the right kind and amount of food is large. It has been estimated that only eighteen in one hundred are getting as much as a pint of milk a day; that nearly two thirds do not include either fruit, vegetables other than potatoes, or an egg, in their daily dietary. Because the effects of a faulty diet do not show at once, the problem of choice of food does not seem to many people an important one. For an adequate treatment of this subject, the reader should consult a standard book on nutrition. The easiest way to supply the necessary calcium, phosphorus, and vitamins A and B, is by providing a quart of milk a day for each child.

This amount of milk, supplemented by a normal allowance of other foods, will furnish the necessary requirement of at least one gram of calcium per day or the growing child. Milk is also a good source of protein and energy. If an egg a day, lettuce and other green vegetables, whole wheat bread, and some fruit is added to the quart of milk, the essentials of an adequate diet are guaranteed. A simplification of menus is desirable. Although the amount of food is increased, the kinds of food in a given meal need be no more numerous than those planned for the pre-school child. A breakfast of fruit, cereal, toast, and milk is still suitable. A luncheon of vegetable soup, egg salad, milk, bread and butter provides sufficient variety. A dinner of potatoes, carrots and peas, meat or fish, bread and butter, and a fruit or milk dessert furnishes enough different foods for a primary child. Some of the reasons why children do not eat the good food provided for them, have been summarized by Neff as follows:

- Nervous parents. An over-anxious, excitable, nagging parent is not conducive to good eating habits in children. Few adults would enjoy their food as they were admonished with every mouthful.
- Nervousness. A high-strung, delicate child frequently has difficulty in setting down to a meal.
- Illness. A sick child does not possess his normal appetite.
- Faulty habits of eating acquired early.
- Eating between meals.
- Quarrelling, fault-finding, criticism, and threats of punishment. These conditions interfere with food intake.
- Suggestion and imitation. Children are quick to imitate likes and dislikes of other members of the family and to maintain their reputation for being finicky.
- Interest in other things greater than interest in eating.
- Too close housing and overheating.

Preventing Measles

Measles is a common disease of the primary period. It begins with symptoms resembling an ordinary cold-sneezing and coughing, running nose, reddened eyes, and fever. The rash appears after three or four days. Symptoms appear about ten or twelve days after exposure to the infection. Prevention of this and other communicable diseases is best secured by being quick to detect the initial symptoms and isolating the child, and by quarantining the patient and not allowing the children exposed to the disease to attend school for two or three weeks. Children who have been exposed to measles may be protected by having the physician inject into the child a small amount of blood serum obtained from convalescent measles patients. In this way about 80 per cent of children can be protected entirely from measles during a period of four or five weeks and the rest will have it in a very mild form. Measles and other so called children's diseases should be prevented if possible, because of the complications and the large number of deaths resulting from these diseases.

Preventing Eyestrain

A few simple precautions will do much to decrease eyestrain in the primary period. In the first place proper lighting should be provided in the classroom and at home. Glare will be avoided if the light is placed at an angular position of 25° or more, in other words, if a line drawing from the eye through the object makes an angle of 25° with a line drawn from the yet through the light. Glare also may be minimized by having the surroundings of approximately the same brightness as the light on the book or other work. Indirect or semi-indirect lighting is the best kind to eliminate glare. Indirect or semi-indirect lighting is the best kind to eliminate glare.

In the second place seats and desks should be adjusted so that the work may be comfortably placed at least 12 inches from the eyes, and so that the light will come from above and behind the person. In the third place, the periods of time requiring short distance focusing of the eyes should be limited. Periods of reading, writing, and arithmetic should alternate with periods of physical activity, story telling, and dramatization.

Other Emotional Problems in the Primary Period

Love

Should a child love his teacher? Yes, if by love is meant

the kind of liking and admiration one gives to born leader. No, if by love is meant an intense personal affection between teacher and child. Admiration and respect for the teacher aid immensely the formation of good habits in this period. Antagonism and conflict between teacher and child result in a negative attitude on the part of the child to even the most reasonable and necessary requests. A child frequently obeys a command of a person whom he genuinely likes and refuses to obey the same command given by a person whom he dislikes. On the other hand a child who is all bound up in his teacher finds adjustments to a new teacher very difficult, and has not gained interests and motives which are independent of a single personality.

The motive of pleasing the teacher is not one that is permanently useful. It fails to function when a new teacher comes, or when the child's attitude toward the former teacher changes. As soon as possible, the motive for good work should be one that in inherent in the work itself, and the motive for desirable social behaviour, the satisfaction the child himself feels in such behaviour. Is this too idealistic an aim for the primary period? A teacher's strong affection for one child is likely to interfere with her judgment of the child's behaviour, and to lead to favouritism, a type of injustice children keenly resent. An intense desire to please the teacher may result in a temporary spurt which is usually followed by a slump. It interferes with efficiency in the long run.

Fear

What causes some children to be afraid in school? The first days of school frequently call forth this reaction in the case of the spoiled, or shy, or too dependent child. The strangeness of the room, the teacher, and the children, and the absence of the mother combine to make such a child afraid. Later, a difficult lesson, an impending examination, a threat of punishment may cause fear of failure and of the social disapproval and perhaps physical pain which may result. Previous training may be the cause of a six-year-old putting her head on the desk and crying continuously the first few days of school. The wrong associations may have been built around the child's ideas of school and teacher: school-a place where children do not like to go; teacher-someone who will whip you if you are naughty and do not learn your lessons; school children-children who will tease you or hurt you.

Frequently these ideas constitute a child's conception of school instead of the desirable associations: school-a place where you learn to read stories, play games with other children, and see and hear new and interesting things. The obvious treatment of fear due to wrong first impressions is patiently to associate school with pleasurable experiences. Work that the timid child is able to do and is interested in should be offered to him. Doing something successfully is a pleasant experience. Success in school activities is one of the best ways of changing children's attitudes toward school and driving out fear. The people who have previously been responsible for the wrong associations should retract their statements. Since excessive and persistent timidity may often be traced to poor physical condition of the child, attention should be given to securing a healthful school program and to cooperating with the parents regarding the food, sleep, and other health habits which must necessarily be carried on at home. Excessive timidity may be the result of brutal treatment at home.

In this case the child can be led to see that his fears of punishment, which at home are well-grounded, have no similar foundation in school. Our knowledge of how fears are acquired suggests the following steps in dealing with any irrational fears:

- The detection and correction of physical causes. The discovery of the specific causes of a given fear response.
- The preventing of the fear-provoking stimulus from occurring or systematically trying to attach a different and desirable response to the situation which at one time called forth fear.
- The detection and correction of physical causes.

In the case of rational fears, the cause is usually obvious and unavoidable. A serious accident, a severe thunderstorm, a fire in the school building, being incommutable for typhoid fever or diphtheria are causes of fear that may occur. The first requisite in the control of these fears is that everyone know exactly what to do under the circumstances. If an accident occurs, first aid materials should be ready for use by one or two people who have been trained to use them. The others should go on with their own work away from the injured person. Starting the children on some interesting work is a good means of relieving tension and fear.

In the case of fire, the method of leaving the building must be thoroughly learned. When everything has been done that is possible, the attitude of courage in the face of danger and inevitable pain must be built. Younger children imitate the attitude of those about them. It is important that the teacher maintain a clam, unemotional attitude. Fear is infectious. With older children stories of bravery may help build an attitude of courage. The habit of taking every pre-school bump and scratch and disappointment with fortitude is the best way of building a courageous character.

Anger

A group of primary teachers listed the following specific situations which had in their experience made primary children angry:

1. Stimuli to anger which cannot be avoided entirely by the teacher. The child's attitude toward the situation, however, may be changed.

- One child is chosen to be it in a game. The child not chosen becomes angry.
- A child loses in a game.
- A child wants something that belongs to someone else.
- One child does better work than another child.
- A child interrupting the class work is reprimanded.
- A child wants to play a game which the majority of children do not want to play.

- One child teases another child.
- A child is not permitted to read because there is not time enough for everyone to take part.

2. Stimuli to anger which should have been avoided by the teacher.

- Seizing hold of a child.
- Having no regular schedule in which the child may know when to expect a change in activity.
- Giving a child work that is beyond his capacity, with the result that he is constantly failing in it.
- Making a promise to a child and not keeping it.
- Becoming angry herself.
- Interfering with a child's activity when he is interested and able to carry it on by himself.

3. Some causes of anger which are due to influences outside of school.

- The child's environment is one which furnishes constant thwartings and irritation.
- The child is suffering from some physical irritation or from malnutrition or fatigue which makes him easily provoked.
- An attitude of suspicion has been built which causes the child to go about with a chip on his shoulder most of the time.
- Parents fail to control their anger.
- The child has found that he can get what he wants by flying into a range.
- The child has inherited an unstable nervous system and consequently disappointments and annoyances which others would hardly notice, result in violent outbursts of temper in his case.

The kind of treatment natural depends on the cause. Attention to the child's physical condition is always a wise first step. Unnecessary provocations to anger should be avoided. Anger at not being it and at not being given certain privileges, such as a chance to read to the class, may often be prevented by posting several days in advance the names of those who will take part in certain activities. The children will not when their names appear and look forward to the opportunity coming in the near future. The child who becomes angry when he is excelled is some activity by another child, may be interested in competing with his own past record. The child who becomes angry or sullen when his conduct is criticized should be shown how social approval may be won by acting in a different way.

A child who becomes angry when he cannot have something that belongs to another persons, should be re-educated in his sense of ownership. Diverting the attention is worth trying, especially with young children. With an older child, active exercise a game he enjoys, a race upstairs, carpentry work, some special commission takes the mind away from the cause of the injury, keeps him from brooding over it and picturing himself as a suffering hero, uses some of the energy released by the emotion, and demonstrates to the child a method of gaining self-control. Helping the child to see a funny side to the situation is also a constructive method of dealing with a tense situation. After the anger has subsided, the child may be reasoned with the some extent, given a picture of the other fellow's point of view, and interested in the person who annoyed him. If the habit of becoming angry in order to get what he wants has become established, firm consistent treatment is necessary.

The child should be calmly told that he is annoying the rest of the class and that if he wants to act in that way he must go by himself. No one should pay attention to him temper. This treatment may have to be repeated frequently, but the method of always attaching dissatisfaction to undesirable responses is a sound one and should be used persistently. Finally it is most important that the teacher who is face to face with an angry child should herself keep calm and impersonal.

11

Dilatory and Precocious Children

Some children having a small proportion are mentally deficient. They cannot profit to any appreciable extent from the instruction given in the ordinary schools. These children are now provided for a special school, and the ordinary teacher has no longer to concern himself with them. But there remains among the children attending the ordinary school a comparatively large proportion of backward children. And it has been pointed out that these deserve-what they have not in most cases obtained-even more attention than the mentally deficient. For, on the one hand, they are much more numerous, and on the other, they will repay for more than the mentally efficient for the care bestowed on them.

Thus Professor J. A. Green writes as follows: Whilst a great deal of energy is being misspent in wrongly directed effort to educate mentally deficient children whose social value must in the great majority of cases be something less than zero, we have been in this country content to let the problem of the backward child remain with the struggling teacher, who can, in general, do nothing more for him than insist upon his repeating the meaningless grind at which he has previously failed. The necessity of dealing more effectively with these backward children becomes all the more obvious when it is shown that of short time prisoners in our goals a very large proportion have been among the backward at school.

If this is true, we are not only failing by our lack of special attention to backward children to get some return for our educative work, but we are saddling society with a positive burden. One of the most striking results of observation of backward children is that a large number of them have some physical defect. Thus Dr. Warner writes: Taking 100 dull boys and 100 dull girls, we find:

- Among children seven years and under: 45 boys, 55 girls have developmental defects; 49 boys, 44 girls have nerve-signs; 23 boys and 30 girls are delicate. Note the large proportion of young girls that are also delicate.
- Among children eleven years and over: 38 boys, 35 girls have developmental defects; 59 boys, 56 girls present nerve-signs; and 7 boys and 10 girls are delicate.
- Among children eight or ten years old: 43 boys, 42 girls have developmental defects; 63 boys, 56 girls show nerve-signs; 14 boys and 16 girls are delicate.

But, in addition to physical defects which are open to observation, there may be many more which are due to past occurrences but which have left no obvious external mark on the child. Only an investigation into the past history of the child could bring these to light. This was undertaken in the case of the backward pupils of the Manchester Grammar School by the School Medical Officer. And the Headmaster reports: There are some cases in which there has been grave illness before the age of four: serious infection like scarlet fever, croup, bronchitis, typhoid, pneumonia. These, so far as our experience goes, seem to inflict an injury on the brain which is more or less permanent.

After that, from five to twelve, there is also an onset of disease which interferes very considerably with intellectual progress. It not only damages the brain, but it also involves a great deal of absence from school, and in those cases where the school attendance has been broken into, you get a backward pupil who has a deficiency in acquirement and very frequently a difficulty in memorizing. Another physical cause of backwardness which is sometimes overlooked is poor feeding. You will be sometimes told that the brain is the last organ in the body to suffer from deprivation of food. Do not believe that. My own conviction is that it is the first to suffer.

It may under starvation retain its plump contour, and show less wasting than other organs, but what of its delicate machinery within? Every brain worker must know the dulling effect of the want of regular meals. And in children any insufficiency of nourishment is promptly reflected in a curtailment of their learning capacity. Parents must by no means be relieved of their parental responsibilities, but all children must somehow be supplied, not occasionally, but always and systematically, with a sufficient amount of food if we are to better the condition of our people. Probably, if we could know all about each case of backwardness, we should find that in every instance mental weakness is correlated with physical defect of some kind.

Wherever possible, therefore, we should do what we can to remove the physical defect. Feeding of poor children has already begun. And medical inspection is also in process of development. It is to be feared that many children in the past have been hopelessly consigned to the abyss of backwardness when a little observation of their physical characteristics would have revealed a cause which could to some extent have been dealt with. Not a few cases have been noted in which children partially deaf or short-sighted have remained stupid for years, when the discovery of the cause could have led either to its partial removal or to simple arrangements whereby its consequences might have been mitigated. The fact remains, however, that in many cases the evil has already been done.

Sometimes, indeed, it has not been during the lifetime of the child. Joseph Cook quotes Oliver Wendell Holmes as saying, in response to the declaration that any disease may be cured if a physician is called early enough, that the statement is true, but early enough would usually mean two hundred years in advance. Though, therefore, we may diminish the amount of backwardness in the future by more careful attention to the physical side of the children's lives, we can never hope to remove it entirely, and the problem of the backward child will continue to confront us. The most obvious thing to do with the backward child is to keep him back when the other children are promoted. This is the course which has most frequently been followed.

But it has serious disadvantages. In the first place, it leads to an accumulation of dull children in the lower classes of the school. And these have a depressing effect on the other children and on the teachers, both of whom could get on more smoothly and rapidly without them. In the second place, it is partially wasteful for the backward children. For, in spite of their failure to assimilate much of the instruction, there are still many things which either do not need or will not bear repetition. The same songs, the same drawing exercises, the same stories, the same reading books, the same writing tasks are not calculated to inspire the interest which is so pre-eminently necessary in the case of dull children. Often they are distinctly good, sometimes, indeed, considerably above the average, in some parts of the curriculum.

To grind over these again must therefore be a soul -deadening task in many cases. But perhaps the most baleful effect of such a plan is the loss of self-respect which an older boy usually suffers when he finds himself condemned to take a position among other boys much younger than himself. In the treatment of backward children we need above all things to cherish self respect, to find out what a lad can do, and give him opportunities for excelling in it. In the German city of Mannheim, and in some other continental cities, special school, each consisting of a series of classes for backward children, known as the coaching or intermediate series, have been established.

In these the maximum number *of* children is thirty-five, so that greater individual attention can be given. The curriculum is practically a repetition *of* the work done in the main series from which these repeaters or the backward children have been drafted. At the end *of* the year the child may have so far improved as to be able to pass back to the main series of classes, or he may be transferred to the next higher grade of the intermediate classes. In any case he will have lost a year, so that supposing his progress continues to be normal, at the time he reaches the age of fourteen he will only be in grade 7 of the intermediate series. Hence there are only seven grades in the latter series. About 10 per cent. Of the children belong to the Forderklassen. This Mannheim system, though it appears to be doing good work, has serious disadvantages.

If ill-health or irregularity has been the reason for degrading a pupil, he usually makes up leeway and is restored to the main system. But a really backward child tends to remain in the intermediate series. There seems, however, to be little adaptation of the curriculum to the special needs of such children. We shall see, for instance, that a large amount of manual work is good for these children. Another strong objection to this type of school is that the backward children are segregated in institutions whose general character is well known, and which are often called by such names as Fool Schools, Silly Schools, or some such offensive title. But as we have already noted, it is most important with backward children to preserve self respect. Further, a child who has remained through the whole course *of* such a school acquires habits *of* reacting to companions of the same type only as himself. When, therefore, he goes forth into the world, he finds himself at a loss, and largely unable to meet the demands *of* ordinary community life.

It must be remembered that a child often learns as much from his fellows as from his teacher. And while little if any intellectual harm is done to the normal children by allowing the few backward ones to mix in their games and other receptive occupations, a great deal of good accrues to the latter by virtue of such opportunities. In America, therefore, a different system has been adopted. Instead of having a separate school to supply a large district, what is called an Un-graded Class is formed within some ordinary school in every small district in which it is required.

No attempt is made to permanently segregate the amounts in special schools, and in every way possible competition with normal children during recesses, in games, etc., is encouraged, in order that the amount may in a measure mature in the midst of the community in which he must later live. Perhaps the most important difference between the American system and the German is that in the former the attempt is not made to feed the backward children on the same intellectual peplums as is found suitable for the normal children. The backward child is usually inferior to the normal child is sensory discrimination, and responds much more feebly to the stimuli of the outer world.

In other words, his perception are much more imperfect; and since perception is the foundation of all further intellectual progress, everything possible must be done to improve its efficiency. In this case the teacher must first awaken the sensory mechanisms, or teach the child to feel, taste, smell, hear, and see. For this purpose the teachers of the Un-graded Classes use the kindergarten methods of sense training, but use them to a degree which would be overuse for a normal child.

Above all, the self-activity of the child must be aroused, and this is done by finding out the things which he is interested in doing, and selecting from among those things which can be made educationally profitable. This is precisely what Madame Montessori did in Rome in the case of the feeble-minded, with whom she was so successful that they were able to equal the normal children in tests of intelligence. And though her system may have to be considerably modified when applied, as she is applying it, to normal children, there is little doubt that some of its essentials infused into our ordinary curriculum would do a large amount of good.

It, then, this system as a whole is excellent for the feeble-minded, and to a certain extent necessary for the normal children, it follows that a large portion of its principles, if hot of its details of method, should be adopted with those who are neither intelligent enough to be called normal nor stupid enough to be classed as feeble-minded. It is obvious that this fitting of the work to the needs of the individual child cannot be done with large classes. Accordingly, the size of each Un-graded Class in America is limited to fifteen in average attendance. As in Germany, the Un-graded Classes are considered as special coaching classes, and some of the children are returned or promoted to the ordinary grades. To sum up, the activities of the children are co-ordinated and developed:

(i) by games and exercises to music;

(ii) by simple folk dances and gymnastic drills; and

(iii) by manual work, with a large share of emphasis placed upon the particular form of annual training for which each child shows an aptitude or preference.

Similar classes have been formed in some English schools. Thus in 1909 a class known as a practical class was formed in Brighton under the superintendence of Dr. Duncan Forbes at Richmond Street school. Some of the remarks made upon it are extremely interesting, as they emphasise still more strongly what should be the general nature of the work and organisation. The following extracts are taken from Dr. Forbes report upon the class. This aim of Mr. Mulrenan, the headmaster, is to make the curriculum fit each boy. Unfortunately, although classed together, the individual boys differ widely from each other in capacity in anyone subject, so that much individual attention is required. The class joins with the others at prayers, opinion and closing of school sessions, scripture and play.

They interchange rooms with other classes for reading, writing, and drawing, etc., at those times their classroom is available for the teaching of manual work to classes from the school proper. This makes the carrying out of this work economical. Method of teaching - This has been elaborated by Mr. Mulrenan, the headmaster, to whom the success of the class is almost entirely due. All things are taught in a practical manner. For instance, when the class started, only two boys could read the time from a clock. The boys we set to make dials, to put on figures and hands, and now each boy in the class with one exception can tell the time. Similarly, with weights and measures, the boys actually measure objects, they weight out quantities, they make out headed bills for small amounts of well-known food stuffs, and handle the money supposed to be paid.

When history is taught, they make models of the various things mentioned. Work of the same kind, though on a somewhat higher plane, was provided for the backward boys of the Manchester Grammar School By R. J. L. Paton, the High Master. Thus he tells us: They rise very readily to the idea of making the properties for the school play-the throne, settee, balcony, the spears, and shields, and so forth-and we get here a beautiful correlation between art and handicraft. They will rise to making their rarely physics apparatus. They will do their levers and pulleys and their wheel and axle and work them out in a practical was, just as they will work out their kite of Pythagoras in work for the mathematical master. In short, these backward children are catered for by providing for them much more of that handwork which has already been found essential for normal children.

This additional handwork involves and neglect of some parts of the usual subjects taught. And the parts neglected and the more abstract ones, such as the more complex operations in arithmetic, grammar, the theory of music, and so forth. But the additional handwork provided must be such as interests each individual. Further, it must not be a mere isolated occupation, but a real part of the boy's curriculum, more or less connected with the other lessons, and involving definite intellectual progress. Unless the workshop becomes the laboratory for the class-room, it simply remains a joiner's shop, and has no more education in it than a joiner's shop. Such are the best things that have up to the present been done for backward children. But these classes cannot be formed in all schools.

For instance, small schools in outlying districts would not have sufficient backward children to warrant the formation of a class. What then is to be done? The answer is simple. We must try to do as much as possible of the same kind of thing for the backward children within each class. We must allow these children to drop out of certain subjects in which they cannot keep pace with the rest, and to do further handwork on lines which interest them. In this way, they will recover their self-respect; they will find that there is something that they can do well; and they will become happy and tractable members of the school community. Further, the pleasure which they derive from their successful activity will stimulate them to heightened activity.

It has been found that backward children show a great improvement in energy and brightness when put on to manual work of a kind which appeals to them. And when they are engrossed in this work, the teacher will have little trouble with them; he will thus be able to devote most of his time of the more numerous normal children. While we find mentally deficient and backward children at the lower end of the scale of intelligence, we are compensated at the upper end by precocious children and geniuses. True geniuses are so rare that we need not concern ourselves with the problem of making special arrangements for them. But the number of supernormal children is comparatively great.

Little, however, has been done up to the present in the way of giving special attention to their education. At the outset, it is necessary to distinguish two broad classes of supernormal. We have those who display remarkable ability in only one branch, e.g. in music, in art, in mathematics, or in literature. Extreme cases of these are often spoken of as infant prodigies. But we have also those who, without displaying transcendent ability in anyone subject, are very intelligent indeed in almost all branches. These, if their early promise is fulfilled by continued development, will, under favourable conditions, become the really great intellects. Infant prodigies are often merely cases of very rapid development which comes to maturity early and hence produces no very remarkable result.

But, even when a better fate might await them, they are often spoilt by being dragged before the public eye, by the pampering and one-sided development which they obtain, and by the injury to body and mind which is a necessary consequence of the artificial life they are constrained to follow. Some of those who are highly gifted in one special branch are fortunate enough to have parents or patrons who take them in hand and wisely arrange a special course of education in which their whole nature is developed as harmoniously as possible, while their special gift is at the same time cultivated by the instruction and guidance of expert teachers. But this is at present largely a matter of chance.

For one individual who attains distinction and who benefits the community by his talent in this way, there may be, among the millions of children in our primary schools, some hundreds whose talent is never appreciated, and who are forced into the same routine as that of the normal children. A single illustration of this fact: A few years ago a prominent educator in Munich, Kerschensteiner, undertook his well known experiments upon some 50,000 children of pupils had to make free-hand drawings of specified objects, both from memory and from nature. Among the drawings were found some of remarkable artistic merit, and these were found by Kerschensteiner to be, almost all, the work of children of very poor patents.

Moreover, in most cases, this exceptional talent in drawing had not been properly appraised by the school, and in some cases it had not even been noticed at all. Kerschensteiner saw to it that these children were assigned to art schools or to arts and crafts schools, where they found an opportunity to develop and realise their special gifts. But what would have become of these children had not Kerschensteiner chanced to make his experiment? And how much similar talent may smoulder unrecognised in other places where no one thinks of making such tests? And should we not expect similar discoveries of talent to result in any other place where like tests were made? What Kerschensteiner did for these children of Munich should be done for the specifically endowed of all other cities.

Where, however, they are sent to special schools care should be taken that their general development is not sacrificed. Thus is a special school of art for such children, arrangements should be made for some instructions in literature, in science, in geography, in history, and in arithmetic. But it may not be necessary in many cases to segregate such children completely from their fellows. May be possible to arrange special talent classes, which the pupils attend for advanced instruction in the particular subject, while for the remainder for their education they work with the normal children. It is hardly necessary to add that the same arrangements could be made, mutatis mutandis, in the case of other talents beside the one mentioned, e.g. for pupils of exceptional ability in music, in language, in mathematics. While awaiting such developments of education, it is every teacher's duty to be on the alert for exceptional ability in his pupils in any of the branches of the curriculum.

And when he has found it, he should do all in his power to foster it. In the lessons on the subject in question, the pupil might be allowed special opportunities of developing his talent. This will be within somewhat narrow limits while he remains in the same class with the normal. In some subjects a brilliant boy can be allowed to assist in the teaching rather than act as a pupil. Thus a boy who is a fine musician might accompany the songs on the piano or violin, and even conduct the class from time to time; if his ability runs in the direction of singing, he might also sing many solos, and very often he could be called upon to give the class a model for the rendering of a difficult passage.

In drawing, somewhat similar use could be made of the talented boy. So, also in other forms of manual work. And even in arithmetic, a good deal could be done in the way of getting the smart boys to supervise and assist the duller boys. But it is important that any arrangements of this kind should not develop into a systematic attempt merely to exploit the talent of such boys. The first thought in the teacher's mind should be the progress of the boy, not the use to be made of him. In schools where the time-table for the subject in question in synchronous, it would be possible to place the brilliant boy of a lower class into an upper one for this part of his instructions.

Where, however, this is not possible, or where the boy has outstripped even the oldest of the normal boys, he might be allowed to work on by himself. And if one of the staff is specially qualified in the subject, that teacher might be asked to give him some assistance. The great differences which are being noticed as the result of more careful observation, even among what are called normal boys, are leading some educationists to advocate far more attention to individuals and far less collective work, in which all go at much the same pace, than has been the case in most modern schools during recent years. Although it is impossible for the teacher to carry this change very far with his numerous pupils of the normal type, he should nevertheless regard it as an essential part of his duty to devote as much of his time as possible to the encouragement and development of special talent in particular branches.

We come lastly to the case of those boys who are distinctly above the average in almost all of the work. Until quite recently, with promotions occurring no more frequently than the end of each school year, no special arrangements were made of these boys. To a large extent they marked time. The work of the normal boys presented no difficulties to them. There was little to grip their attention. Bored to death, they were frequently a nuisance to the teacher instead of a source of satisfaction. Here, then, was the most valuable product of human progress wasting and spoiling for lack of proper instruction. With the terminal and half-yearly promotions of recent times, these boys can pass up more quickly into a more profitable intellectual environment.

And the system of scholarships by which they can rise rapidly from the elementary schools to the secondary school forms an incentive as well as a means for higher endeavour. But this system has its disadvantages. Although these specially gifted boys are promoted frequently, they work during the intervals between their promotions with normal boys. And although they could easily go much faster. Further, it is to be borne in mind that, although a boy of great gifts may be more than the intellectual equal of normal boys who are much older than himself, he is not their equal in other matters. He is, of necessity, smaller than they. And there is a certain general ascendency, largely dependent on age and size, which contributes to place such a gifted boy at an obvious disadvantage. Intellectually he is superior.

But socially he has to take a position of inferiority. And this is likely to be harmful to the development of his character in strength and independence. In has, therefore, been proposed by some educationists to establish select classes for these exceptional boys. These have been called by Dr. Stern Elite-classes, and he writes of them as follows. Into the elite-classes should be transferred only those pupils who were surely gifted with superior general intelligence; moreover, the super-normality, to justify enrolment, must be of an extraordinarily high degree, so that these classes should represent the strictest selection. These classes would not, of course, be very numerous and they would not be formed for very young children, since it would take some years for a child to show sufficient superiority to warrant selection.

One writer, for instance, proposes that in the secondary schools of Berlin not more than 20 of the most gifted pupils of the Quinta should be selected each year, these being formed into an elite-class which would continue the work more rapidly and more thoroughly than is possible in the ordinary secondary school. From the elementary schools, however, a larger number of pupils could be selected. For among so great a body of children, many more especially gifted ones would be discovered. Precautions would have to be taken against the development of intellectual arrogance among such children.

The classes would not be publicly called elite-classes, and strength of character. Much attention would be necessary to the health of such children. In particular it would be important to guard against the dangers of over-working. The method of selection for these classes would require vary careful attention. Examinations which test mere knowledge would not be sufficient. Mental tests would have to be elaborated. Such tests have already been devised by the French psychologist Binet, and improved upon by others. They have been tried upon a considerable number of children of different ages. But they are by no means completely satisfactory at present. With further progress in this matter.

Particularly in the direction of framing tests to distinguish the specially gifted, it should soon be possible to make reliable selections of supernormal children. If suitable teacher are found for such classes and schools, and if they are not made too large, their achievements may be quite extraordinary. By following a very different pace from the ordinary classes, by broadening and deepening the culture material, by minimizing drill and mechanical aids to memorization, by cultivating especially the habit of independent mental review and assimilation of the subject matter and by free election within the subjects of instruction, the superior capacities of these pupils would be given the possibility of development for which their birth had fitted them; moreover, by reason of the quite unusual demands made upon them, self-discipline and the spirit of conscientiousness would also be developed in a manner totally impossible for such pupils in the ordinary school.

And there would be developed for society a class of leaders equipped with really deeper and broader training. Thus would Plato's dream of a class of perfect guardians be realised. The golden minds would be distinguished from those of copper and iron, and would receive all the refinement of which they are capable. No longer would a child destiny be decided chiefly by the birth or position of its parents. For even the rulers themselves would have to obey this law-viz. That if a child be born in their class of copper or iron, they are to have no manner of pity upon it, but giving it the value that belongs to its nature, they are to thrust it away into the class of artisans or agriculturists. This may to some appear inhuman.

But in reality it is the greatest kindness. For what can a parent do better of this son than to see that he has the education most suitable for him, and then that he enters the trade or profession in which he can do the best work? The greatest follow which parents can commit is to force their children into callings for which they have no aptitude. It is a step that can seldom be retraced with safety or advantage.

12

Physiological Considerations

Physical activity is an important consideration during the growing years if normal growth and development of children are to be maintained and encouraged. This fact has long been recognized. In recent years a new phenomenon has emerged in many countries. With the national and international prestige presently attached to athletic success, we are seeing more and more training and sport programs being developed for progressively younger children. Some of these programs are of extreme intensity and duration. Indeed, some young children today are involved in training programs that are more intensive than would have been believed possible even for adults 25 years ago. Do these programs have an effect on the dynamics of human growth?

When are children ready for the rigours of intense sport training and competition? Are there critical times during which a training stimulus may be more important in terms of functional capacity? These and many more questions are waiting for answers. But answers are not easy to come by for a variety of reasons, including the difficulty in isolating the training stimulus from the multiplicity of other factors that affect the growing organism. There are, however, certain things we do know about the affects of sport training on physiological function in growing children. This research paper will touch on some of these.

Children Are Not Miniature Adults

The ability to sustain physical performance while competing in or training for a sport activity depends to a large degree on the ability *of* the organism to transfer oxygen from the atmosphere to the working tissues. Maximal aerobic power represents the greatest volume *of* oxygen that can be utilized per unit of time under conditions of maximal exertion. To this end, maximal aerobic power is considered to be the best measure of cardio respiratory efficiency because it dependent on the interrelationships of all the body systems concerned with oxygen transport and is independent of motivation. Compared to adults, values for relative maximal aerobic power are high in children.

However, if one looks at metabolic reserve - that is, the difference between maximal oxygen uptake and oxygen uptake needed for a given task - children are shown to be at a disadvantage. The higher oxygen cost in young children in performing a given task is probably the result *of* mechanical inefficiency. The relative oxygen cost of walking or running is higher among children. MacDougall and others found that an 8-year-old child running at a pace *of* 180 meters per minute is operating at 90% *of* maximal aerobic power, while a 16-year-old running at the same speed is operating at only 75% *of* maximum.

Thus, in comparison to an adult, the child is not as aerobically efficient as might be expected from looking at the high relative maximal aerobic power values. Curiously, in spite *of* the above consideration, children grade physical effort lower than adolescents and adolescents perceive the same effort as being less strenuous than adults, do. Bar-Or conducted a study on over 1,000 male subjects, ranging in age from 7 to 68 years, who performed an identical cycle ergometry test. The younger the individual, the lower the subjective perceived effort, although the relative intensity of effort demonstrated by heart and circulatory reactions was equally great.

These data suggest that a given physiological strain is perceived to be less stressful by children than by older individuals, which raises a disturbing question: Is it possible that young children under external pressure may be pushed too far? There are also differences between children and adults with respect to the anaerobic energy system. This system can be employed by the working muscles in the absence of oxygen. Work that results form anaerobic reactions can only be sustained for short periods of time, in contrast to aerobic work, which can be carried on for many minutes, even hours. Accumulating evidence supports the contention that the ability to derive energy from the anaerobic lactate pathway is not as developed in the pre-adolescent child as it is in the adult. A detailed discussion of child-adult differences with respect to the individual components of the aerobic and anaerobic systems has been provided elsewhere.

It is sufficient here to refer to a statement by Astrand and Rodahl: It may be concluded that children are physically handicapped compared with adults. When related to the child's dimensions, its muscular strength is low and so are its maximal oxygen uptake and other parameters of importance for the oxygen transport. Furthermore, the mechanical efficiency of children is often inferior to that of adults.

Overview

Form a physiological point of view, concern has been voiced from some quarters that the stresses imposed by certain competitive sport-training regimes, particularly those of an endurance nature, may make excessive demands on the cardiovascular systems of children or early adolescents. In healthy children there is little evidence to substantiate this concern. Under certain circumstances heavy exercise can have deleterious effects on a child's health, but these can usually be categorized into sport injuries or overuse syndromes, conditions.

It is true that there have been cases of sudden death or cardiac arrest in young athletes during or immediately following games or practices, but, invariably, underlying pathology has been identified as the cause of death. Even in young cardiac patients sudden death during exertion is not as high as might be expected. Lambert, Menon, Wagner, and Vlad examined pooled data from nine countries on cardiac deaths in girls under age 21. Only 10% died while engaged in sport, 32% while playing, and 58% during sleep or at rest. The investigators concluded that catastrophe was not prevented by the avoidance of physical exertion in young cardiac patients. For this age group at least, Jokl's contention that exercise never caused death in a normal heart is probably correct. Similarly, there is little reason to believe that the physical demands of sport have any deleterious effect on growth and development of physiological function in the young athlete. Numerous studies have verified that in the absence of injury or disease, the dynamics of growth do not seem to be adversely affected by athletic participation.

A comprehensive review of the growth and maturity characteristics of young athletes is beyond the scope of this research paper. In general, it can be said that young athletes of both sexes grow as well as non-athletes. The experience of athletic training and competition does not harm the growth and development of the youngster. There is one area of concern that is currently receiving considerable attention: the skeletal integrity in extremely active young women experiencing menstrual dysfunction. Chronic exercise can result in delayed menarche and amenorrhoea in some young women. The situation has led to a concern that bone loss, secondary to an oestrogen deficit, is a potential cause of stress fractures in the short term and osteoporosis in later years.

The topic of exercise induced amenorrhoea and bone density will be discussed later in this research paper. For the present, it can be said that healthy children have few adverse physiological responses to exercise; on those rare occasions when they do occur they are usually reversible and can be minimized with proper precautions. The body of a youngster is a wonderful machine with sophisticated built-in controls and instinctive limit-defining sensors. In the absence of externally created pressure or stress, a young body functions very effectively.

Menstrual Dysfunction and Skeletal Integrity

Disturbances of the menstrual cycle have long been associated with high levels of physical activity, both in growing girls and mature women. Until recently, these disturbances have generally been regarded as benign because the dysfunction is readily reversible with a reduction in training intensity. However, it is now clear that athletic amenorrhoea is associated with a significantly reduced trabecular bone density, thus increasing the probability of stress fractures in the short term and osteoporotic fractures in the long term. This problem is of direct relevance to those concerned with growing girls because the incidence of athletic amenorrhoea is closely linked to activity patterns during growth. In particular, the factors predisposing to athletic amenorrhoea are

(a) Delayed menarche,

(b) Onset of training close to menarche,

(c) Menstrual dysfunction before training,

(d) High training intensity, and

(e) Low body weight and fat.

The high incidence of eating disorders in teenage girls further aggravates the problem, as very low caloric intakes, even without athletic activity, can induce amenorrhoea, leading to the general hypothesis that amenorrhoea is a "functional adaptation to a negative energy balance, whether it is induced by low energy intake along or increased energy expenditure together with low energy intake". It is likely that, as in postmenopausal women, most of the bone loss resulting from oestrogen deprivation occurs in the 5 to 10 years immediately following loss of menses. If this is so, athletic amenorrhoea in teenage girls should be viewed with serious concern for three reasons.

It may reduce the peak bone mass attained in early adulthood and therefore lower the age at which the osteoporotic fracture threshold is reached. It significantly increases the incidence of stress fractures. And, perhaps most important of all, it may affect skeletal development in a qualitative fashion. This hitherto unexamined possibility should be given high priority by researchers. With continuing amenorrhoea, bone loss is difficult to reverse. Despite claims to the contrary, calcium supplementation has not proved effective in middle-aged women and has not been tested in young women. Fortunately, those girls at risk can be readily identified by their late menarche, high training intensity, and low body fat level.

Adaptation of Children to Sport Training

Sport competition and training subjects the developing organism to a variety of stresses that may give rise to any number of significant responses. Whether adapting to repeated training sessions or to a single game situation, the growing child undergoes changes. The magnitude of these changes varies with the timing, duration, and intensity of the training stimulus. It should be noted that the physical exertion associated with sport training is only one of many factors that may affect the growing child. Thus, our knowledge of children's adaptation to exercise is difficult to define and not completely understood. Not withstanding, when the literature is critically analyzed, some facts are apparent. It is clear that regular sport training has no apparent effect on stature in growing youngsters. Also, skeletal maturity as assessed in growth studies does not appear to be influenced by physical training in young adolescent boys and girls.

The regulation and maintenance of body weight, however, are affected by regular physical activity. Youngsters regularly engaged in sport programs, be they formal in nature or recreational, and have proportionally more lean body mass and less fat than those who are not regularly involved. One question remains open: Do these training associated changes in body composition persist into adult years?

In studying the physiological response of the oxygen transport system to sport training, another dimension is added beyond simple quantitative change. Qualitative changes may occur in children during growth and/or training with or without quantitative alteration. Qualitative changes at the cellular level are not easily observed or measured; therefore major gaps exist in our understanding of the processes involved in the physiological response to exercise. The traditional approach to studying the influence of sport training and physical activity on functional growth of the oxygen transport system has been to compare athletes with non-athletes or trained subjects with untrained subjects. Most of these studies have been of short duration involving pre-test and post-test measurement and many have failed to control for maturational differences.

Taking into consideration all the constraints and limitations inherent in studying training-mediated responses in growing children, what conclusions can be drawn? A consistent finding is that sport training has a small or limited effect on maximal aerobic power prior to adolescence. The preponderance of evidence suggests that the trainability of aerobic power in young pre-adolescent is lower than expected in spite of improved athletic performance. Because most sporting take at this age are performed at less than maximal work rates, it has been suggested that the use of maximal aerobic power as a measure for evaluating the efficiency of the oxygen transport system in prepubescent children may be misleading.

Sport training or a high level of physical activity has been shown to lead to improvements in sub maximal efficiency that is independent of changes at maximal effort. In adolescence, the effect of sport training on aerobic power is less clear, and it is difficult to draw any firm conclusions. Some studies report expected improvements following training during the adolescent years and other studies do not. It has been suggested that the effectiveness of aerobic training may be greatest at or around the time of peak height velocity in boys.

Biologically, this would seem reasonable in view of the marked changes taking place in endocrine function during this state of development, but further investigations are needed to confirm this hypothesis. What happens when training ceases in growing children? Here again there are no clear answers, although it appears that, as in adults, adaptations to short-term training are not permanent.

Similarly, the aerobic response to long-term training in children appears to be lost in adult years with the cessation of training. A major consideration in studies looking at the effects of sport training in children is the role of heredity. Early data from twin studies suggested that the principal determinant of variability in maximal aerobic power among individuals who lived under similar environmental conditions was genetic.

However, recent studies are more cautious in the interpretation of the environment-heredity interaction. Details of the genetics of aerobic power and adaptations to work have been provided elsewhere. Why it is our understanding of the growing child's response to sport training is still as fragmentary in spite of the surge of interest in the child as a sportsperson? The gaps in our understanding are primarily attributable to an inherent methodological constraint that has been and continues to be a major challenge for investigators working in this area.

Is Earlier Better?

On the theory that is some training is good, vast amounts must be better, we are seeing youngsters at increasingly earlier ages being subjected to intensive training regimes in the hopes of developing world champions. In some countries of the world, exceptional talent is identified at an early age, and children are put through intensive programs in hopes that they will eventually arrive at the top. We are not told what happens to the youngsters who do not make it. The theory that the younger we start a child, the better the chances of his or her becoming an adult champion deserves close scrutiny.

Some studies have suggested that early success offers no promise of the same later on. Clarke found that outstanding elementary school athletes may not be outstanding in junior or senior high school and vice versa.

Could it be that intensive participation and competition in the under-11 age group is not the great spawning ground it is purported to be? True, there are examples of child athletes who later set world records, but the examples are not nearly as numerous as we have been led to believe.

Many world-class runners, for instance, were not outstanding internationally as juniors-names like Double, Wottle, Viren come to mind. Before discovering the gift of running, Keino, Temu, and Gammoudi primarily played soccer until their late teens. It is abundantly clear that future champions and world record holders do not have to be outstanding childhood athletes. In fact, it can be argued that success too early makes future success more doubtful. As in human endeavour, there are exceptions to this observation, but the exceptions are rare enough not to discredit the hypothesis. Sweeney documents the case of a New Jersey junior high school track team called the "4:47 team"- team with seven boys who ran the mile in under 5 minutes, with an average time of 4:47. Surely, here was a team that would create a dynasty in their new high school.

Three years later only one member of the 4:47 team was still participating for that school. In the ninth grade he had run 4:27. 7 and as a high school senior his best time was still only 4:23. What happened? The reasons run the gamut from too much early success to not enough later on, or from an overlay active, highly concerned coach to a rather remote one. The point to be made is that all that can safely be said about fast young runners is that they are fast young runners. Early success has only a distant relationship to future stardom. Dr. Gabe Mirkin, medical editor for Runner's World magazine and co-author of The Complete Sports medicine Book for Women has documented the case of his young running son.

As a 9-year-old, the body ran the mile in under 5 minutes. He held 12 age-class world records before he was 10. He is now 25 and has not run since he was 10 years old. Mirkin's observations as a sports medicine physician and as a former advocate of running training at an early age are pertinent to this discussions: Kids burn out. They don't get injured. Of the hundreds of kind who came through, I didn't see a single long term injury. Some of these kids were running 70 or 80 miles a week, hard. You'd see a few injuries then-but, boy, and drop-out rate was frightening. Too much too soon. Swimming is often cited as an example of what can be accomplished if training is started at an early age.

Shane Gould of Australia, for example, was only 15 when she held every world freestyle record form 100 to 1500 meters, an unparalleled achievement. But swimmers not only start early, they also tend to quit early as young as 18 or 19 in the case of top women performers. The assistant United States swimming coach at the Montreal Olympics is quoted as saying. "In some ways, the age-group program is backfiring. Sure it gets young kinds into swimming, but it also burns them out before they're even close to their potential peak." It is certainly reasonable to hypothesize that more success would be achieved if the people involved in the sport stayed with it longer. Even granting the opposite point of view-that is, to get a world beater of tomorrow we must train and crown young champions at an early age-and further assuming that it is possible to identify and select potential champions at an early age, the primary mandate of people working in children' sport programs should still be to respond to the longer-term activity needs of all children.

If athletic potential can be identified at an early age, it is logical to assume that a lack of potential should be just as easy to identify. If this is the case, should we not devote more time to the unskilled youngsters who have no motivation or encouragement toward physical activity? Perhaps what is needed in programs for the very young is to pay less attention to the selection of athletes and provide more encouragement to all youngsters to take an active interest in sports, games, and activities.

If this occurs, every child has a change to realize his or her potential, and the talent pool will be enlarged. In North America a significant number of children who are late maturing and following a slower-than-average developmental timetable are denied a chance to even try to participate in sport because most competitions for youngsters and adolescents are based on chronological age. Because size is an important determinant in many activities, youngsters who are small for their age are often discriminated against or discouraged, though they may have potential and may eventually be of average or even above-average adult size.

Thermo-regulation in Children

Not all sporting events or training sessions are held under ideal climatic conditions. In many regions of the world, climate can play a crucial role in terms of an individual's ability to perform. Climate is an especially important consideration in regard to sport programs for children where many activities are performed outside in sometimes quite hostile weather. In general, it can be said that children are not as efficient as adults in terms of temperature regulation, especially under conditions of extreme heat or cold. A child has a smaller absolute surface area than an adult.

However when surface area is expressed per unit of body mass, the situation is reversed. Because heat loss is related to surface area and heat production to body mass, children should, theoretically, be at a disadvantage in a cold climate and favoured in a warm one. However, there are other considerations that place children at a disadvantage in a hot climate as well, in spite of their relatively large surface area. Children have a lower sweating rate than adults; consequently, their evaporative capacity is deficient.

The effect of deficient evaporative capacity is to raise skin temperature and create a less favourable temperature gradient between the body core and the periphery, which, in turn, inhabits heat transfer by convention. The lower sweating rate in children is apparent both in absolute terms and when normalized per unit of body surface area, and results from a lower output per sweat gland rather than a reduce number of glands. Sweat excretion per gland is 2.5 times greater in the adult compared to the child.

In summary, although low sweat production conserves water in the exercising child, it inhibits heat transfer in a hot climate. Another age-related difference in adaptation to exercise in heat is the rate of acclimatization. The process of adaptation to heat takes considerably longer in children than in adults. Further, children do not instinctively drink enough fluids to replenish fluid loss. Bar-Or reports that children exercising in dry heat will voluntarily become dehydrated even if allowed to drink and libitum.

Summary

Only selected aspects of the physiological response of the child to the rigours imposed by sport training and competition have been considered in this research paper. Other areas of research are undoubtedly relevant and important. For instance, there is a need for a more detailed examination of hormonal responses to sport training, especially as they relate to bone mineral content in young female endurance athletes. Further studies are obviously necessary as there are still many gaps in our knowledge of the underlying biological processes involved in the response of the growing child to sport participation.

Form a physiological perspective, the following quotation, drawn from a position statement on children in competitive sports prepared by the Canadian Association of Sports Sciences, summarizes material presented in this research paper and represents an appropriate guideline for adults involved in sport programming for children. Form a physiological and medical point of view, it should be recognized that each child is different in his/her response and tolerance to exercise due to a great range of variability in growth rates, anthropometric indices, gender and state of health, even in children of a similar chronological age. Younger prepubertal children should be encouraged to participate in a wide variety of motor skills, whereas older post-pubertal children can become more specialized in their training and sport participation.

A child's performance and adaptation to training should not be directly compared to an adult's as significant differences exist, especially during the years of accelerated growth. Environmental exercise tolerance is also more limited in children than adults. Are young children ready for sport? Perhaps the question should be rephrased. Are adults represented by parents, coaches, teachers, and spectators, ready to be involved in children's sport? While sport participation can be healthy for children, it is unfortunately not always the case.

Adult involved in sport situations for children, be they local recreational leagues or elite championship venues, have a responsibility to ensure that a child's happy participation is not jeopardized by unrealistic adult expectations. It is imperative that adults make the distinction between encouraging children to gain satisfaction from doing their best, and pushing children beyond their capabilities and levels of interest.

13

NUTRITIONAL VALUES

Adequate nutrition is a vital health factor, important to nations as well as to individuals. With it, health, vitality, working efficiency, contentment, and the enjoyment of life are increased. Thus the diet of nations has personal, economic, political, and international significance. From the day of your birth your body can get only from food the substances which it need for

- Heat and energy,
- Growth and repair, and
- Regulatory control.

Green plants can live upon water and minerals salts from the soil, plus oxygen, carbon dioxide, and nitrogen from the air. Man cannot. Plant chlorophyll can use the sun's energy to build simple elements and compounds into highly complex plant substances. Man must get such substances from food, taking them either from plants directly or from animals which have fed upon plants. The living tissues of the body consist of millions of microscopic cells, each of which is a chemical mechanism.

Each cell must get, indirectly from the food we eat, those substances which it needs for fuel, growth, maintenance, and special functions, such for example, as the contraction of muscle cells, the transmission of impulses within nerve cells, or the manufacture of chemical products by gland cells. Nutrition is the sum of the processes by which the body takes in and utilizes food.

It is the story of food and what happens to it in the body. It includes diet, digestion, and metabolism. We choose our diet. Digestion takes apart the food and converts it into simple substances which can be used by the body in metabolism. Metabolism includes all the chemical and physical changes which take place in the body tissues. This are, in general, of two kinds:

- The building and maintenance of body structures, and
- The destruction and oxidation of the constituents of protoplasm with the production of energy and simpler products.

The chemical elements of which the body is made include oxygen 65 per cent, carbon 18 per cent, hydrogen 10 percent, nitrogen 3 per cent, calcium 2 per cent, phosphorus 1 percent, and smaller amounts of sodium, chlorine, magnesium, potassium, sulphur, iron, and copper, with still smaller amounts of manganese, iodine, fluorine, cobalt, and zinc. All these elements come to the body from food, in suitable chemical form for digestion and subsequent use. Let us see what substances the body needs. Then, with the needs in mind, we can better consider the planning of an adequate diet.

The Body's Need for Water

The body's need for water is more urgent than that for anything else except oxygen. Man can live a month or more without food, but only a few days without water. Living cells require water for both structural existence and the carrying out of their functions. Water makes up about two-thirds of the body weight, and three-fourths of the weight of active tissues such as muscle. It is the basis of the body's liquid carrier system which carries food and oxygen to the tissues and waste products away from them. It is important in every healing process. It regulates body temperature. The chemical changes which take place in the body are carried out by dissolved substances. Kidney function may be impaired if the liquid intake is sharply curtailed. Water is so essential that a loss of 10 per cent of the body's water produces serious disorder and a loss of 20 per cent results in death.

Such dehydration takes place when water or other liquid is not available. There may also be excessive loss of water through sweat, or through prolonged vomiting or diarrhoea. Excessive sweating will cause loss of salt as well as loss of water, with the development of weakness and "heat cramps," often accompanied by nausea and dizziness. The frequent taking of small quantities of water containing a level teaspoonful of table salt to a quart of water is commonly recommended for preventing or correcting this condition. A less serious amount of dehydration may take place gradually.

A deficiency of water in the diet is a common and rather serious fault. The body then functions less well. Increased water intake is commonly recommended for the person who has a cold on the theory that it assists in the more rapid elimination of the injurious substances produced by the cold germ.

Classes of Food

You have long known the important types of food substances; namely, proteins, carbohydrates, fats, vitamins, and inorganic salts or minerals. An interesting approach to the food needs of the body is to consider the substances which, along with water, pass through the walls of the digestive tract. They are

(i) Products of protein digestion,

(ii) Simple sugars,

(iii) Products of fat digestion,

(iv) Minerals, and

(v) Vitamins.

Until the first decade of this century it was believed that

water, proteins, fats, carbohydrates, and minerals would meet all the needs of the body. At that time Frederick Gowland Hopkins, of Cambridge University, England, carried out some animal feeding experiments which showed that other substances are essential to life and health, although they are needed in very small amounts. His laboratory animals ceased to grow and thrive upon mixtures of purified proteins, fats, carbohydrates, and minerals; but they did thrive when a very small amount of milk or the alcohol extract of certain vegetables was added to the diet.

From these studies a host of investigations led to the discovery of the vitamins and demonstrated their essential functions in the body. Animal experimentation has contributed materially to our understanding of human nutrition. However, as different species vary in their nutritional requirements, great care must be used in applying the results of animal experimentation directly to human beings without adequate investigation. The absence of a vitamin from the diet may produce a definite deficiency disease, perhaps death.

Its presence in the diet in insufficient quantity may produce a lowered state of health. We must, therefore, study these substances carefully. We must also recognize the difference between buoyant health with optimal nutrition and merely passable health with only adequate nutrition.

Carbohydrate Requirements

The simple sugars which the body secures from the digestive tract are the products of carbohydrate digestion. They are excellent fuel or energy-producing foods because, when they are oxidized or burned in the body, they are completely broken down into carbon dioxide and water, both of which are easily eliminated waste products. These simple sugars and all other carbohydrates are composed of carbon, hydrogen, and oxygen, there always being two times as many hydrogen atoms as oxygen atoms, just as there are in water, hence the term carbohydrate or hydrated carbon. Glucose is the form of carbohydrate that is transported and used in the body, and animal starch or glycogen is the storage from.

Approximately 1 per cent of the weight of muscle is stored glycogen, available for instant use. A reserve supply is kept in the liver. The blood usually contains from 0.08 to 0.12 per cent sugar, but the body is free to draw upon its reserve when more energy is needed. The amount of sugar in the blood is thus increased when fear, anger, or other emotions press the body for vigorous action. If the blood sugar falls below normal, a condition called hypoglycemia develops with symptoms of irritability, nervousness, and weakness. The body needs a constant supply of carbohydrates for fuel.

Protein Requirements

Muscles and other soft tissues are composed mainly of proteins. The word comes from the Greek verb meaning "to take first place." These substances all contain nitrogen, carbon, hydrogen, and oxygen. Some proteins contain sulphur; some phosphorus, iron, or other mineral elements. The process of digestion changes proteins into chemically simpler fragments called amino acids. There are at least twenty-two different amino acids. Each of the innumerable proteins contains a particular combination of many amino acids in its large and complex molecule. Amino acids are sometimes called the building stones of tissue substances because they recombine inside the body to form the typical proteins of body tissue.

They are especially needed for the muscles and for the blood. They are used in the formation of haemoglobin, various enzymes, immune bodies, and hormones. Studies indicate that protein deficiency may lower resistance to infection and delay wound healing. Today we feel that at least eight amino acids must be provided· in the proteins of the diet since the body cannot synthesize them. They are called the nutritionally essential or indispensable amino acids.

If they are all present in suitable quantity the body can form the other amino acids from them. Proteins which contain all of the essential amino acids are called complete proteins. Animal proteins such as milk, cheese, meat, fish and eggs are complete proteins. Gelatin and the various cereal and vegetable proteins are incomplete. The diet usually contains many proteins so that they supplement each other. Excess protein is used as fuel. A gram of protein gives as much energy as a gram of starch. But proteins do not burn completely as starches do. The excess of nitrogen is removed through the kidneys in the form of urea.

Mineral Requirements

In considering the mineral needs of the normal adult it should be remembered that there are differences in individuals. Moreover, certain minerals are needed in extra large amounts by growing children and expectant or nursing mothers and in various disease conditions. Some of the minerals are of special nutritional importance.

If the body requirements for the above minerals are met, the other minerals which the body needs are pretty certain to be provided in sufficient quantity. Some of these other minerals also have important functions in the physiology of the body. The normal beating of the heart, with its contractions and relaxations, depends upon a balance between the salts of calcium and those of sodium and potassium. Sulphur is an important constituent of many body proteins. Cobalt, manganese, and zinc are believed to be essential but their functions in human nutrition are not well understood.

The Need for Fats and Lipids

Fats are changed to fatty acids and glycerin in the digestive tract. These simpler substances pass through the intestinal wall to be used as fuel, to be stored as body fat, or to be changed into carbohydrates and stored as glycogen. Stored fat has value in addition to its availability as fuel. It is stored just below the skin and serves as insulation against cold as well as contributing to the smoothness of the skin itself. It also helps to round off the angular contours of the body. Some of the stored fat is packed around the kidneys and gives these vital organs some protection. The fats, like the carbohydrates, contain the elements of carbon, hydrogen, and oxygen, but the proportion of oxygen is less.

Consequently, they may be regarded as fuel foods in a more concentrated form, since the same weight requires more oxygen for combustion and, therefore, is of greater heat value. Fats produce about 2¼ times as much heat as equal weights of carbohydrates and proteins. The diet contains many food fats from animal sources and from vegetable sources. Fats are carriers of fat-soluble vitamins. They are rich and postpone hunger because they stay in the stomach longer than other foods. Fat is interchangeable with carbohydrates in the diet to a large extent but not completely.

Vitamins and Health

Vitamins are vitally needed by the body although in minute quantities. Their deficiency causes grave conditions and their protective qualities are far-reaching. The amounts needed in the diet are so small that they are measured in milligrams or in agreed-upon standard International Units. Certain conditions such as pregnancy, lactation, rapid growth, and infectious fevers increase the body' need for most of the vitamins. A severe deficiency of some of the vitamins causes acute disease or death.

Limited amounts maintain a passable health, while in many cases optimal amounts have been found to contribute to vigorous health with an accompanying high morale and work output. We should be as much concerned with the common, mild, or subclinical conditions as we are with the less frequent deficiency diseases.

Vitamin A

Vitamin A is a colourless, fat-soluble substance found in animals but not in plants. The orange-yellow colouring matter of plant tissues has been found to contain precursors of vitamin A, the carotenes, which give rise to vitamin A in the body. Although it is related to the health of the mucous membranes, vitamin A is not a specific in warding off infections. Xerophthalmia is a vitamin A deficiency disease that is common in the Orient. It was widespread in Denmark in 1914 to 1918 due to the excessive exportation of butter, which was the most important source of the vitamin.

It is characterized by failure of the tear glands to function, followed in the severe cases by dryness, bacterial growth, and ulceration of the cornea. Night blindness is an affliction characterized by an inability to see in dim light, especially after the eye has just been exposed to bright light. The condition disappears shortly after vitamin A is supplied. This vitamin is necessary, for it is part of the visual purple, a compound in the retina of the eye which plays a vital part in the process of seeing. A severe deficiency of vitamin A may also produce skin changes. The body is capable of storing a supply of vitamin A for several months.

Vitamin B Complex

If we go back to 1920 we find three vitamins, A, B, and C, described in the literature, since then many other vitamin substances have been discovered, several of them related to the original concept of vitamin B. We now speak of the B group of vitamins or the vitamin B complex. These vitamins are very important to the normal functioning of body cells. The most important ones are thiamine, riboflavin, and niacin, but there are several less important ones including pyridoxine, pantothenic acid, choline, biotin, folic acids, and vitamin B12.

Thiamine

Thiamine has a wide distribution in natural foods, but it is often deficient in the diet because people eat so much artificially refined food from which this vitamin has been removed. Considerable thiamine is lost in the cooking process.

It has been called the anti-neuritic vitamin because its absence produces beri-beri in man and a similar disease in experimental animals. The disease beri-beri is found in Asia among people who make polished rice a large part of their diet. It has also been found in Newfoundland and Labrador among people who subsist largely upon white flour. Many cases and several deaths occur in the United States each year. The dry type of beri-beri is characterized by progressive emaciation; the wet type, by swelling in the limbs and trunk due to the accumulation of fluid in tissues and cavities. Infantile beri-beri occurs among nursing infants when the mother has insufficient thiamine, regardless of whether the symptoms are demonstrable in her.

It is one of the leading causes of infant mortality in oriental countries. Up to the year 1883 it was common for more than one-fourth the sailors on Japanese battleship to suffer from beri-beri. A navy physician, Dr. Takaki, suspected that the disease was of dietary origin and proved it by changing the diet on one ship. The addition of barley, vegetables, fish, meat, and canned milk to the ration, which had previously consisted largely of white rice, eliminated the disease. Takaki's work, however, did not then command as wide attention as it deserved. Medical authorities generally regarded beri-beri as an infectious disease until army medical officers in charge of the Bilibid prison in Manila in 1902 demonstrated that it could be cured by dietary means. A condition called polyneuritis has been induced experimentally by feeding birds on polished rice.

The birds showed inactivity, loss of weight, and museular contraction; but when fed with an aqueous extract of rice bran, they immediately recovered. Beri-beri in human subjects in prevented by using unpolished rice or by introducing a mixed diet.

Riboflavin

This is a greenish-yellow, water-soluble pigment, widely distributed in plant and animal tissues. It is relatively stable to heat, mineral acids, and oxidizing agents but is sensitive to alcohol and is easily decomposed by light. It is an important factor in health maintenance although symptoms of a deficiency are rather slow in developing. They include general weakness, deterioration of muscle tone, and poor condition of the eyes and skin. There may be burning, itching, and irritation of the eyes, with sensitiveness to light and visual fatigue with dimness of vision.

Soreness of the lips, tongue, and the corners of the mouth are characteristic skin symptoms. Cracking of the mouth is characteristic skin symptom. Cracking of the lips at the corners of the mouth and the growth of blood vessels in the cornea of the eye are the liaisons most commonly related to this vitamin deficiency. Niacin deficiency is apparently a cause of pellagra, although deficiency in thiamine and riboflavin further confuses the clinical picture.

This disease is usually characterized by the three D's--depression, dermatitis, and diarrhoea. Bronzing of the skin on exposed surfaces, sore mouth, and gastric disturbances are characteristic symptoms. As the disease progresses, these three conditions become increasingly serious. Pellagra occurs in many parts of the world. In the United States pellagra or the less serious subclinical stage of the disease appears where poverty or ignorance leads to the fat pork, corn bread, soda biscuit and syrup type of diet. The person with pellagra is usually a sufferer from a deficiency of riboflavin as well as of niacin.

Vitamin C

When suitable amount of ascorbic acid is absent from the diet, scurvy results. This disease has been serious and widespread at many times and places, before our newer knowledge of nutrition told us how *to* prevent and cure it. It was a scourge of the Crusaders. The explorer Vasco de Gama lost more than half of his crew from scurvy in his voyage around the Cape of Good Hope. The explorer Cartier lost one-fourth of his men from scurvy in 1535 before the natives game him a remedy in the form of decoction of evergreens twigs and needles. The Russians used pine needle infusions during the World War II. It has been shown by various studies that mild subclinical scurvy is still common, although the more severe form of the disease is now rare.

An interesting instance of such a situation occurred in a

large boys' school in England. In mid-winter the boys complained, and became irritable and listless. They exhibited a decline in athletic ability and in the quality of their work. Investigation showed that the diet was without raw fruits and vegetables, and that a nearby fruit ship, which had been generously patronized in previous years, was now closed. The condition of the boys improved immediately upon the introduction of fresh fruit into the diet. As ascorbic acid deficiency becomes more severe, lassitude, weakness, and irritability may be followed by pains in the muscles and joints, tiny haemorrhages in the skin, swelling and bleeding of the gums, rapid heartbeat, and shortness of breath; the teeth become loose and infection and ulceration of the gums may develop.

Since pasteurized milk contains little or no vitamin C, orange juice or tomato juice or some other source of ascorbic acid is now added to the bottle-fed infant's diet before he is one month old. Scorbutic babies suffer pain and tenderness in the legs. The ends *of* the bones often become enlarged as they do in rickets. There is considerable difference between individuals at any age both in their requirement of ascorbic acid in the body and in the particular symptoms of ascorbic acid deficiency which manifest themselves. The body has little ability to store ascorbic acid. It must, therefore, be supplied in the diet daily.

Vitamin D

This vitamin is not a single substance. There are several closely related compounds which have the same ability to prevent rickets. The provitamin from which they are derived belong to the group of chemical substances called sterols. Ergosterol is found in yeast and other plants, but not in animal tissues. Animal sterols can be activated to for vitamin D substances by the action of the sunlight or ultraviolet light upon the sterol in the skin. Fish liver oils furnish a particularly rich source. Proper skeletal development can take place only when the blood contains sufficient calcium and phosphorus in proper proportions, and vitamin D.

When one or more of these is lacking, rickets may develop. Vitamin D seems to be essential to aid the body in its use of the minerals in the formation of bones and teeth. It not only makes a better skeleton but also improves the rate of growth. Rickets has been known for centuries as a common disorder of early childhood in the temperate zones.

It was not until 1922 that its cause and prevention became known. In that year McCollum showed that it could be prevented by the addition of certain oils to the diet. The disease develops more rapidly during the winter months because the child is less exposed to sunlight and because the vitamin in the dietary is low. It usually appears during the early months of life, developing especially in the premature, the artificially fed, and even the rapidly growing breast-fed baby whose mother's diet is inadequate in vitamin D.

He becomes restless, wakeful, constipated, and sweats profusely, especially on the head. In severe cases the head enlarges and becomes misshapen. Knobs or beads so-called rachitic rose appear at the junction of ribs and costal cartilages. Similar knobbing occurs at the ends of the long bones, producing enlarged wrists, ankles, and knees. The long bones of the legs may not be equal to the task of supporting the weight of the baby; they may curve, giving the child bow legs and knock knees. The thorax may seem flattened on the sides, and the sternum depressed or protruding, forming the typical pigeon breast. Muscles and ligaments seem too lax to hold the body together.

The child sags, grows pot-bellied, hollow-chested, and round-shouldered; the result is a child with poor posture. He is slow in teething, slow in walking, slow in developing. The successful preventive treatment of rickets should begin early in the life of the infant by the administration of daily doses of fish-liver oil, or vitamin D milk, and by exposing the child's body to the direct rays of the sun. Vitamin D milk is produced by irradiating the milk, by mixing purified concentrates of animal vitamin D, or by feeding irradiated yeast to the cow. Children living in the arctic regions, where whole fish and fish-eating animals constitute the chief diet, seem immune to this disease. These foods contain a provitamin of vitamin D.

Vitamin E

This vitamin is an antisterility factor in experimental animals, where its absence leads to muscular, nervous, endocrine, and growth-disturbances. It has not yet been proved to be essential to human health. It is plentiful in the germ oils of wheat and other seeds, and is fairly widely distributed in other foods.

Vitamin K

This vitamin occurs in more than one form of closely related fat-soluble substances. Its importance to the prevention of serious haemorrhage, lies in the fact that it is part of the prothrombin molecule. It has important and valuable uses in medicine, especially for pregnant women and newborn infants.

Summary

We have found certain substances to be needed for metabolism within the body. They are water, amino acids, simple sugars, glycerin, fatty acids, minerals, and vitamins. The planning of diets in health and disease is based upon our knowledge of the body's need for these substances and upon other considerations.

is in part the husband's responsibility. He must see that proper medical care is provided for his family when it is needed.

Community Standards of Maternity Care

The responsibility of the community or the state in providing the proper facilities for suitable maternity care is set forth in the following list of requirements, suggested by various authorities.

1. All midwives to be required by law to show adequate training, and to be licensed and supervised.

2. Maternity or prenatal centres, sufficient to provide for all cases not receiving parental supervision from private physicians. The work of such a centre should include:

- Instruction in hygiene of maternity and supervision throughout pregnancy, at least monthly visits to maternity centre until end of sixth month, and every who weeks thereafter. Literature to be given mother to acquaint her with the principles of infant hygiene.
- Complete physical examination by a physician as early in pregnancy as possible, including pelvic measurements, examination of heart, lungs, abdomen, and urine, and the taking of blood pressure; examination of urine every four weeks during early months, at least every two weeks after six months, and more frequently if indicated; Wassermann or other blood tests.
- Hospital care or nursing service at home at the time of confinement and during the lying-in period.
- Employment of sufficient number of public health nurses to do home visiting and to give instruction to expectant mothers in hygiene of pregnancy and early infancy; to make visits and to care for patient in confinement; and to see that every infant is referred to a children' health centre.
- Examination by physician six weeks after delivery before discharging patient.
- Daily visits for five days, and at least two other visits

during second week by physician or nurse.

- Confinement in a hospital or at home by a physician or a properly, trained and qualified attendant.
- Sufficient rest in bed after a normal delivery, with enough household service for four to six weeks to allow mother to recuperate.

3. Education of general public in problems presented by maternal and infant mortality and their solution.

4. Clinics, such as dental clinics and venereal disease clinics, for needed treatment during pregnancy.

5. Maternity hospitals or maternity wards in general hospitals, sufficient to provide care in all complicated cases and for all women wishing hospital care; free or part payment obstetrical care to be provided in every necessitous case at home or in a hospital.

6. Adequate income to allow the mother to remain in the home through the nursing period.

Problems of Maternal Care

The special problems that accompany maternity and make expert supervision necessary are particularly concerned with the diet, with the elimination of body waste, with the size of the birth canal, and with the mother's general physical condition. Since the baby grows within the mother's body and obtains all its nutrition from the mother's blood stream, the mother must take care to provide herself and the developing infant with all the essentials of an adequate diet in sufficient quantity. If she fails to do this, both she and her child will suffer. The baby requires much calcium, phosphorus, and vitamin D in laying the foundation for the bony framework of the body.

If the mother's diet does not supply these in sufficient quantity calcium will be absorbed from her own bony structures. In addition, the baby's teeth, which begin to form in the third month of prenatal life, may be of poor quality. Studies on white rats clearly suggest that a poor maternal diet contributes to poor teeth in the offspring. The outstanding research studies of Stuard and Burke at the Harvard School of Public Health, and of Ebbs, Tisdall, and Scott in Toronto, to mention only two, show a positive correlation between the mother's diet during pregnancy and her health and the health of her new baby. These studies present evidence that good prenatal diet affects the mother by reducing the incidence of toxaemia and other complications.

It lowers maternal mortality, and makes greater the likelihood of breast feeding. The benefits of good prenatal diet for the baby are better growth and development and improved physical conditional birth. Good prenatal diet also appears to reduce the incidence of stillbirths and premature births. Every mother should be under the care of a competent doctor as early in pregnancy as possible. Instruction in good nutrition should be included as a part of good prenatal care. In general, a good prenatal diet is as follows:

- Fruits and vegetables- 5 to 7 servings including leafy green or deep yellow ones and citrus fruit or tomatoes daily.
- Milk- one quart or its equivalent in whole milk cheese, each day.
- Eggs- one a day.
- Lean meat, fish, or poultry- about 4 ounces; liver or other glandular meats are recommended once a week.
- Butter or margarine- some on bread and vegetables.
- Iodine- iodized salt when suggested by the physician.
- Vitamin D- a doctor will usually recommend a fish liver oil concentrate or other approved source of vitamin D.
- Breads and cereals - 3 servings or more a day; whole grains are best, but if refined flours are used be sure they are enriched.

Additional foods as needed to control weight

The above is a general outline of the foods which will provide a good diet during pregnancy but each mother should consult her doctor about her individual needs. Good diet during pregnancy does not mean so much an increase in quantity as it does an increase in quality. The need for proteins, minerals, and vitamins is increased to a greater extent than the need for calories. The evidence is so great now that diet during pregnancy affects both the new infant and the mother that every program in maternal and child health should have as one of its main objectives the assurance of a good prenatal diet for every prospective mother. Modern thinking in public health is also emphasizing that women should enter pregnancy is a good nutritional state.

Nutrition education in high schools and colleges can make an important contribution to the health of future mothers and fathers. The elimination of waste material for the fetus puts an added burden on the mother's organs of excretion during pregnancy. It is particularly important that the condition of the kidneys be watched, for they must remove all the nitrogenous waste. Any abnormality that occurs in these organs should be detected early and suitable treatment is prescribed. It sometimes happens that the bones of the pelvis are narrow, making the normal birth of the child difficult or impossible. By careful pelvic measurements this can be determined in advance and suitable steps can be taken for making birth possible.

This may consist of controlling the size of the child or of arranging for birth by cesarean section, in which the delivery is made by way of an incision through the abdominal and uterine walls. General medical supervision, if begun early, enables the physician to start treatment in time if anything is wrong. Early blood tests for the Rh factor and syphilis, chest x-rays, urinalyses, and blood pressure determinations enable him to prepare mothers for safe deliveries of healthy babies. The physician has an opportunity to give definite instruction in hygiene and to make effective preparations for proper care through hospitalization or otherwise at the time of childbirth. It is important to the health of the baby that the mother should avoid infectious disease during the first months of pregnancy, particularly the second month.

There is clear-cut evidence that German measles at this time produces defects in the central nervous system of the infant. Other infections at this stage of pregnancy are suspected of injuring the fetus. Thousands of babies are delivered by midwives every year. Health authorities have been carrying on an important and beneficial campaign for some time to raise the requirements for the practice of midwifery. Trained midwives are capable of attending normal deliveries and of recognizing those conditions that require the care of a physician. Where adequate hospital and medical resources are available, medical attendance at childbirth has proved preferable. Then dangerous delays are avoided in any emergency which may arise.

The Preschool Child

The preschool child is the child from 1 to 6 years of age. This is a time when habits that are vital in the mental and physical life of the child are being formed for good or ill. His increased activities multiply his exposures to communicable diseases and his opportunities for accidents. Because he is growing and developing so rapidly, he has continuing nutritional, emotional medical, and dental needs. Much parent time is still needed to give the child necessary training. It may not be provided by some parents because they do not understand the child's requirements. The public health program now seeks to focus much needed attention on this previously neglected age.

Mental Health of the Preschool Child

While physical health is important during the preschool period, mental health is an increasingly vital problem. The fifth White House Conference held in 1950 chose to shift its emphasis from physical health, the theme of previous conferences since 1909, to that of the development of children in mental, emotional, and spiritual qualities that will foster a happy childhood and lead to responsible citizenship. Habits of thinking and feeling established during this formative preschool period eventually result in adult attitudes toward life.

The judicious use of praise for desirable acts and the withholding of approval or attention for those which are objectionable are most important in child training. Regularity also helps in the formation of habits. Some of the basic needs of the child are affection, companionship, understanding, a feeling of security provided by a happy home, a kindly parental authority, and a feeling of belonging which he gains from participation in the work and play of the family.

Health Program for the Preschool Child

Though the mortality rates among children from 1 to 6 years are lower than those for infants, continued medical supervision of the preschool child is desirable. A health examination twice a year by a physician who has had experience in the care of children will enable the parent to learn of any abnormalities that need attention, to know whether the child is growing properly, and to determine whether his nutritional needs are being amply met. Deviation from normal in eyesight or in hearing can be most satisfactorily corrected if found and treated before the age of 6 years.

Defects of adenoids and tonsils may need medical attention. The dentist should watch the growth of the teeth, clean them, and fill cavities. The deciduous teeth are vary important in the development of a normal jaw and in bringing in the permanent teeth with proper alignment. It is a mistake to allow these to be neglected on the score that they are only temporary teeth. The term temporary teeth is no longer regarded by the dental profession as a desirable one in view of the great importance of these teeth in normal growth. A visit to the dentist at every six months or as often as the dentist deems necessary, is important from the time the child is 2 years old. Communicable diseases usually show a higher fatality during infancy and the preschool period than later in life.

So far as possible the young child should be protected

from them. Persons who are sick should keep away from young children. The common cold, often discounted as only a cold, may have serious consequences for the child. Children of this age can be taught to avoid contact with those who are sick, to cover a cough or sneeze, and to use a handkerchief when needed. Throughout the preschool years nutrition plays a vital role in physical, emotional, and social growth and development. The toddler's diet should be composed of the essential foods-milk, fruits, vegetables, meat, eggs, bread, cereals, and butter or margarine plus an approved source of vitamin D.

If he takes adequate amounts of these foods, he has little room for the less important foods-such as candy, sweet cookies, cakes, soft drinks, and rich desserts. Good food habits are about as important in the development of the preschool child as food itself. As he takes more interest in this new world of his, is interest in food often slackens. This is a time when forcing or bribing a child to eat may make him a fussy, finicky eater for years to come. The toddler is growing less rapidly and be may not want or need as much food at 18 months as he did at 1 year of age.

The main aim at this time is to make eating a happy experience. No food is worth a battle. Forcing food is undesirable. Many times foods which are forced on children are those which are hated later on. Small helpings, regular meals, attractive good-tasting food served at a table of comfortable height, with eating utensils suitable for his age, will do much to aid in the development of good food habits. Too much emphasis should not be put on good table manners. Food jags are not uncommon during the preschool period; for day a child may want one food over and over. If it is a good food, there is probably no harm in letting him have it. No moral values should be attached to food.

Desserts should not be used as bribes. If a child is told to eat his proverbial spinach so he may have ice cream, this makes ice cream very desirable, and spinach the opposite. The connotation is that spinach is good for me and therefore does not taste good. Both spinach and ice cream are good foods and both can taste good. The child is more willing to try them when he is hungry and when he sees other members of the family enjoying them. The habit of eating slowly and with enjoyment also is most easily acquired when parents set an example of making meal time a happy experience. When the child enters school, during either his fifth or sixth year, he is once more subjected to a new set of exposures. He needs to be revaccinated for smallpox.

If his diphtheria protection was not secured by his first year immunizations it should be secured now. Most states recommend a diphtheria booster shot at this time. The Schick test is the accepted criterion of adequate protection. Protection against tetanus is becoming more important at this age and immunization should be provided if it has not been secured previously. As stated previously, many paediatricians now include immunization against tetanus when they immunize against diphtheria. The commonly recommended procedure is to give booster shots of tetanus toxoid one year after the first immunization, and every three years thereafter until the end of grammar school. This covers the period of greatest danger.

If typhoid fever is common in the area, or if the child is traveling where it is likely to be present, he should be given typhoid vaccine. In addition to these special protective measures, care should be given to the sanitary quality of water and food supplies. Raw milk should never be used. Children should not eat food bought from street vendors or from counters where it has been exposed to dirt, dust, and flies. The preschool child needs a well-planned regimen with attention given to sleep, play, and exercise out of doors, as well as to diet. He needs to be guided in the formation of habit of cleanliness and elimination. Help with the problems of child training may be given by the family physician or public health workers.

The Infant

Infancy is the first year of a child's life. It is a period

fraught with great dangers. At no other year in life until extreme old age is the death rate so high. Sirrthur New Sholme said: Infant mortality is the most sensitive index we possess of social welfare. If babies were well born and well cared for, their mortality would be negligible. The general trend of infant mortality in the United States has been markedly downward during the past half century and more. The rate varies in different communities, depending upon the extent to which hygienic and sanitary practices are carried on by the people and upon the economic status of the population.

The chief causes of infant disease and death can be largely controlled by intelligent care of the infant and the mother. Prematurity, acute respiratory diseases, acute gastro-intestinal disease, and congenital debility lead the list of specific causes of death. State health departments help to make baby incubators available for infants born prematurely. Public health progress has tremendously reduced communicable disease. Increasingly, mothers are maintaining good maternal hygiene, due to health education received from the physician, health literature, and classes for expectant mothers given by health departments. Special problems are attacked as soon as a solution is found.

For example, at the time of birth, babies eyes have for years been treated routinely with two drops of 1 per cent silver nitrate solution. This has practically eliminated ophthalmia neonatorum or babies sore eyes, which frequently used to cause blindness. A more recent development has been the control of fatal infant anaemia associated with the Rh factor.

Infant Feeding

Breast feeding is usually preferable to bottle feeding if the mother is properly nourished and is able to supply sufficient milk. It is the choice for the infant both physiologically and psychologically. We should remember, however, that a deficient maternal diet may seriously interfere with the quality of mother's milk. The adequate diet during lactation is about the same as during pregnancy. Additional small mid-meals may be suggested by the physician. In bottle feeding the possibilities of infection and of digestive disturbances are greatly increased. The greatest of care is needed in keeping bottles and other equipment sterilized.

If cow's milk is used, it should be pasteurized milk and given subsequent protection from contamination. In communities where pasteurized milk is not available, directions for making raw milk safe at home may be obtained from a physician or the department of health. Vitamin D milk is widely used and other vitamin D supplements are regulated according to the advice of a physician. Any form of cow's milk must be modified to make it suitable for infant feeding. When using dried milk instead of fresh, it is important to select whole milk. Skim milk lacks the butter fat required by the baby. Unsweetened evaporated milk can be properly modified to meet the infant's individual needs.

It is economical and, by virtue of its method of preparation and marketing, free from contamination. The first additions to the infant's diet are fish liver oil or other approved form of vitamin D and citrus or other source of vitamin C. Then follow cereal, egg yolk, strained fruits and vegetables, strained or scraped meats at the time the doctor recommends them. As teeth develop, foods to chew on are added. By the time a child is 1 year old" he is taking some form of all the foods recommended for an adequate diet.

Infant Care

The hygienic practices particularly needed by the infant are feeding, rest, and cleanliness. The formation of correct habits, almost from the time of birth, is important to the child's physical and emotional health. During the first months, when the flame of life is feeble and most rapid growth is taking place, it is exceedingly important that the mother learn from her physician, from the health centre, or from literature on infant hygiene, the essentials in caring for her baby. The young infant should be vaccinated against small-pox before he is 1 year old regardless of whether or not smallpox is prevalent. Immunization against diphtheria, telanus, and whooping cough is usually given at the age of 6 months or so on thereafter.

Six months later the Schick test should be given to determine whether protection against diphtheria has been established. Measles and whooping cough are both highly fatal in infancy. As indicated, a vaccine is being used successfully against whooping cough. In the case of measles if the baby is inoculated within a week after exposure with immune or gamma globulin serum, the disease can be prevented or made very mild. Gamma globulin is prepared as a clear colourless solution of the protein substances from human blood which contain the immune bodies against infectious disease.

It appears to be of value also in preventing, whooping cough, complications from mumps in adults, and possibly some other infections. Babies should be kept away from any person who has tuberculosis, even though it is the father or mother. Babies are very susceptible to colds and should be isolated from any person with one. Acute respiratory disease is always a leading cause of infant deaths. Care should be taken to avoid all possibility of conveying germs from the nose or mouth to the baby, since some persons carry infection although they show no symptoms. Training given during infancy in regular habits of eating, sleeping, and elimination are important to the immediate and future health of the child.

This no longer consists of forcing every infant into the same time schedule. Present recommended procedures are to adapt the schedule to the baby's individual needs. Parents ask, do we pick the baby up or let him cry it out? Opinions of experts vary on the answer. If the baby finds the easiest way to get attention is by crying, he will probably develop the undesirable habit of doing so often. There is no doubt, however, of the infant's need for attention and a feeling of security. Physicians have been known to write prescriptions for TLC as well as for medications. It is often urged, for example, that bottle-fed babies be held when fed and that all babies be shown loving attention at that time. Daily playtimes encourage happy babies. Caring for a baby is so important that it requires not only intelligence but also preparation and guidance. Health agencies have made excellent helpful literature available.

Community Standards of Infant and Child Welfare

The duty of the community is set forth in the following set of suggested standards for child welfare relating to infants and preschool children:

1. Children's health centre to provide or to cooperate with sufficient number of public health nurses to make home visits to all infants and children of preschool age needing care-one public health nurse for an average general population of 5,000. Visits to the home are for the purpose not of bedside care, but of instructing the mother in

- Technique of bath, sleep, clothing, ventilation, and general care of the baby, with demonstrations.
- Technique of nursing.
- Preparation and technique of artificial feeding.
- Prevention of disease in children.
- Value of breast feeding.
- Dietary essentials and selection of food for the infant and for older children.

2. Complete birth registration by adequate legislation requiring reporting within three days after birth.

3. Dental clinics; eye, ear, nose, and throat clinics; venereal disease clinics; and other clinics for the treatment of defects and disease, for persons for whom care from private physicians is not available.

4. Prevention of infantile blindness by making and afforcing adequate laws for treatment of eyes of every infant at birth and supervision of all positive cases.

5. Children's hospitals, or beds in general hospitals, or provision for medical and nursing care at home, sufficient to care for all sick infants and young children.

6. Sufficient number of children's health centres to give health instruction under medical supervision for all infants and children not under the care of a private physician, and to give instruction to mothers in breast feeding and in care and feeding of children, at least once a month throughout the first year, and at regular intervals throughout preschool age. This centre to include a nutrition and dental clinic.

7. General education work in prevention of communicable disease and in hygiene and feeding of infants and young children.

8. State licensing and supervision of child-caring institutions or homes in which infants or young children are cared for.

It will be interesting for the student to investigate the extent to which these standards are met by his own community.

15

Adolescent's Behaviour and Problems

There are many questions concerning development during the adolescent period which cannot be fully or satisfactorily answered because of lack of scientific knowledge and because of the complex factors involved in the case of a particular adolescent boy or girl. Although there has been no study of adolescence comparable to the studies already made of the small child, the investigations relating to adolescence have been well summarized in a recent book. An individual girl or boy rarely has all the characteristics ascribed to adolescents in general.

This section aims merely to present sufficient facts to complete a bird's-eye-view of the entire period of childhood. Those who are especially interested in the adolescent period will find a more adequate treatment in the references listed throughout and at the end of the section. Some of the questions which may be answered in part are: At what age do most children show the signs of puberty? What physical and mental changes occur in early adolescence? What changes in social behaviour, in interests, and in attitudes? What progress should be made in memory, imagination, and reasoning? What emotional reactions are normal? There is no fixed age at which boys and girls show the characteristic signs of physiological maturity.

In general, girls mature earlier than boys. Crampton's, Baldwin's, and other studies show a wide range in the ages at which individuals show the first signs of physiological maturity. The first menstruation of some girls is as early as nine, and of others, as late as twenty years. The average age is the thirteenth year. In the development of boys Crampton found a similar range, but an average of a year later in the age at which they show the characteristic pubescent growth and pigmentation of fine hair.

Certain Physical Abilities

Physical abilities found by Rogers among two hundred and ten high school boys ranging in age from thirteen to nineteen years, the average age being sixteen and one-half years.

Changes at Puberty

Physical changes occur at puberty which explain to a considerable extent many other changes in the social environment and in the behaviour of the adolescent. The acceleration in rate of growth and the increased maturity of form result in wearing adult clothing, in being treated as adults, and in being introduced into wider social circles. These environmental changes in turn result in an increased desire for independence, a growing interest in vocations, and frequent difficulty in meeting successfully the new responsibilities. A summary of the physical, environmental, and behaviour changes in three parallel columns shows relations more clearly than a treatment in paragraph form.

Physical Changes

- Bodily proportions change. The more rounded curves of girlhood are especially noticeable.
- The different parts of the body grow at an unequal rate-nose, hands and feet enlarge, arms and legs grow more rapidly than other parts of the body.
- Growth in height is rapid, and is followed by increase

in weight. There is an increase in lung capacity, strength, and vigour.

- The boy's voice deepens, sometimes dropping an octave in pitch. The girl's voice acquires a richer quality.

- The reproductive organs increase in size and capacity to function. Menstruation in girls occurs.

- Tendency toward skin eruptions is increased.

- The individual becomes capable of reproducing the species. Changes in internal glandular secretions occur.

- A rise in mental development of girls between the ages of 11 and 13 has been noted; and in superior boys, between the ages of 12 and 14 years.

- Except in the case of superior individuals, intelligence probably reaches its maximum height in adolescence, at about 16 years of age.

- Growth of hair on the body is noticeable.

Change in the Environment

- The adolescent begins to wear adult clothing. Other people treat the adolescent more like an adult: they ask his opinion, admit him to adult discussions, engage with him in adult subjects of conversation.

- He is introduced to a wider circle of acquaintances and often to a world that is strange to him; he may go away to school, join new clubs.

- The adolescent is accepted on a different basis of understanding and expectation.

- Undesirable sex information is often obtained through contact with older boys.

- Adults sometimes ridicule and call attention to the child's awkwardness.

- He plays different games with more complex rules.

- Greater freedom of action and participation in social events is permitted.

- There are more opportunities for association between

the two sexes.

Changes in Behaviour

- He may discover the conflict and contradictions between his childhood standards and those of the wider social group with whom he comes in contact. Choice and individual initiative and responsibility are required to a larger extent.

- There is a broadening of interests, especially interest in vocations, his future, and the assumption of new responsibilities.

- The adolescent feels a new freedom: he resents restraint and being treated like a child; he is likely-to accept things on their merit rather than on outside authority. Social values replace parental precepts. There may be outbursts of strength and vigour that lead to physical combat.

- The boy frequently feels embarrassment concerning his voice.

- He desires to choose his own companions.

- He engages in team games requiring an increasing amount of cooperation and subordination of the individual to the good of the group. He becomes willing to follow as well as to lead. Desire for individual success is overshadowed by desire for the success of the team.

- He may have a feeling of inadequacy and insecurity in the face of the many new situations which he must meet.

- Loyalty to a small gang may be widened to loyalty to larger groups-school, community and to causes.

- Movements and posture are frequently awkward and clumsy. Old habits of muscular coordination are interfered with. The adolescent's self-consciousness is increased, and is sometimes manifested in shyness, and sometimes in exaggerated self-assertiveness.

- Certain forms of emotional instability may be directly related to glandular disturbance.

- Girl is interested in older boy companions.

- Self-awareness is increased. The adolescent is more conscious of his body. Attention is frequently too much directed to the adolescent himself rather than to objective conditions.

- Sex excitement on the part of the adolescent is aroused by the changes in the sex organs and by the social situations in which he is placed. Social awkwardness often results from lack of knowledge of how to meet new situations.

- Interest of boys and girls in each other replaces the earlier antagonism between the sexes.

- Morbid curiosity results if normal curiosity is not satisfied.

- Social attitudes and values are largely fixed in this period.

- Highly intelligent children have moral, social, and religious doubts and questions.

- There should be an increased comprehension of abstract words and principles.

- Emotional feelings are often expressed in music, art, social service, religious aspirations, or some other worthwhile creative activity.

Adolescent Changes are not Sudden

All the changes taking place in adolescence are, in at least half the cases, gradual rather than sudden, and should be, in a still larger proportion. Someone has aptly said that the adolescent stands with one hand stretched out to childhood and the other to adulthood. The shift into adult attitudes and feelings is gradual and takes place with much fluctuation between childish and adult interests. Adolescents are still much interested in childish things. One fourteen-year-old girl was reading in the same week modern adult fiction and the St. Nicholas Magazine. On the same day she played jacks and bridge. No two days are alike.

The adolescent is neither a child nor a man. Adults should recognize the mood in which the boy or girl happens to be and should deal with it appropriately. No one phase should be taken too seriously by adults, as it is likely to be a passing occurrence that will fade out of its own accord. All the important changes represent a development of abilities already present rather than a new birth of abilities previously non-existing. Ability to cooperate on a team does not appear suddenly. In the pre-adolescent period the child should have learned some cooperation. Competition is not suddenly abandoned. In fact it is still intense in the teens. The rules of games become more complex, and the element of gaining approval of the opposite sex for athletic prowess is dominant.

Adolescence is not Necessarily a Period of Storm and Stress

These changes are not necessarily sudden or violent. Whether adolescence is the stormy period usually pictured depends on at least four factors. The first is the extent to which the child has been prepared to meet a variety of social situations. Children who from the age of eight or nine years have gone away to summer camps or boarding school, who have been accustomed to associating with their parents' friends and with a large number of children of their own age do not find difficulty in adapting themselves to the larger world which opens to them gate of adolescence.

They have already had practice in a variety of social situations and have acquired the knowledge necessary to meet most situations in which they will be placed. The second factor is the extent to which the child has developed independence and the ability to think through his own problems. The child who has learned to rely on himself and to solve his own difficulties will have little difficulty in gradually assuming adult responsibility. Miriam Van Waters labels a parent bad who will not let a child grow up; who does all the talking, makes all the decisions, and meets all the issues. A third factor is intelligence.

The more intelligent children are concerned with problems of science, philosophy, ethics, and religion which children of lower mentality do not even recognize as problems. The number of adolescents who have keen intellectual doubts and religious anxiety is relatively small. A fourth factor determining the difficulty of adjustment in the case of a given adolescent is the complexity of the environment in which the boy or girl is placed. To require many new adjustments at one time, to crowd the day and night with social events, to live with parents who make many, conflicting, and unreasonable demands, to attend a school which requires a different type of study and behaviour from that of the school previously attended-this very complexity results in strain and stress.

Reasoning and Memory

Reasoning, which was present in a simple form in the first year of life, develops into the ability

(i) to solve arithmetic problems, such as "If a man's salary is \$20 a week and he spends \$14 a week, how long will it take him to save \$300?"'

(ii) to see the most significant common element rather than trivial differences in two things such as a king and a president;

(iii) to make a generalization on the basis of careful and selected observation of a series of events;

(iv) to detect cause and effect relationships, such as are indicated by the ability to construct the entire situation from the details given in the following paragraph in the Binet test:

My neighbour has been having queer visitors. First a doctor came to his house, then a lawyer, then a minister. What do you think happened there? Rote memory increase up to the fourteenth year but shows little further improvement. At seven years of age, average children can repeat five digits in the order in which they are given; at ten years, six; and at fourteen years, seven digits.

Drawing

At adolescence, drawing will probably have met one of two fates, it will have been dropped entirely, or else it will have been developed as a vocational or a vocational interest. In high school, art is usually an elective study, and may be pursued along practical lines, such as interior decorating, pottery-making, costume design, mechanical drawing, and other forms of applied design. Interest in art is well worth developing as an outlet for emotional drives that in our present civilization must seek delayed satisfaction and as an insurance against loneliness and unavoidable losses, as well as a convenient form of expressing ideas and a vocational pursuit.

Language and Reading

The vocabulary increases from an estimated average of 3,6000 words at eight years of age to 5,400 at ten; 7,200 at twelve; and 9,000 at fourteen years. There is a shift in interest to books of the more romantic type, although interest in adventure, surprise, and plot is still strong and fiction predominates. Jordan found in his study that some of the favourite books of boys from fourteen to sixteen were The Call of the Wild, Treasure Island, Boy Scout Series; Tom Sawyer, Ivanhoe, Huckleberry Finn, Tale of Two Cities, When a Man's Man, White Fang, Freckles, and Penrod. Some of the favourite books of girls of the same age were Little Women, Pollyana, Girl of the Limberlost, Freckles, Ivanhoe, Tale of Two Cities, Laddie, Rebecca of Sunnybrook Farm, and David Copperfield.

Mental Growth

Mental development is also gradual. Some authorities say that general intelligence reaches its maximum in the teens. Thorndike estimates that the growth limit of intelligence is higher-about twenty years of age. He believes that individuals after sixteen years of age may be expected to do increasingly difficult types of abstract thinking as well as to reason with equal skill along more lines as rapidly as they acquire the facts with which to reason. There is no evidence of a sudden sharpening of the senses, of an increased memory span, or of sudden acquisition of reasoning ability at adolescence.

Emotional Changes

The change in emotions likewise is in degree and intensity, rather than in quality. In the adolescent's environment, there are more stimuli than formerly to call forth various emotional responses. Fear, love, rage are manifested in the first year of life. In adolescence, emotional control should have been attained in the case of fear and anger. The observation has been made that fear of large animals, of small creepy things such as bugs and spiders, and of social blunders increases; while fear of other physical things decreases. In the case of love, the natural expression of this emotion is denied during the long period of delayed marriage.

Boys and girls in most communities do not at puberty launch immediately into adulthood, as they do in primitive tribes and in some of the more primitive sections of our own country. Early marriage is not the rule in this country. From four to twelve years are frequently spent in preparing for and gaining headway in a profession. During these years of preparation, sex impulses must be suppressed. These impulses may be aroused by anyone of four types of stimuli:

(i) direct excitation,

(ii) indirect physical means, such as irritation in the bladder and rectum, too warm a bed, climbing a pole, riding a bicycle,

(iii) violent emotions of dread, anger, horror as well as sex emotions,

(iv) imagination dwelling on romantic thoughts or on sexual acts.

There should also be a gradual change in the perception of stimuli and consequently in the emotional responses which these stimuli call forth. Participation in social situations should evoke responses of increased sympathy with the understanding of people, and a higher type of comradeship. History, literature, art, and music should arouse sentiments of sympathy, reverence, admiration for whatsoever things are true, whatsoever things are honest, whatsoever things are just, whatsoever things are pure, whatsoever things are lovely, whatsoever things are of good report.

Individual Difference in Intelligence

A wide range of intelligence is found in adolescents, as in younger children. The present tendency seems to be for many children to go to high school regardless of their mental capacity for academic work. Adolescents with a mental age of less than 15 years will usually not be able to do the abstract work set for their fellow pupils. Training suited to the capacity of these children should be provided so that they can become economically independent. The satisfactory vocational adjustment of this group would prevent many social problems.

A boy or girl of average or below average intelligence will find the usual high school work unsuited to his or her capacity. Failure results in unhappiness, sullenness, day dreaming, boastfulness, or defiance of authority. When these children continue in high school, a bore and tolerate it only because their friends are there. The boy or girl of average ability in a family of superior intelligence or a child in a family eager to give him the advantages which they lacked is in an especially difficult situation. The most important pre-requisite for mental health-work suited to his capacity is denied him. Such boys and girls should be sent to high schools which offer work which they can do well-courses in sewing, cooking, art, business, the manual arts, practical English, hygiene, and civics.

This type of high school should give the pupils a wider development on their intellectual level, prepare them directly for the positions which they can fill-positions which do not require much initiative, originality, or abstract thinking and establish habits of hygienic and moral behaviour. To accomplish these aims the high school must make the school situations as similar to life situations as possible. This means that the sewing, cooking, business, and other technical courses should teach the very things that these students will be required to do; that the English and civics courses should deal with practical situations and be conducted as socialized recitations; that hygiene should consist of a study of concrete health problems which the pupils are meeting now and will probably meet later; that extra classroom activities should furnish practice in using leisure wisely, and in associating with other boys and girls, children and adults, in a happy and at the same time constructive way. Work suited to his capacity is equally important for the child of high intelligence. Such a child, if not given work that challenges him, often lapses into habits of idleness, day dreaming that is an end in itself, or other unwise use of time.

Standardized Tests

Pintner suggests the following intelligence tests for high-school and college students:

- Chicago group intelligence test.
- The Otis group intelligence scale.
- Champman and Wells high school intelligence test.
- Trabue mentimeters.
- Thurston's Psychological examination.
- Terman group test of mental ability.
- Miller mental ability test.
- The army alpha.
- Thorndike intelligence examination.

The tests most frequently applied in the junior high school of the Lincoln school of teachers college have been the otis self-administering intermediate examination and the term group test; in the senior high-school graduates, the otis self-administering high examination and the army alpha. Some use has been made of the brown-woody civiles test and the much-polypnoea general science tests.

Habits in the Adolescent Period

The laws of learning are the same for adolescents as for younger children. A boy or girl is continually learning something. Habits either desirable or undesirable are constantly being formed. One group of teachers listed habits which they definitely knew to have been formed in high school. Both good and bad habits were mentioned. This limited list could easily be supplemented by the reader, but it is sufficiently large to call attention to the fact that adolescents are forming habits every day, and that the environment should be controlled and the child guided in ways that will result in a maximum of desirable habits.

Special Problems of Adolescence

Many problems with adolescents reported by parents and teachers have been created by the parent or teacher by thwarting activities which are themselves valuable and necessary for normal development. In subordinate, boy- crazy, too amorous, asks foolish questions, lawless, and disobedient are terms which describe adolescent faults frequently mentioned by parents and teachers.

Other faults, such as those indicted by the terms posing, trying to be cute, attracting attention, smart Alec, exaggerated idea of own importance, lazy, indifferent, are merely symptoms of some underlying difficulty, often of a feeling of insecurity and inadequacy in meeting the new situations with which he is confronted. Using smutty words, painting and powdering excessively, and dodging work may be due respectively to a lack of understanding of the role sex plays in normal life, and of the best way to secure the desired attention, and to the assignment of work unsuited to the capacity of the individual. A discussion of some of the more fundamental problems follows:

Intellectual Independence

Another type of independence which should be established during the high school period is intellectual independence. While in high school, the pupil should learn to budget his time and of his own accord to set aside certain periods for each subject. He should recognize standards of achievement and know when he has reached them. He should no longer require the periodic prodding of teacher and adviser to sustain his effort and keep him progressing in intellectual achievement. The teacher or parent can aid the pupil

(i) in seeing clearly the objectives of habits, knowledge, and attitudes which he personally can and should attain;

(ii) in appraising his progress by showing him how to judge his achievement objectively; and

(iii) in gradually assuming responsibility for independently pursuing his intellectual interests.

Among the twenty administrative reasons why high school pupils fail which Edmonson lists are large classes, failure to set up standards for each pupil according to is capacity and previous education, and lack of cooperation of teachers and pupils with parents in regard to the time required and conditions favourable to home study.

Emancipation from the family

Psychological weaning at adolescence is as important as dietetic weaning at the end of the first year of life. To keep a child so dependent on his family that he cannot be happy anywhere else is cruel. Sooner or later when the child goes away to college, establishes a home of his own, or loses his parents by death-such dependence results in an emotional wrench which is frequently tragic in its intensity. To make more difficult the child's struggle to achieve adult independence by ridiculing or punishing his attempts to assert himself, by making docile, dependent behaviour satisfying to him or by appealing to personal devotion and obligation to his parents is most unwise and usually results in more or less intense antagonism between parent and child.

The better course for the parent to pursue is to be ready to give facts, to point out the probable consequences of certain specific acts, and to leave the intelligent child to make his own decisions. Control of the adolescent depends largely on showing him what society demands of him-that is, of giving him a correct perception of the situations he faces. As it is, parents frequently increase rather than lessen their demands and the closeness of their supervision. The wise use of freedom does not suddenly develop at fourteen or gradually accustomed to independent action-to sleeping alone, to playing alone occasionally, to making his own decisions, to going away from home for shorter or longer periods on visits to relatives, to attending summer camps or boarding schools.

In these ways the child becomes accustomed to thinking and acting for himself. This desirable independence is not achieved if the separation from the family is in space only, and not in spirit. One girl sent away to college was still emotionally dependent on her mother, who encouraged and probably enjoyed the emotional parting at the termination of every vacation. The mother planned the daughter's wardrobe, did her laundry work, and wrote frequent letters telling of the enjoyable activities going on at home. As a result, the child, though many miles away, was still tied to her mother's apron strings. Her infantile reactions persisted. One way in which the mother can guard against being all wrapped up in her child to the extent of making impossible the child's achievement of normal independence and self-reliance, is to cultivate interests apart from her family.

The discovery that her children no longer need so much of her time and care is painful. A plan of life which a number of modern women favour is, first, professional training and some experience in her chosen work before marriage; second, a middle period occupied with the care of children, home activities, and part-time interest in the profession selected; and finally, a full-time return to her chosen work when the children are old enough to establish their own independence and do not need her intimate care. Another means of aiding the boy or girl in establishing his independence and developing self-confidence is to help him secure remunerative jobs for a few hours a day or during summer vacations.

A one-act play by McCauley presents very clearly how a mother attempts to restrain her adolescent daughter, upbraids her for indifference, and emphasizes her obligations to her parents, thus making difficult her emancipation from the family and assumption of adult responsibility. To summarize: emancipation from the family requires:

(i) a separation from the family in spirit, if not in space;
(ii) a willingness on the part of the parents to have the child break away from the dependence on them which is frequently so satisfying to parents; and
(iii) an opportunity for the child to test his newly acquired potentialities. In the case of primitive people, the time of puberty was the occasion for an important ceremony in which the boy or girl definitely became a member of the clan. Today, likewise, adolescence should be the time when adjustment to life outside the home is completed.

Establishing Hetero-sexuality

The antagonism, or at least indifference, between boys and girls which is frequently shown in the pre-adolescent period should, in this period, be replaced by interest. Stanley Hall recognized the importance of emotional adjustment during adolescence when he says that book is probably a bad sign in a girl or boy. Undoubtedly book is a bad sign if it indicates a lack of interest in the opposite sex, because if boys and girls do not learn to make a satisfactory adjustment to the opposite sex during adolescence, the chances are that they will never work out their mating impulses in a thoroughly satisfactory way, but will remain in the infantile stages of being interested in their own bodies and in members of their own sex.

The problem of crushes is probably due to lack of a normal outlet for the sex impulse and to the social training in which a girl is definitely warned against men. This type of prolonged intimacy of one girl with another may result in inability to make a normal hetero-sexual adjustment during an entire lifetime. Where two girls are seen constantly together, arms entwined, interested exclusively in each other, four things may be done to break up or modify this intimacy: one of the girls may be sent away to a co-educational institution; both of the girls may be introduced to and interested in associating with boys; both may be encouraged to widen the circle of their acquaintances and interests; or they may be helped in developing their relationship on an intellectual and social rather than physical level, by engaging together in debates, school publications, dramatics, athletic events, or other school activities. Several factors are important in maintaining and promoting a normal relationship between the sexes.

The first is opportunity for boys and girls to associate with each other in social and intellectual activities group work and recreational opportunities should definitely be provided. Cooperation in such projects as school publications, dramatics, athletics, and subject-matter clubs, helps to establish wholesome relationships as well as to neutralize self-consciousness and too strong tendencies toward introversion. Separating boys and girls at a time when they are most interested in each other has given rise to some serious problems.

One of these problems is attachment to persons of the same sex. This is harmful in so far as it serves as a substitution for a healthy relationship with both sexes and interferes with adjustment to the opposite sex. One investigation indicates fewer divorces and a better type of family life in the case of people graduating from co-educational schools than among graduates of men's and women's colleges. The methods of disuse-removing the stimuli to emotional reactions-cannot be applied successfully to problems of adolescent emotional adjustment. Segregation and strict rules do not produce the hoped-for results.

On the other mean, co-educational boarding schools have been maintained successfully. One English co-educational school developed public opinion which discouraged undesirable silliness and flirtation and achieved a spirit of unselfconscious comradeship and wholesome friendship among all the pupils. Boys and girls should have much opportunity for social intercourse and for play activities in 'which both sexes participate. The more opportunity there is for choice of a mate, the better. Fundamentally, co-educational schools seem to be a wiser solution to the problem than segregation. Association with the opposite sex in work and play broadens young people's interests, supplies a natural outlet for their energies, and directs attention away from themselves. Too much social activity can be guarded against by the agreement among the parents. In one community, the parents agreed to limit evening entertainment to certain hours on non-school nights. After various experiments the following schedule was found satisfactory:

For Monday, Tuesday, Wednesday, and Thursday

3-5 PM - recreation

5-7 PM - study and dinner

7-9:30 PM - study if necessary; if not, reading, games, or music at home.

This arrangement prevented much of the anger and resentment so often felt by adolescents when permission to attend a certain party is refused by their parents and all the rest of the crowd are allowed to go. A second factor in establishing normal hetero-sexual relationship is the realization that sexual life is the natural order of the universe and not a taboo subject; that it is a perfectly wholesome phase of life. Sex curiosity is aroused in this period also and should be satisfied. Frankness and fair dealing on the subject should be the policy with adolescents as with small children.

They should be shown that their impulses are natural and may be directed wisely. Adolescence is the time for frank discussion of the many problems of sex in the life of the individual which are from time to time suggested by literature, by daily life, and by moving pictures, plays, and newspapers. In this incidental way insight into the social and moral meaning of marriage may be gained. At present there is no school in which an individual can learn about this important subject. His conception of marriage is largely obtained from observation of his parents' married relationship.

In cases where this relationship has been happy and wholesome, the child is most fortunate; in cases where the

is necessary in order to direct him to the school which will give him the education he needs, or to point out the vocational opportunities open to him if he must early embark on his vocational career. Franklin found that two-thirds of the 1500 children whom he asked to name the one occupation that they would most like to enter, had the same preference at the end as at the beginning of the year. Children' preferences, however, are not necessarily a reliable indication of the work that they can do or that is open to them.

The two occupations preferred by the largest number of the 1590 girls in Woodruffs investigation were music and dancing, in both of which fields there are relatively few vocational openings. The ten other occupations most frequently mentioned were typewriting, stenography, acting, art, drawing, teaching, dressmaking, expression, costume design, and painting. There is some indication that too few boys are choosing to enter the fields of agriculture, mining, and transportation, and too many the field of professional service. From the army intelligence test, so much overlapping was found in the intelligence of different vocational groups, that it is impossible to classify vocations according to the intelligence required.

There may be, however, a critical point of intelligence below which success in a given coalition becomes doubtful. In general, it was found that the professional men stood highest in intelligence, business men and clerical workers next, craftsmen next, semi-skilled labourers next and unskilled lowest. Occasionally there were found unskilled labourers with high scores, but rarely professional men with very low scores on the intelligence tests. Vocational guidance includes giving information about vocations, analysing the vocational possibilities of the individual, helping to connect the individual with a job for which he is suited, and helping him to progress in the chosen occupation. Vocational information is given in a number of ways: through specially prepared pamphlets and books describing certain vocations, through visits to industrial plants; through interviews with typical representatives of a vocation; through special vocational guidance programs in which successful members of different vocations speak specifically of their work; through writing themes on occupations; through actual participation in the occupation after school hours or in the summer vocation; through pre-vocational courses in junior high schools, and through various other methods.

All of these methods help the individual to understand the kind of work, the salary, the training needed, the opportunities for securing a position and for advancing in the occupation, and the advantages and disadvantages of a number of occupations in which he is interested. The analysis of the individual is preferably made in terms of what he can do, rather than in terms of qualities and traits which he is supposed to possess. Intelligence tests, opportunities to try out his ability on the job, and a review of similar kinds of work which he has done in the past, give the most direct and accurate estimate of his ability. Special tests of vocational ability are, on the whole, unsatisfactory in discovering the particular task for which an individual is fitted.

If the occupation is analyzed in terms of the specific work to be done, and the individual is analyzed in terms of the specific things he can do, the problem of fitting the person to the job is somewhat simplified. Helping the individual to progress in his vocation in an important phase of his education which is too frequently neglected. Proctor found that arranging pupils courses of study by using psychological tests, elementary school marks, pupils preferences for subjects, future educational plans, and vocational ambitions, pays. Of two groups practically equal in intelligence, only one-third as many of the guided as of the unguided pupils were out of a job during their first year of work and only approximately half as many failed in one or more school subjects.

Thorndike has said that there should not be a horizontal split between learning and doing. Ideally here should be no time in the person's life when he should stop learning, and therefore, no time anywhere on the educational ladder when he will be learning something for the far distant future. The continuation schools which supplement the individual's work with a few hours of systematic instruction each week, the vocational schools which prepare for a specific vocation, the instruction given in many industrial concerns, and the Antioch plan of providing students with alternate periods at the college and on the job, are some attempts to help young people make more satisfactory progress in their chosen occupations.

Education for Parenthood

Instruction concerning the way life begins and the bodily changes that occur at puberty is necessary in order to

(i) satisfy normal curiosity,

(ii) to prevent the bewilderment and fear that occurs if the changes come upon the child unexpectedly, and

(iii) to substitute accurate knowledge for distorted and vulgar impressions gained from other sources.

Natural curiosity, as has already been pointed out, occurs in the early pre-school period; and the questions asked by three-year-old concerning where babies come from and what is the difference between little boys and little girls should be answered simply, accurately, and without embarrassment. Similarly, questions about sex asked by individual children of any age should be answered by giving a true matter-of-fact statement, or referring them to someone who can give them the desired knowledge. Explaining to the pre-adolescents the changes which may be expected to occur and the organic basis of their vague emotional unrest is a more difficult task, but one which should not be avoided.

The wise family will know when adolescent changes are likely to occur, will recognize them, and will help the child to adjust himself to them. For example, many a boy has suffered from not being allowed to shave as early as he though necessary. Many a girl has been emotionally disturbed by mysterious hints of impending maturity. Accurate information about sex should probably be given before ten years of age because many distorted ideas of sex are acquired about that age. One successful way of giving such information is in connection with animal families at home or in school.

A frequently mentioned program of education for parenthood begins with facts concerning reproduction below mammals, arid leads up to reproduction in mammals and to the generalization that the life of a new individual begins with the fertilization of the female by the male germ cell. A few of the best established and most useful fact of heredity are also included in this program. The high-school girl can be given a normal attitude toward motherhood and an appreciation of the psychological importance of the parents in the child's life. Knowing more about motherhood is an excellent way of building interest in it. More specific training for parenthood is given most economically to recently married women and mothers. As early as 1902 at Ghent, Belgium, Dr. Miele started a school for mothers in connection with the Bureau de Bienfaisance.

At this school, health talks to mothers and training courses for girls as infants nurses were given. Emphasis today is being placed on the education of parents concerning the psychological as well as the physical care of young children in such centres as those at Vassar and Wellesley, and in many parents' classes and associations. Better than any formal sex instruction is the establishment of such an intimacy with the child that he will come to the teacher or parent with questions suggested by moving pictures he has seen, adult discussions he has heard, or articles he has read in some of the magazines and tabloid newspapers. Group sex instruction, unless given by a person who is attractive, refined, and skillful in dealing with adolescents, may do more harm than good.

Correcting Tendencies Toward three Undesirables Mental Mechanisms

Feeling of Inferiority

Because of the many new situations he must face and because of his physical, social, and economic awkwardness, the adolescent's sense of his own inadequacy frequently becomes very acute. This feeling of inferiority is accentuated by being laughed at or criticized, and may take the form of shyness, seclusiveness, unwillingness to attack new problems, or an outward bravado and apparent indifference to public opinion. Miriam Van Waters describes the manifestations of feelings of inferiority as follows: These individuals who are incapable of team-play, and whose, malady takes the form now of bashfulness; shrinking, depression, envy, jealousy and self-pity; again of showing off, boastfulness, aggression, critical scorn of the achievements of others, belittling the value of the players and the game itself, interference, occasional exhibitionism-they should not be blamed.

They are, it is true, a terrific nuisance, but they are almost heroically unhappy. The basic difficulty is their feeling of inferiority. She mentions two remedies for this feeling of inferiority. One is the parent's cultivation of respect for varying personalities, and an objective appreciation for the activities and achievements of children for whom no congeniality is felt.

Excessive Activity

Children of opposite characteristics, on the other hand the so-called extroverts should be protected from too much social activity, should be given opportunity for quiet and solitude, and should be encouraged to think for themselves by the parents showing respect for their opinions, and taking the time to discuss problems with them and interesting them in spending some of their leisure time in contact with nature, music, art, and literature. Richmond tells of an exceedingly active girl leading her classes in college and engaging in all the college activities. Not a moment of her time was left unaccounted for. Her career culminated in a breakdown and was ruined by her eccentricities. Richmond emphasizes the necessity of counteracting the tendency to undue extroversion in our social milieu of haste, speed, and noise.

Seclusiveness

In general, the following recommendations are applicable to the shy, seclusive boy and girl:

(i) Find out something they can do well and see that approval is given for successful performance and enthusiastic genuine praise for their efforts. Advantage rarely comes of sarcasm.

(ii) Show them the attractive opportunities in the world, at the same time helping them to face squarely its harshness and contemptuous accidentalness.

(iii) Remove the children, if possible, from an environment in which they are constantly urged to attempt the impossible and then reproached for their failures or excused and petted instead of being encouraged and stimulated to do the things within their capacity.

(iv) Provide small congenial groups with whom they can engage successfully in interesting activities. Any adult who hopes to have a favourable influence on an adolescent boy or girl must be very careful not to arouse antagonism by sarcasm, ridicule, petty slights or tactless reprimands, or responding coldly to their enthusiasm and affection. The children are repulsed by the person who inflicts these humiliations on them.

Hygienic Living

Menstruation

In the United States the average age at which the menses appear is 13.9 years. The average duration is one to six days at intervals of fourteen to thirty-five days, the average interval being twenty-eight days. The intervals are frequently irregular at the beginning of puberty and when marked changes in physical activity or emotional disturbances occur. A period longer than six days should be referred to physician. Each girl should find out the amount of exercise and the kind of bathing that the best for her. In general, the best practice is to make little change in the customary daily activities.

The vigorous girl can exercise about the same as usual. The tall, thin girl is more comfortable if she stands less and takes less vigorous exercise during the period. Many college girls say that they suffer less discomfort if they take some exercise than if they simply sit or lie around during the period. Richmond gives some excellent concrete suggestions for the hygiene of the adolescent girl. Mosher believes that the headache, weariness, fatigue, nervousness, and more or less severe pain is due not only to malformation and disease of the organs but also to wrong breathing, lack of development of the abdominal muscles, the upright position, inactivity during the period, and the psychic influence of the suggestion that it is a sick or unwell period.

Diet

Special attention to diet and other health rules frequently needs to be given in this period because of the increased temptations to depart from the established routine of childhood, and because of the child's new responsibility for choosing his own food. In the elementary school the children usually go home to lunch. In high school they frequently must either take their lunch with them or buy it at the school cafeteria or neighbouring stores. In one junior high school the boys were buying extremely unhealthful lunches at the two or three candy and ice-cream stores in the neighbourhood. Their usual menu consisted of hot dogs, soda water, and a rich pastry they called Neapolitans.

The hygiene teacher, instead of beginning the course by taking up the organs, as she usually did, began with the problem: What foods should a junior high-school boy choose for his lunch, and where may these foods be purchased in this neighbourhood? Food values were discussed, the effects of deficiency of vitamins and minerals were shown by pictures of animals which had been fed different diets and by graphs of the growth of experimental animals, obtained from the American Journal of Physiology, the American Journal of Public Health, and other scientific books and journal of Public Health, and other scientific books and journals.

The discussion was summarized by the slogan, choose the Big Three-milk, bread or cereals, fruit or vegetables. The next problem was to persuade the little stores in the neighbourhood to sell the big three. One store agreed to sell the small half-pant bottles of milk, to make cocoa using milk as the foundation, and to provide peanut-butter and lettuce sandwiches. Another little store already offered an excellent thick vegetable soup, and the boys were urged to go there frequently on cold days. The pupils also discussed costs and planned a number of lunches which could be purchased for different amounts. Many of the boys brought sandwiches and fruit from home and supplemented these with vegetable soup, cocoa, or milk.

Moral and Religious Adjustment

The small child accepts almost any answers to his questions about God, death, heaven, and the other mysteries. The dull adolescent likewise is little concerned with metaphysical questions. He is willing to believe whatever anyone in authority tells him. The bright adolescent, on the other hand, may be *very* much distressed about the things that no man knows. This latter group, who have the religious doubts and conflicts so often mentioned as characteristic of all adolescents, comprise probably only about 15 per cent of the entire adolescent population.

The biographies of great religious leaders describe the extreme form which religious questioning sometimes takes. One way of helping an adolescent with his religious questions is to review with him the various possible answers to a given question. He may be told: This is what some people believe about it; this is what others believe; still others believe this. You will have to decide for yourself which you can accept as true. This is a better method than dictating to him what he shall believe, or securing his outward assent to a certain point of view through the appeal to personal devotion. Conversion usually means that one of two conflicting trends becomes dominant.

This view of conversion necessitates a review of the past-a conviction of sin a conscious rejection of one path, and acceptance of the other. Another view of conversion emphasizes its developmental aspect-taking the present as a starting point and going forward in one dominate course, ignoring the past. Whether attained as a religious experience or in some other connection, a philosophy of life and a unification of purpose should be acquired in this period. If the individual does not achieve unity of purpose during adolescence, he will probably be at war with himself all during his life.

Burnham emphasizes the importance for mental health of having a purpose, a plan, and greatly aid the adolescent by showing concretely the probable consequences of different trends of behaviour and by helping him to unify his conflicting ideas. Early experience is as important in religious as in other adolescent adjustments. A child who earlier has acquired desirable social habits and altruistic ways of behaving is free to direct his attention to the larger ideals and purposes. In fact, a real understanding of kindness, honesty, courage, and other abstract virtues is impossible unless the individual has already habitually acted in a kindly, honest, and courageous way.

BIBLIOGRAPHY

ALLPORT, G. W. *Personality: a psychological interpretation*. New York: Holt, 1937.

COHEN, M. R. The factional structure of the WAIS between early adulthood and old age. *Journal of Consult Psychology*, 1957, 21, 283-290.

CRANDALL, V. J.; PRESTON, A. and RABSON, A. The development of social compliance in children. *Child Development*, 1958, 29, 429-444.

DARWIN, C. A biological sketch of an infant. *Mind*, 1877, 2, 285-294.

ERIKSON, E. H. Studies in the interpretation of play: I. Clinical observation of play disruption in young children. *Genet. Psychol. Monogr.*, 1940, 22, 557-671.

FREEDMAN, J. L. *Crowding and Behaviour*. San Francious: W. H. Freeman. 1975.

FREEMAN, F. N. Growth in intellectual ability as measured by repeated tests. *Soc. Res. Child Development Monogr.*, 1937,2, NO.2.

GESELL, A. Maturation and infant behaviour pattern. *Psychological Review*, 1929, 36, 307-319.

GESELL, A. Maturation and the patterning of behaviour. In Murchison, C. (Ed.) *A handbook of Child Psychology*. (Rev. Ed.) Worcester, Mass: Clark University Press, 1933.

GESELL, A. The ontogenesis of infant behaviour. In Carmicheal, L. (Ed.) *Manual of Child Psychology*. (2nd Ed.) New York: Wiley, 1954.

GESELL, A. The daily maturation of infant behaviour: a cinema study of postures, movement, and laterality. *J. genet. Psychology*, 1942, 61, 3-32.

GESELL, A. *Infant and child in the culture of today*. New York: Harper, 1943.

GESELL, A. *The child from five to ten*. New York: Harper, 1946.

GESELL, A. and THOMPSON, H. Learning and growth in identical infant twins. *Genet. Psychol. Monogr.*, 1929, 6, 1-124.

GESELL, A. Twins T and C from infancy to adolescence: a biogenetic study of individual differences by the method of co-twin control. *Genet. Psychol. Monogr.*, 1941, 24, 3-121.

GUTHRIE, E. R. *The psychology of learning*. New York: Harper, 1935.

GEWIRTZ, J. L. Studies in word-fluency: I. Its relation to vocabulary and mental age in young children. *J. genet. Psychology*, 1948, 72, 165-176.

GEWIRTZ, J. L. Studies in word-fluency: II. Its relation to eleven items of child behaviour. *J. genet. Psychology*, 1948, 72, 177-184.

GEWIRTZ, J. L. Plans for the construction of a portable one-way observation booth. *Child Development*, 1952, 23, 307-314.

HALL, G. S. The contents of children's minds on entering school. *Ped. Sem.*, 1891, 1, 139-173.

HALL, G. S. *Adolescence*. 2 vols. New York: Appleton-Century-Crofts, 1904.

HILGARD, E. R. *Theories of learning*. (2nd Ed.) New York: Appleton-Century- Crofts, 1956.

HULL, C. L. *Principles of behaviour: An introduction to behaviour theory*. New York: Appleton-Century-Crofts, 1943.

HUNT, J. *Personality and the behaviour disorders*, vol. 1, The Ronald Press Company, 1944.

JAMES, W. T. Variation in social facilitation of eating behaviour in puppies. *J. genet. Psychology*, 1955, 87, 225-228.

JOST, H. and SONTAG, L. W. The genetic factor in autonomic nervous system function. *Psychosomat. Med.*, 1944, 6, 308-310.

KAGAN, J. and MOSS, H. A. Maternal influences on early IQ scores. *Psychological Reports*, 1958, 4, 655-661.

KELLER, F. S. *Principles of Psychology*. New York: Appleton-Century-Crofts. 1950.

McCANDLESS, B. R. Experimental research in child psychology. *Child Development*, 1956, 27, 75-80.

McDOUGALL, W. *An introduction to social psychology*. Boston: J. W. Luce, 1923.

McGEOCH, J. A. and IRION, A. L. *The psychology of human learning*. New York: Longmans, 1942.

MURRAY, H. A. and KLUCKHOHN, C. Outline of a conception of Personality. In Kluckhohn, C. and Murray, H. A. (Eds.) *Personality in nature, society and culture*. New York: Knopf, 1948.

NEWMAN, H. F.; FREEMAN, F. N. and HOLZINGER, K. J. *Twins: a study of heredity and environment*. Chicago: University of Chicago Press, 1937.

OLSON, W. C. Time-sampling techniques. *Child Development*, 1934, 5, 41-58.

ROGERS, C. R. *Client-centered therapy: Its current practice, implications and theory*, Boston: Houghton Mifflin, 1951.

ROGERS, C. R. A theory of therapy, personality and interpersonal relationships, as developed in the client-centered framework. In S. Koch (Ed.) *Psychology: A Study of a science* (vol. 3). New York: McGraw-Hill, 1959.

ROGERS, C. R. *On becoming a person*. Boston: Houghton Mifflin, 1961.

SIMON, R. and THOMPSON, G. G. A study of teacher actions desired by pupils in certain classroom situations: motivating children to overcome problem tendencies. *Journal of Child Behaviour*, 1950, 2, 86-97.

SMITH, J. W. Attitudes of grandmothers and mothers toward child rearing practices. *Child Development*, 1954,25,91-97.

STONE, L. J. A critique of studies of infant isolation. *Child Development*, 1954, 25, 9-20.

Name Index